"Ray Fawkes' *One Soul* was a revelation and one of the most experimental and progressive comics of the last decade. Now with *One Line* he does it again. But this is no rehash of what he's done before—*One Line* takes the language and style he's established and takes it to a whole other level. But what really makes this book so special isn't just the experimentation or boundary pushing, it's that at its core there is a deep humanity and heart in these pages that will stay with you for a long time."

Jeff Lemire (Gideon Falls, Black Hammer, Essex County)

"Both profound and innovative in its narrative, *One Line* elevates the sequential arts medium to a place of poetic brilliance."

David Walker (Bitter Root, The Black Panther Party, The Life of Frederick Douglass)

"Ray Fawkes once again does what only he can do, effortlessly crafting disparate complex relationships across space and through time, towards a beautifully simple conclusion that's at once surprising and— having been reached—seemingly inevitable."

Al Ewing (Immortal Hulk, We Only Find Them When They're Dead)

"Fawkes creates comics like symphonies, with melodies and counter-melodies of narrative dancing in parallel. He uses the grid to show what connects and separates lives, across time and space. It leaves you alive to the world."

Kieron Gillen (The Wicked + The Divine, Phonogram, Young Avengers)

ONE
LINE

by
Ray Fawkes

AN ONI PRESS PUBLICATION

For those beloved gone
And those with us
And those yet to come

R.

ONE
LINE

PART ONE

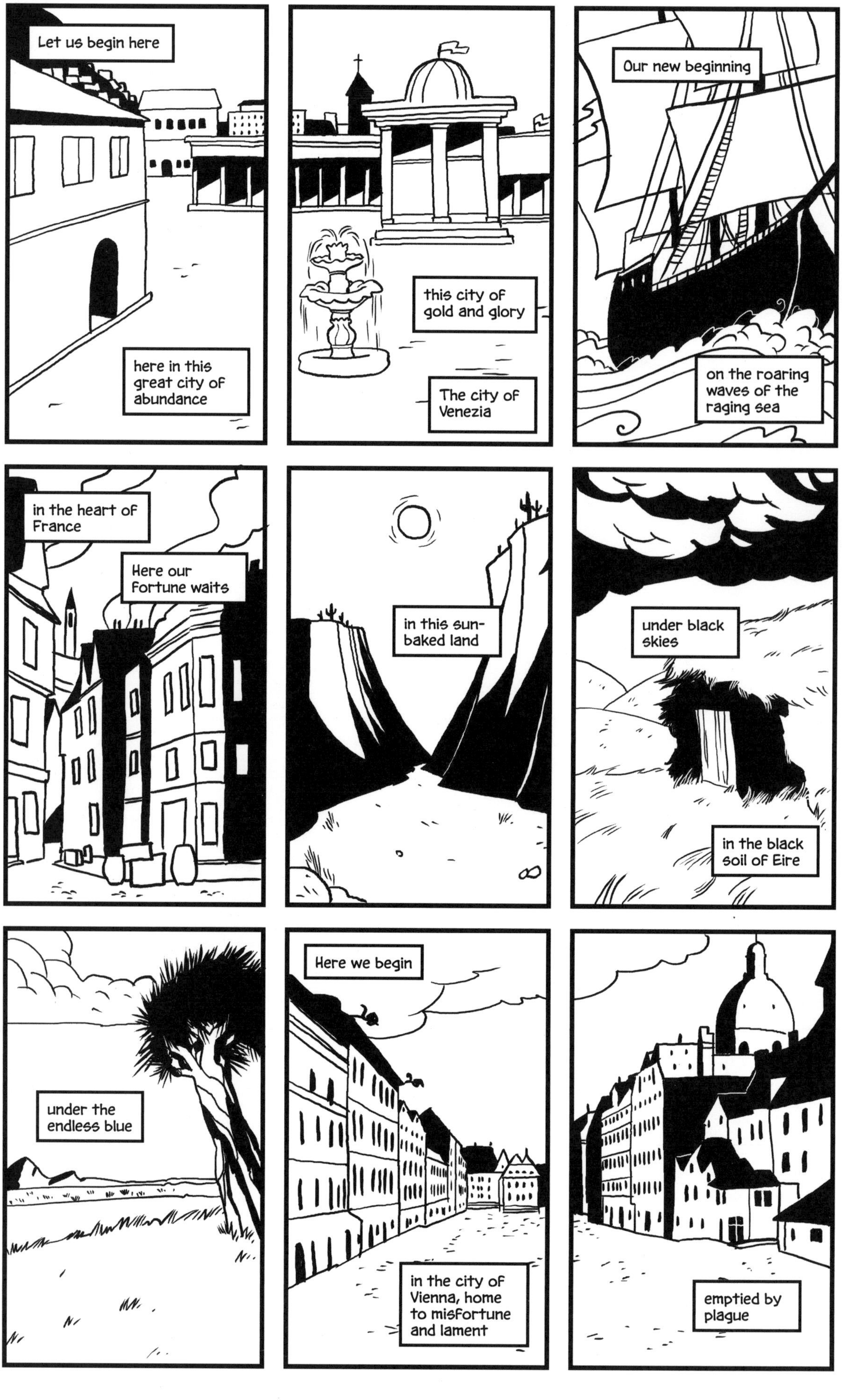
Let us begin here
here in this great city of abundance
this city of gold and glory
The city of Venezia
Our new beginning
on the roaring waves of the raging sea
in the heart of France
Here our fortune waits
in this sun-baked land
under black skies
in the black soil of Eire
under the endless blue
Here we begin
in the city of Vienna, home to misfortune and lament
emptied by plague

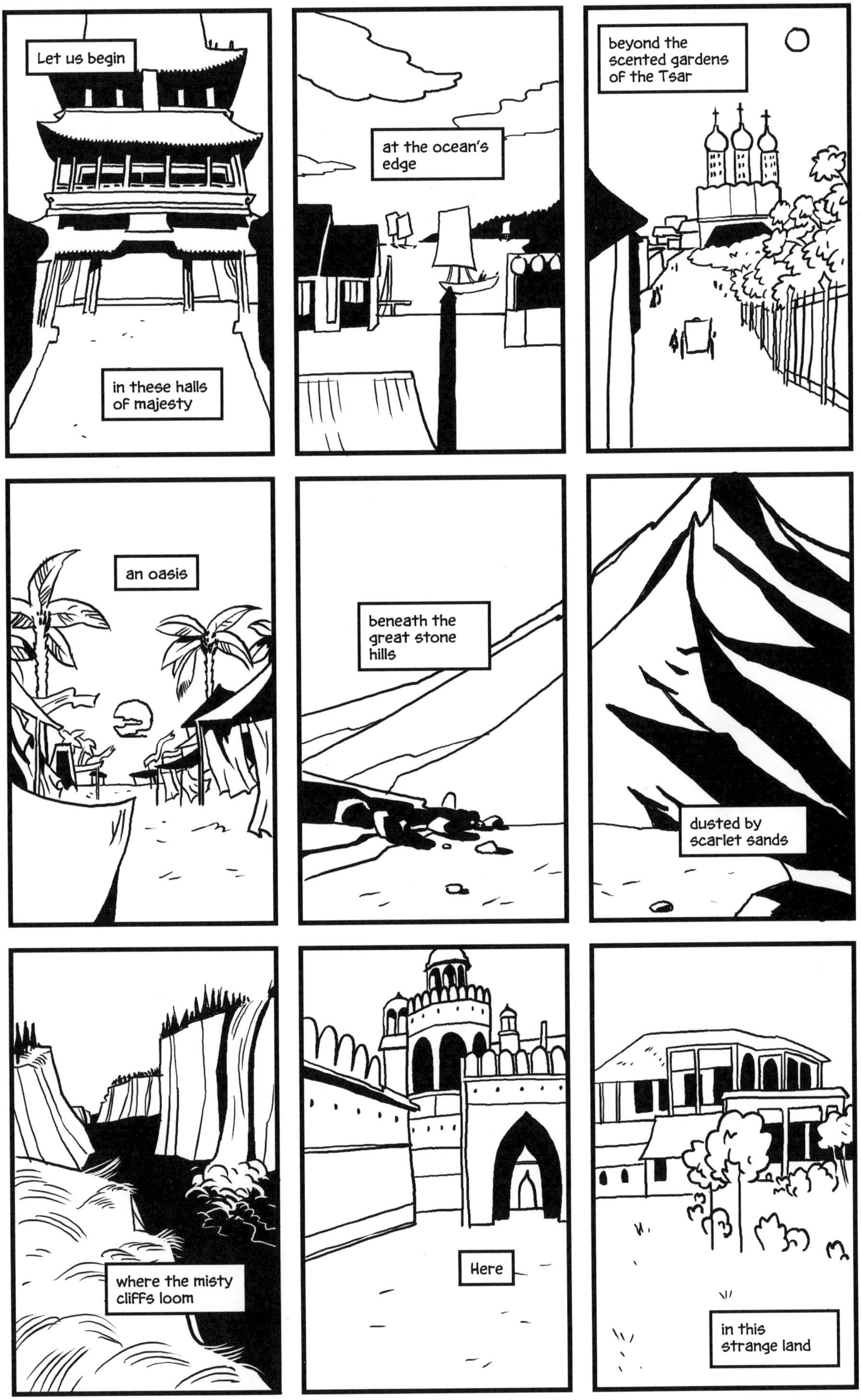
Let us begin
in these halls of majesty
at the ocean's edge
beyond the scented gardens of the Tsar
an oasis
beneath the great stone hills
dusted by scarlet sands
where the misty cliffs loom
Here
in this strange land

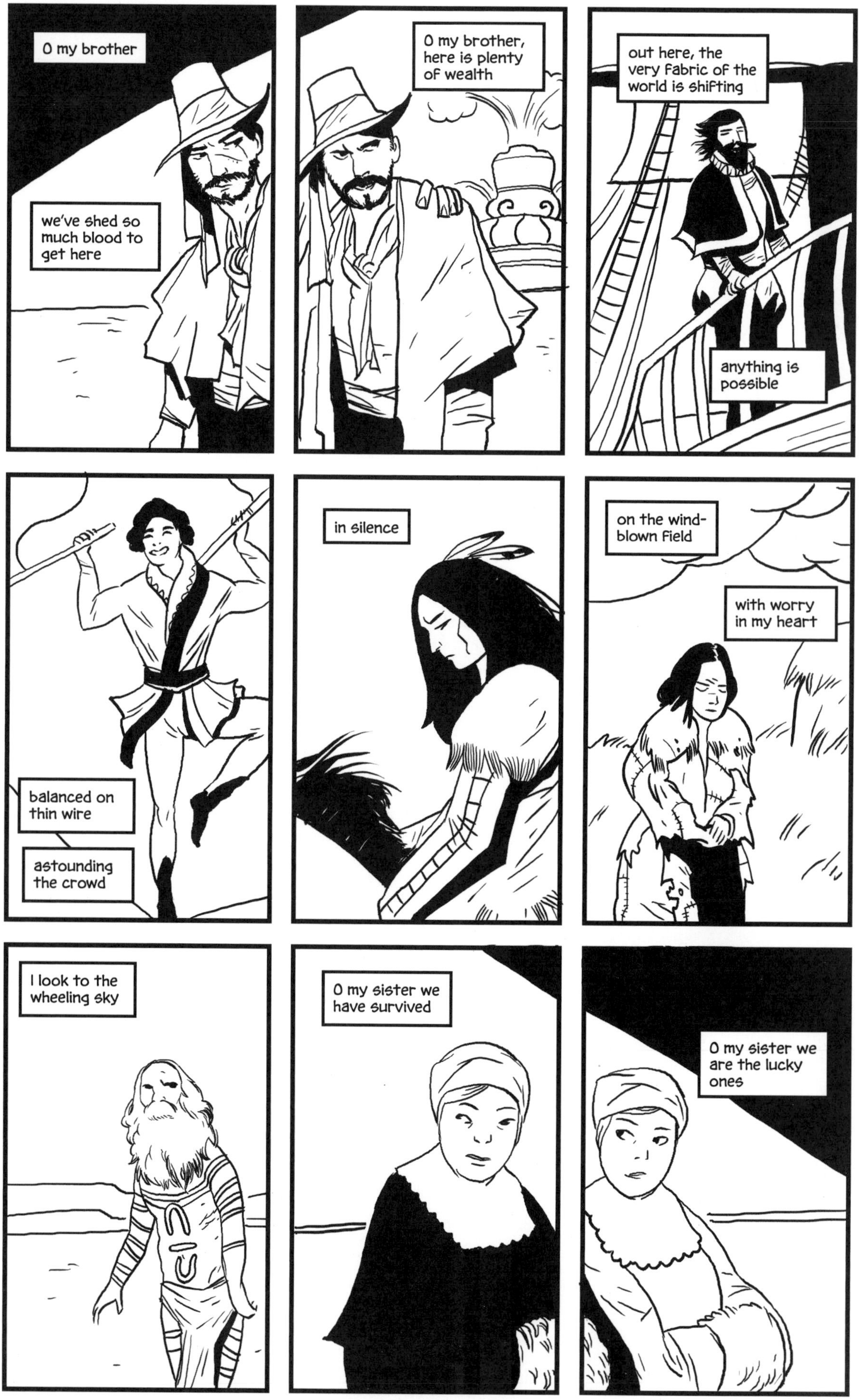
O my brother
we've shed so much blood to get here
O my brother, here is plenty of wealth
out here, the very fabric of the world is shifting
anything is possible
balanced on thin wire
astounding the crowd
in silence
on the wind-blown field
with worry in my heart
I look to the wheeling sky
O my sister we have survived
O my sister we are the lucky ones

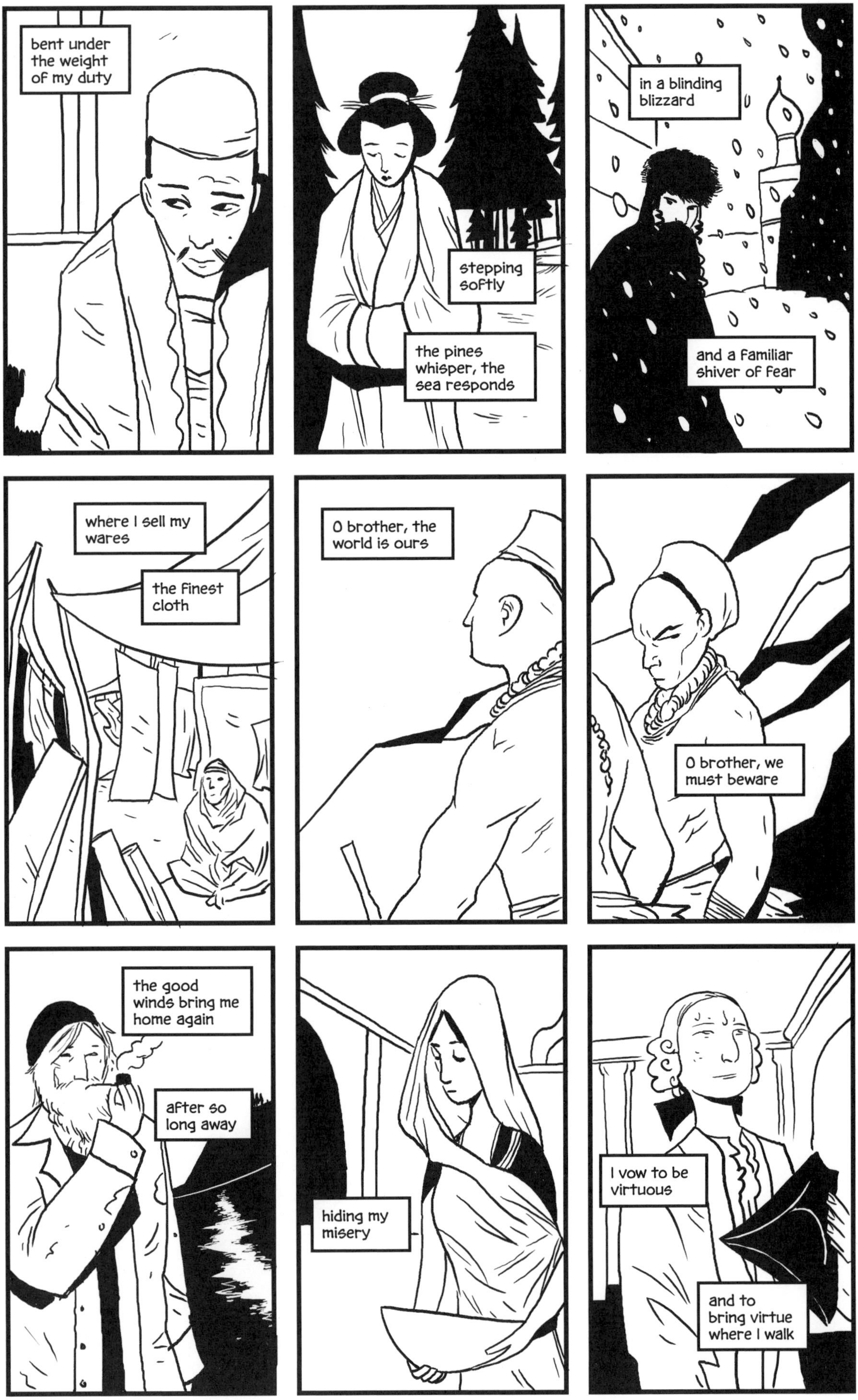
bent under the weight of my duty
stepping softly
the pines whisper, the sea responds
in a blinding blizzard
and a familiar shiver of fear
where I sell my wares
the finest cloth
O brother, the world is ours
O brother, we must beware
the good winds bring me home again
after so long away
hiding my misery
I vow to be virtuous
and to bring virtue where I walk

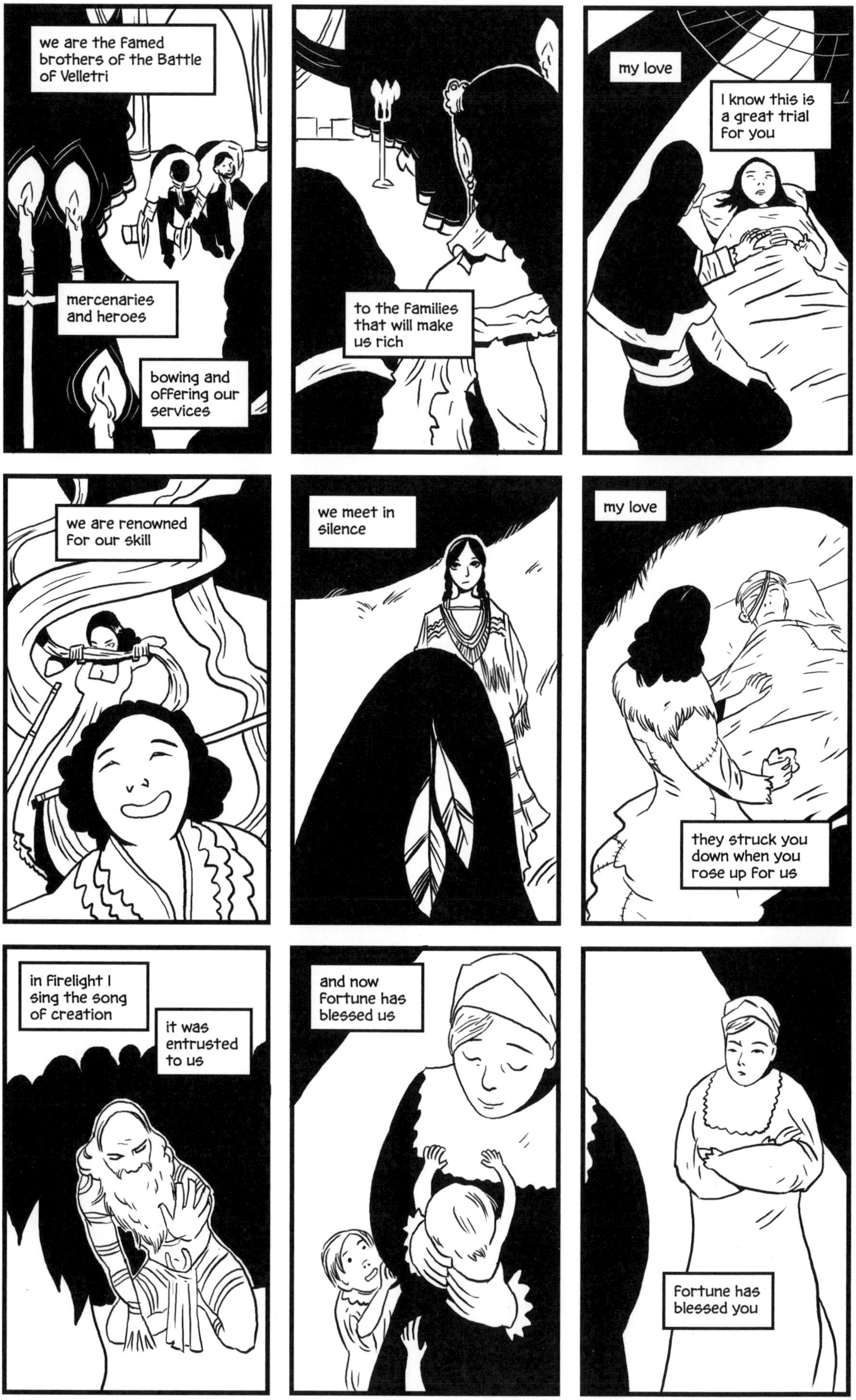
we are the famed brothers of the Battle of Velletri
mercenaries and heroes
bowing and offering our services
to the families that will make us rich
my love
I know this is a great trial for you
we are renowned for our skill
we meet in silence
my love
they struck you down when you rose up for us
in firelight I sing the song of creation
it was entrusted to us
and now fortune has blessed us
fortune has blessed you

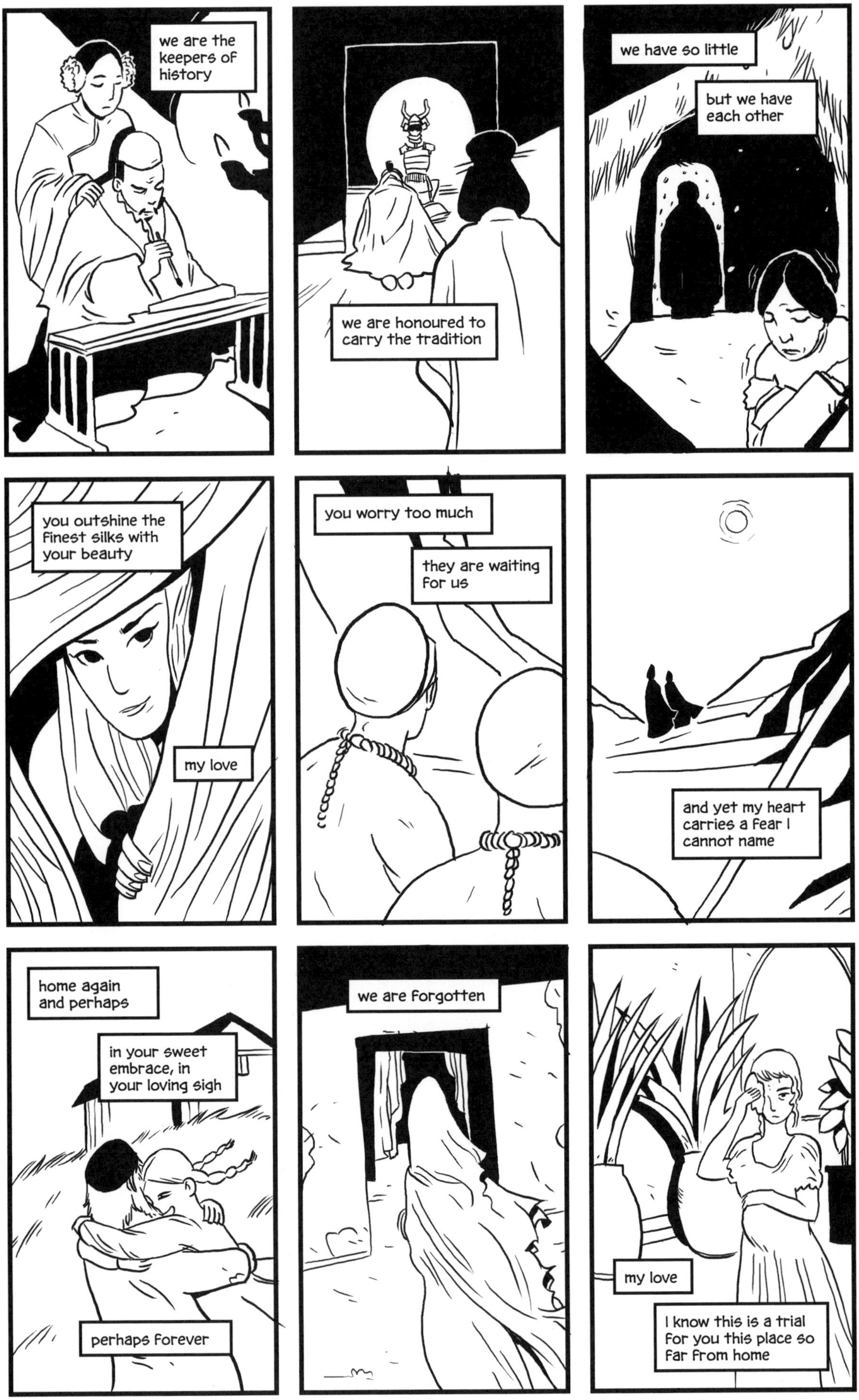
we are the keepers of history
we are honoured to carry the tradition
we have so little
but we have each other
you outshine the finest silks with your beauty
my love
you worry too much
they are waiting for us
and yet my heart carries a fear I cannot name
home again and perhaps
in your sweet embrace, in your loving sigh
perhaps forever
we are forgotten
my love
I know this is a trial for you this place so far from home

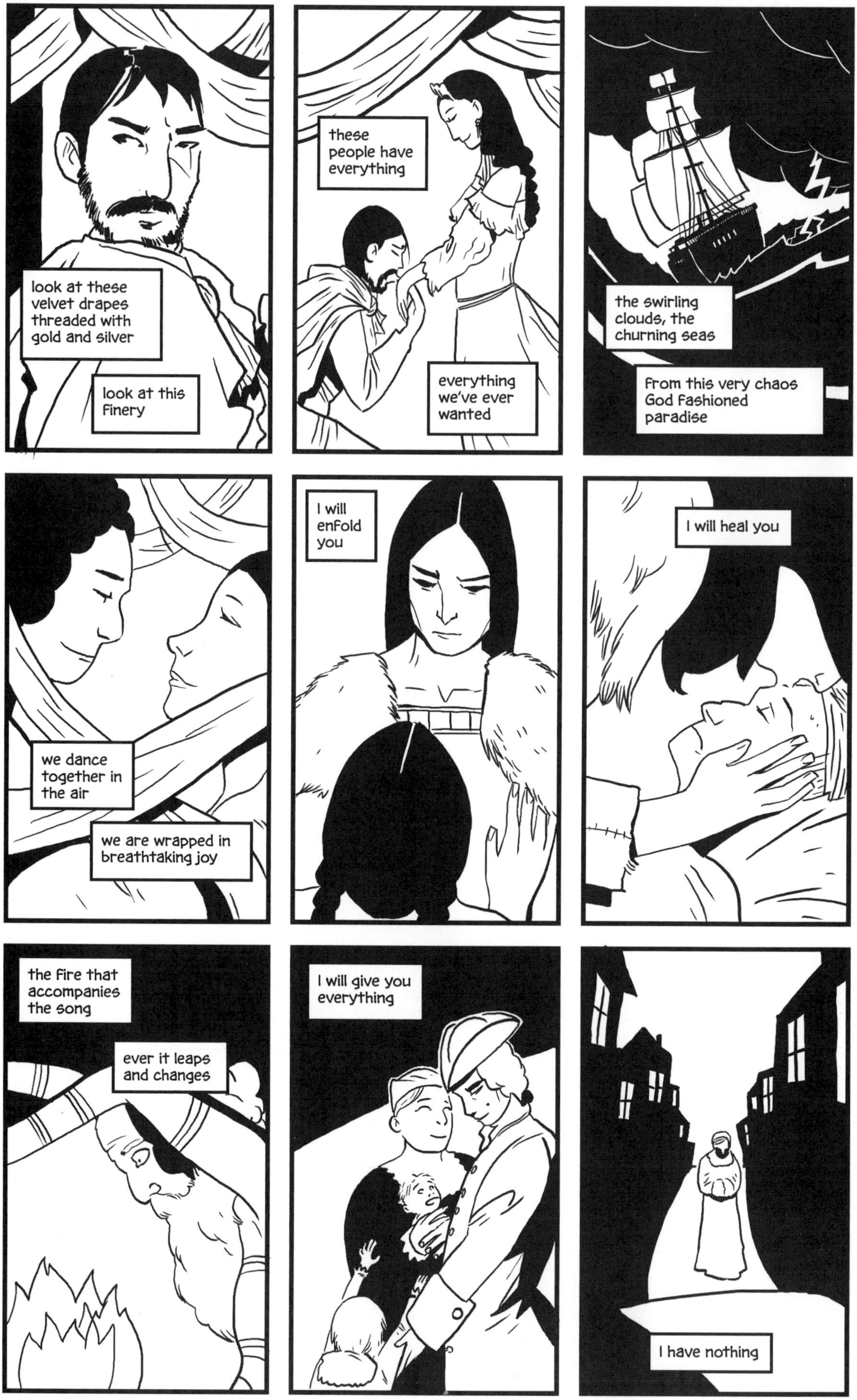
look at these velvet drapes threaded with gold and silver
look at this finery
these people have everything
everything we've ever wanted
the swirling clouds, the churning seas
From this very chaos God fashioned paradise
we dance together in the air
we are wrapped in breathtaking joy
I will enfold you
I will heal you
the fire that accompanies the song
ever it leaps and changes
I will give you everything
I have nothing

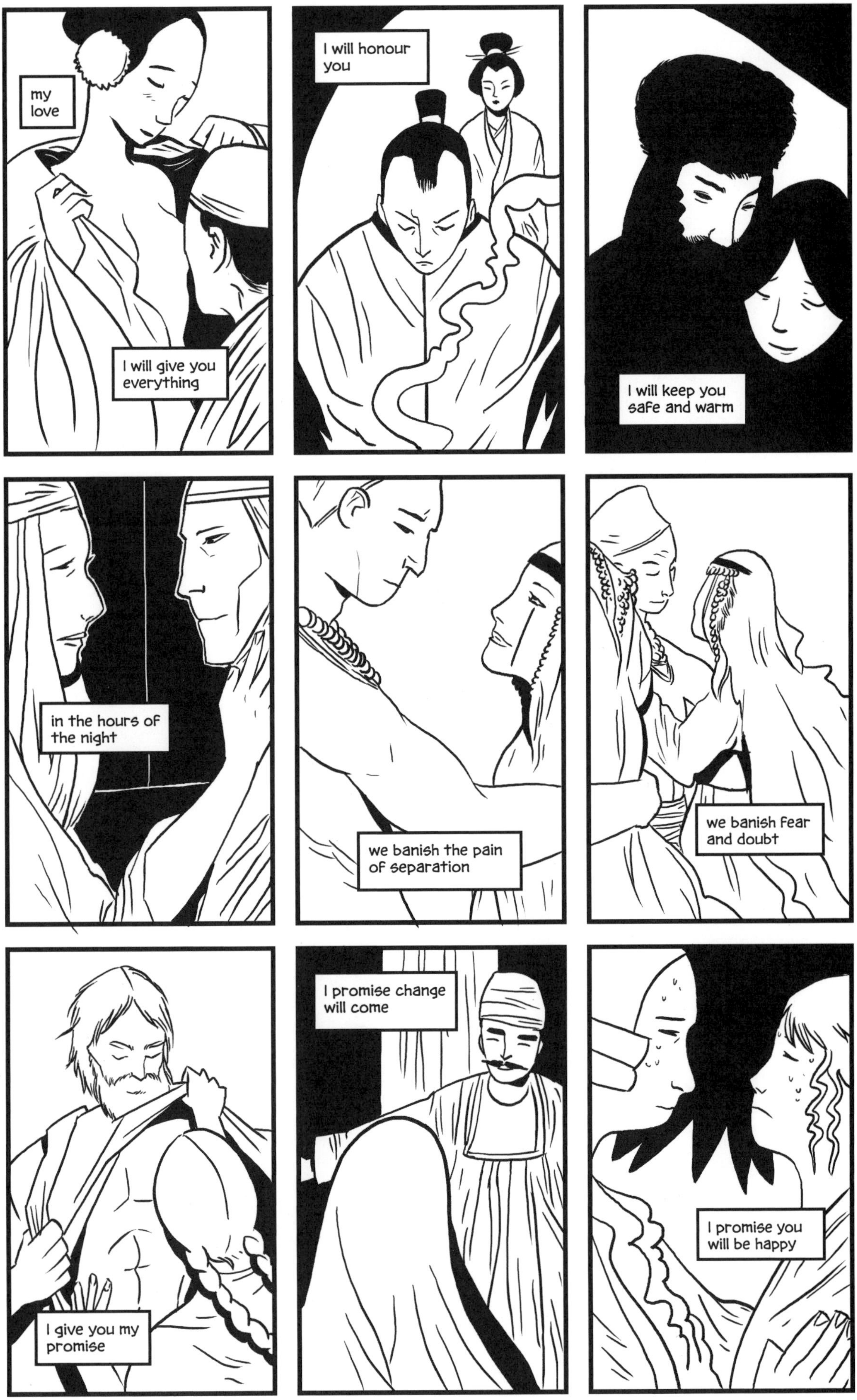
my love
I will give you everything
I will honour you
I will keep you safe and warm
in the hours of the night
we banish the pain of separation
we banish fear and doubt
I give you my promise
I promise change will come
I promise you will be happy

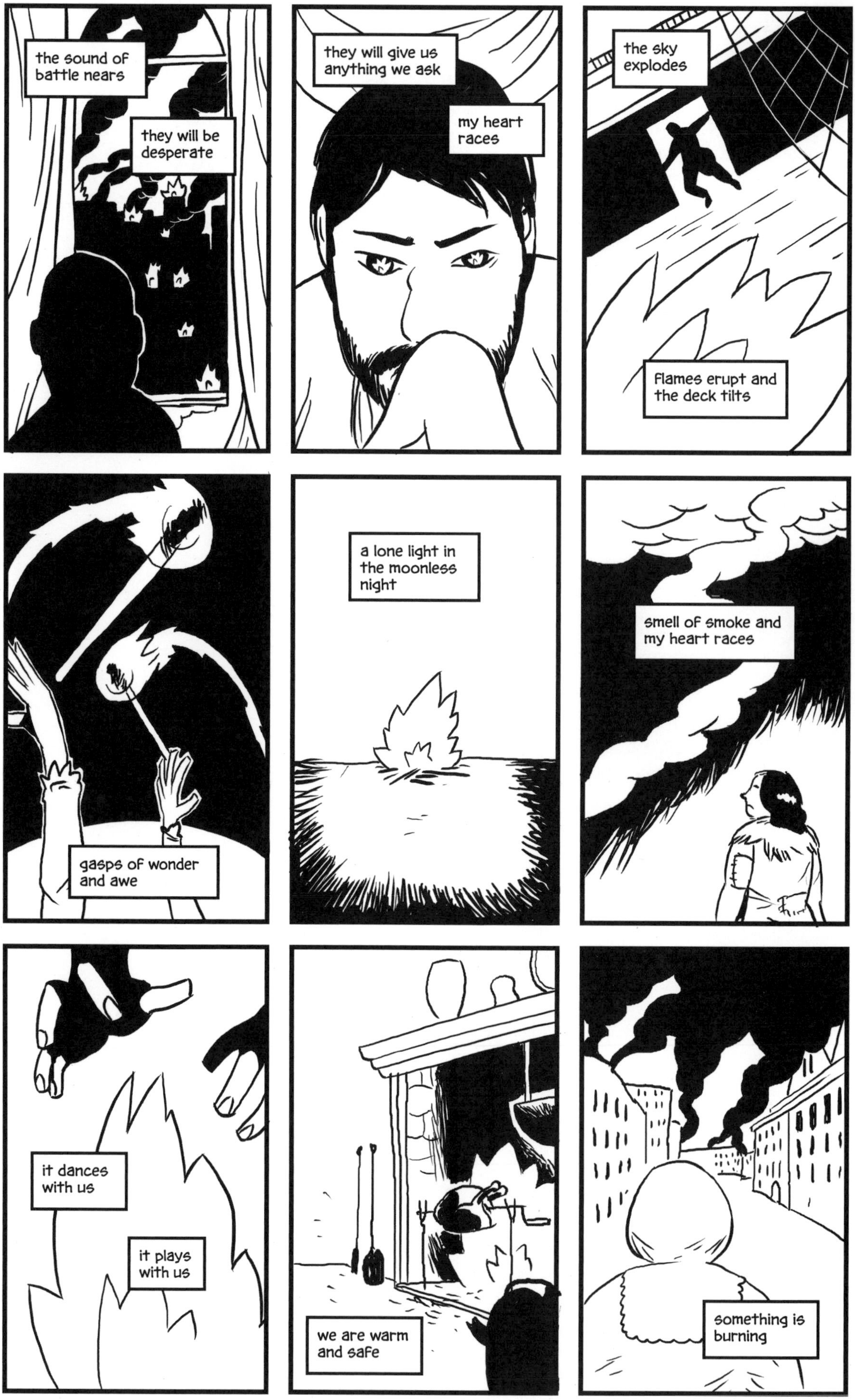
the sound of battle nears
they will be desperate
they will give us anything we ask
my heart races
the sky explodes
flames erupt and the deck tilts
gasps of wonder and awe
a lone light in the moonless night
smell of smoke and my heart races
it dances with us
it plays with us
we are warm and safe
something is burning

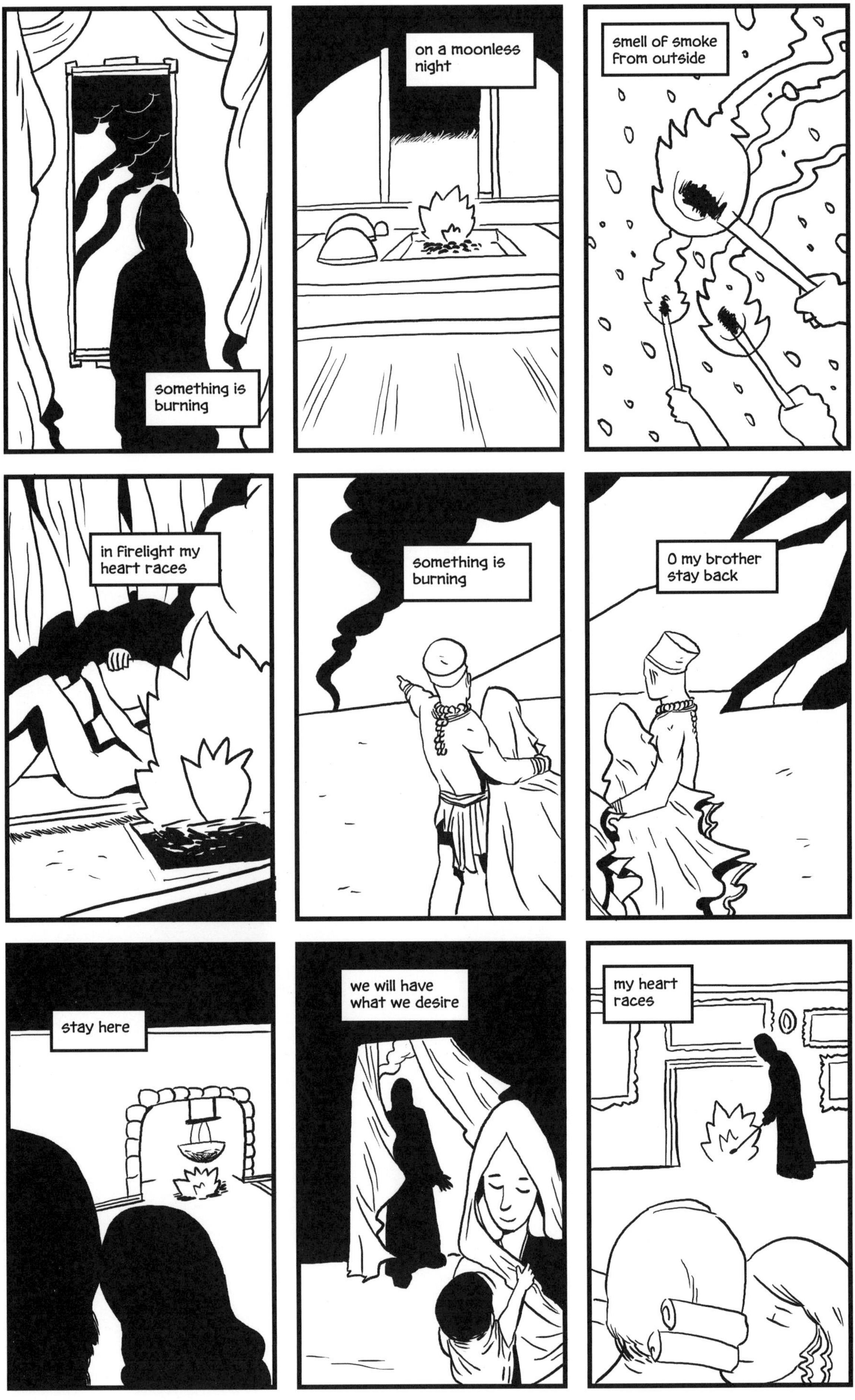
something is burning
on a moonless night
smell of smoke from outside
in firelight my heart races
something is burning
O my brother stay back
stay here
we will have what we desire
my heart races

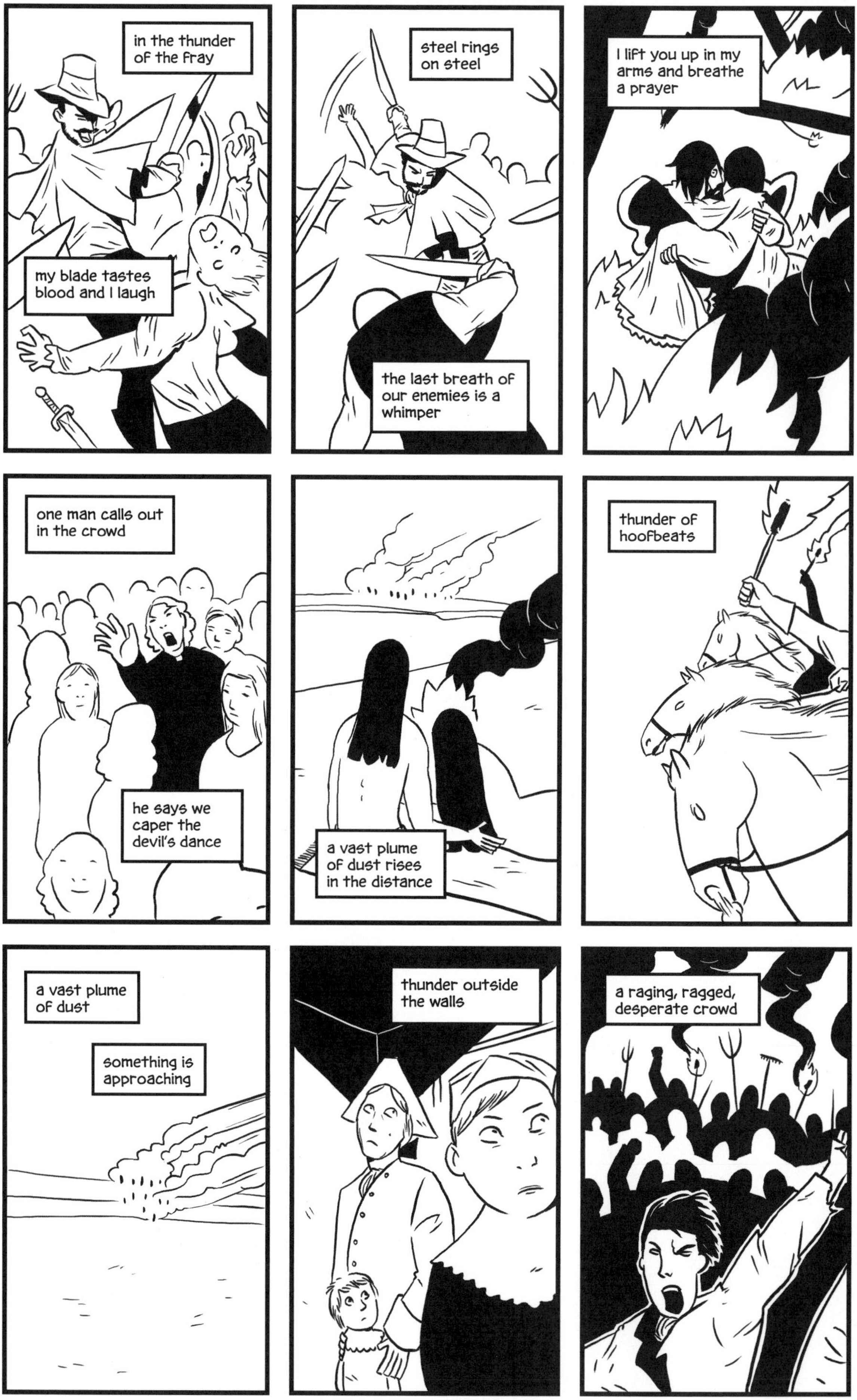

in the thunder of the fray
my blade tastes blood and I laugh
steel rings on steel
the last breath of our enemies is a whimper
I lift you up in my arms and breathe a prayer
one man calls out in the crowd
he says we caper the devil's dance
a vast plume of dust rises in the distance
thunder of hoofbeats
a vast plume of dust
something is approaching
thunder outside the walls
a raging, ragged, desperate crowd

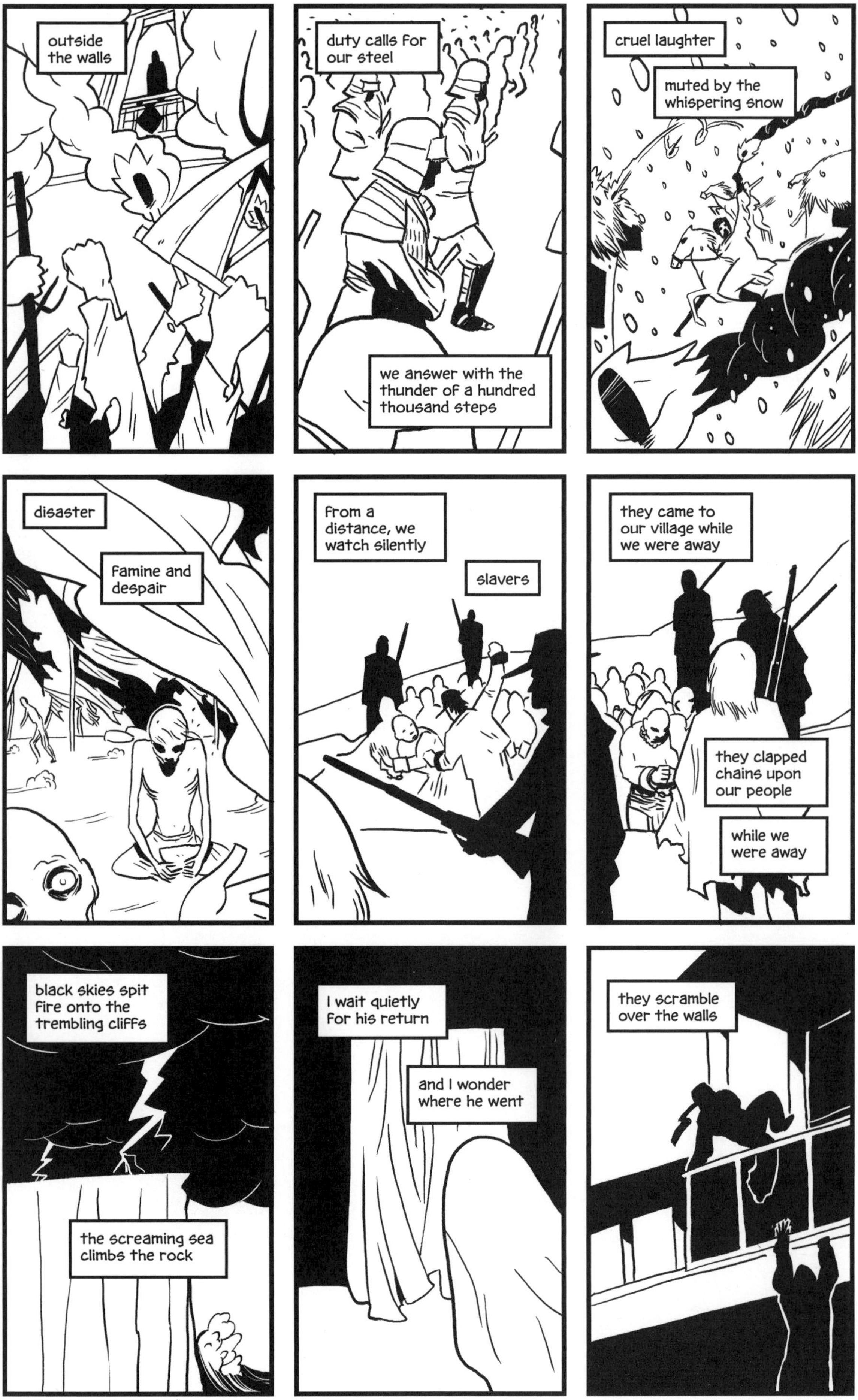
outside the walls
duty calls for our steel
we answer with the thunder of a hundred thousand steps
cruel laughter
muted by the whispering snow
disaster
famine and despair
from a distance, we watch silently
slavers
they came to our village while we were away
they clapped chains upon our people
while we were away
black skies spit fire onto the trembling cliffs
the screaming sea climbs the rock
I wait quietly for his return
and I wonder where he went
they scramble over the walls

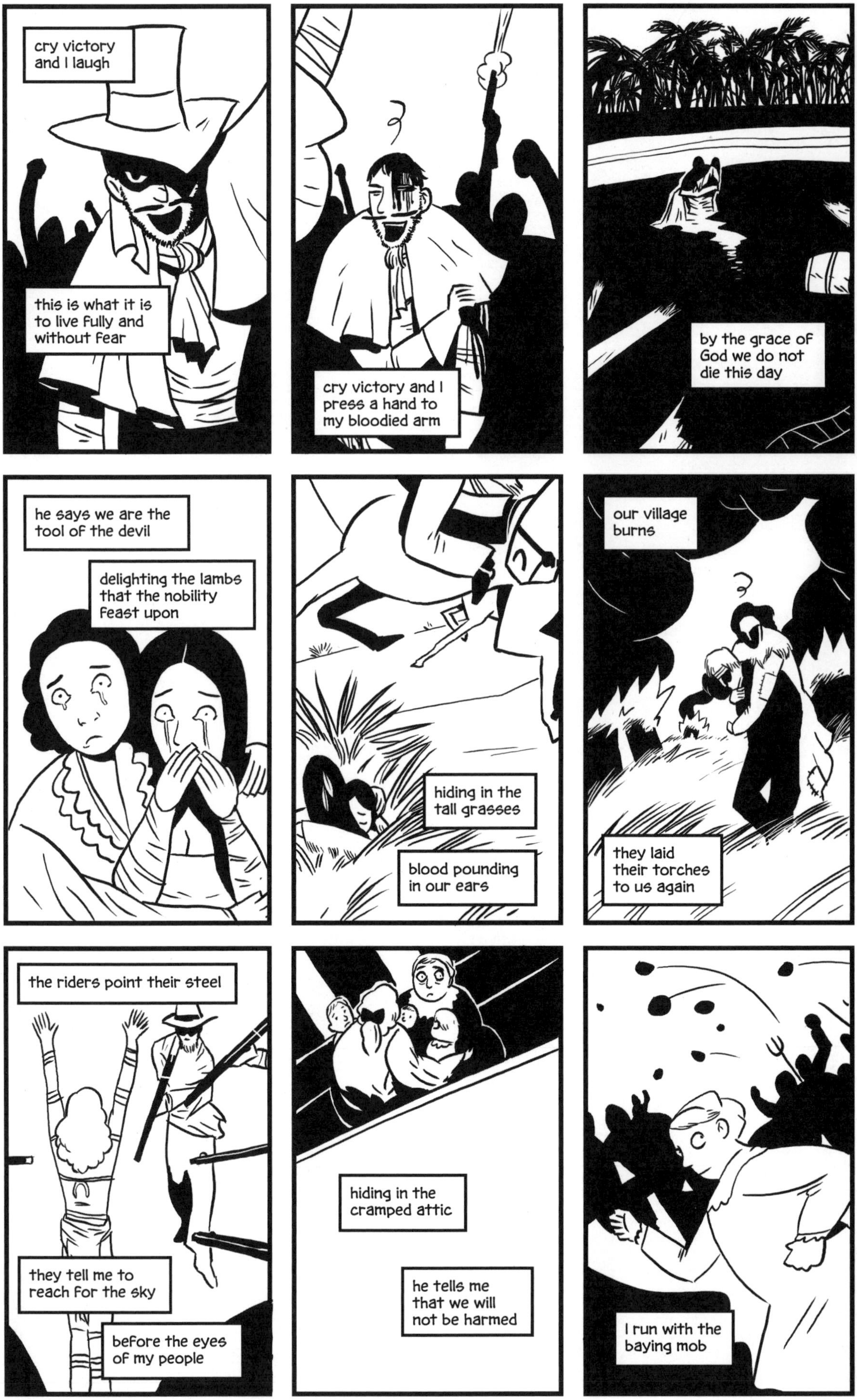
cry victory
and I laugh
this is what it is
to live fully and
without fear
cry victory and I
press a hand to
my bloodied arm
by the grace of
God we do not
die this day
he says we are the
tool of the devil
delighting the lambs
that the nobility
feast upon
hiding in the
tall grasses
blood pounding
in our ears
our village
burns
they laid
their torches
to us again
the riders point their steel
they tell me to
reach for the sky
before the eyes
of my people
hiding in the
cramped attic
he tells me
that we will
not be harmed
I run with the
baying mob

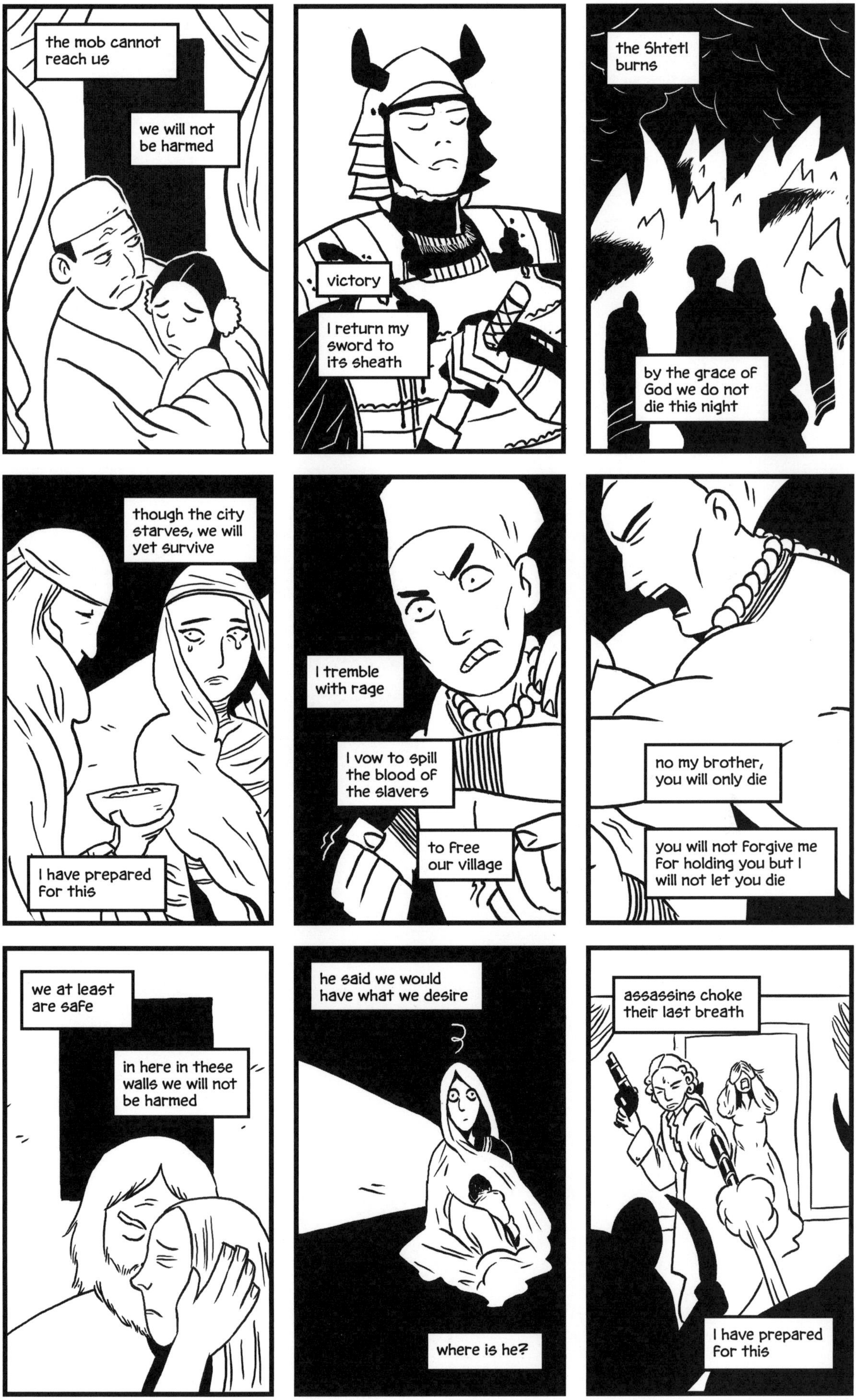
the mob cannot reach us
we will not be harmed
victory
I return my sword to its sheath
the Shtetl burns
by the grace of God we do not die this night
though the city starves, we will yet survive
I have prepared for this
I tremble with rage
I vow to spill the blood of the slavers
to free our village
no my brother, you will only die
you will not forgive me for holding you but I will not let you die
we at least are safe
in here in these walls we will not be harmed
he said we would have what we desire
where is he?
assassins choke their last breath
I have prepared for this

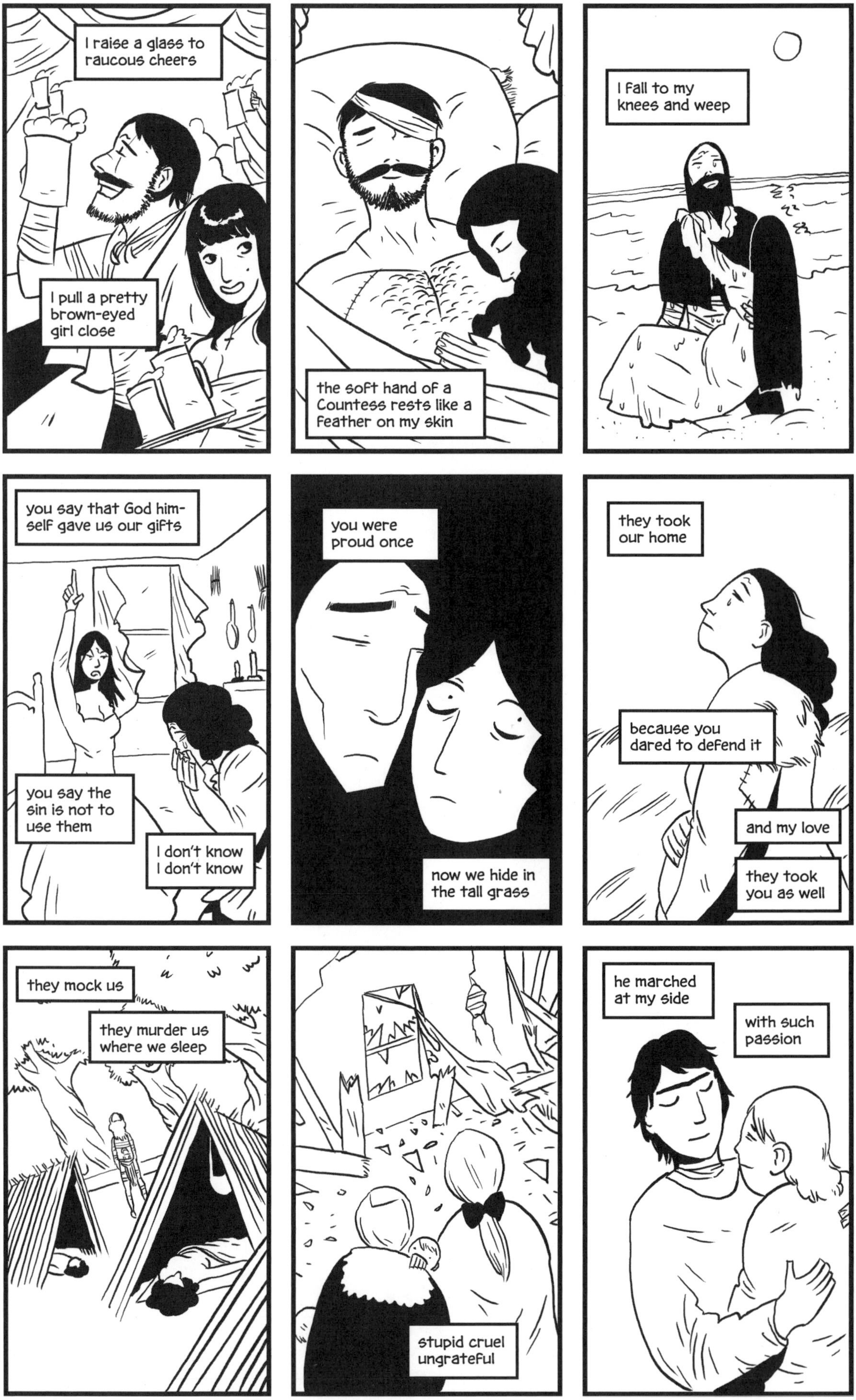
I raise a glass to raucous cheers
I pull a pretty brown-eyed girl close
the soft hand of a Countess rests like a feather on my skin
I fall to my knees and weep
you say that God him-self gave us our gifts
you say the sin is not to use them
I don't know I don't know
you were proud once
now we hide in the tall grass
they took our home
because you dared to defend it
and my love
they took you as well
they mock us
they murder us where we sleep
stupid cruel ungrateful
he marched at my side
with such passion

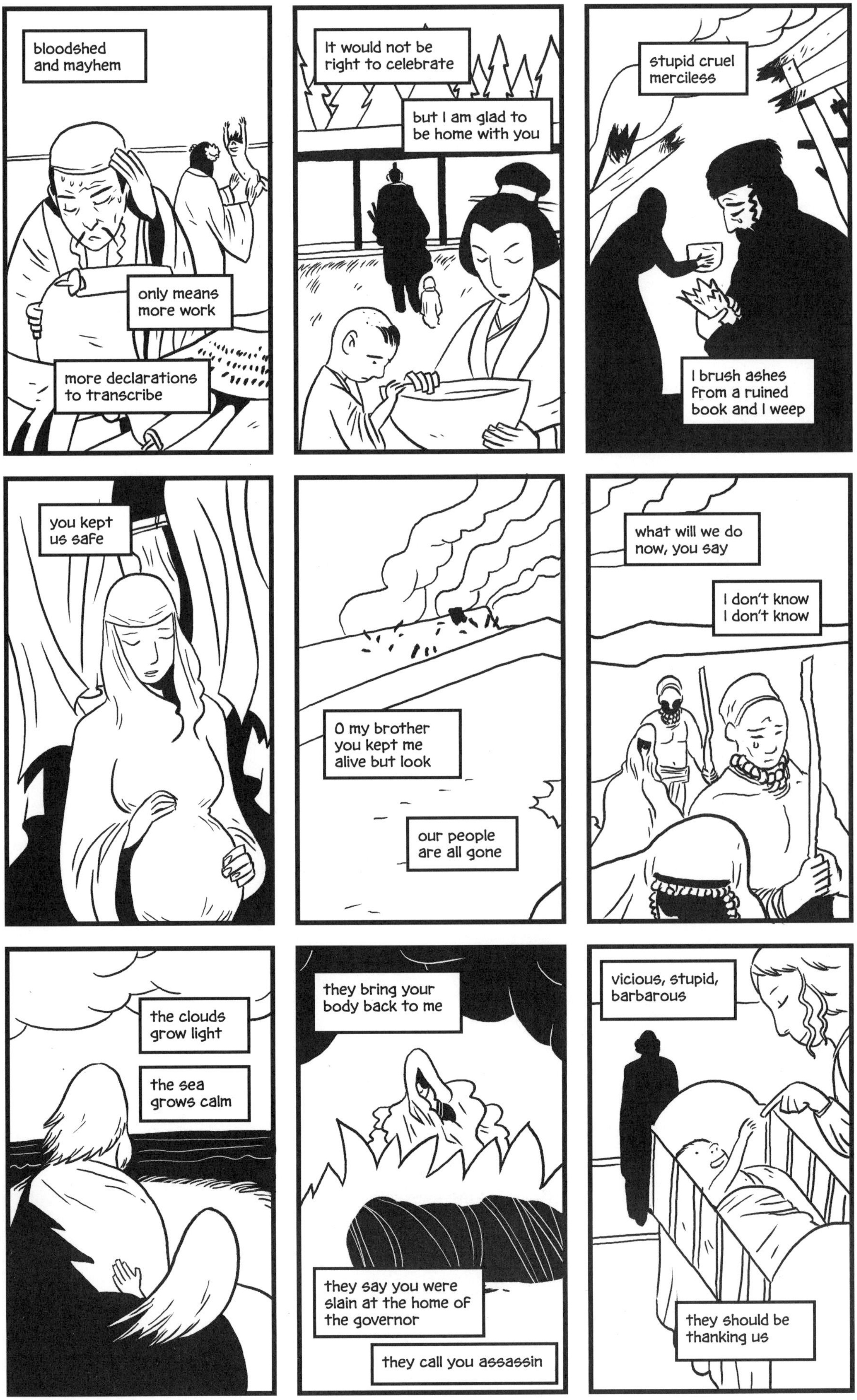
bloodshed
and mayhem
only means
more work
more declarations
to transcribe
It would not be
right to celebrate
but I am glad to
be home with you
stupid cruel
merciless
I brush ashes
from a ruined
book and I weep
you kept
us safe
O my brother
you kept me
alive but look
our people
are all gone
what will we do
now, you say
I don't know
I don't know
the clouds
grow light
the sea
grows calm
they bring your
body back to me
they say you were
slain at the home of
the governor
they call you assassin
vicious, stupid,
barbarous
they should be
thanking us

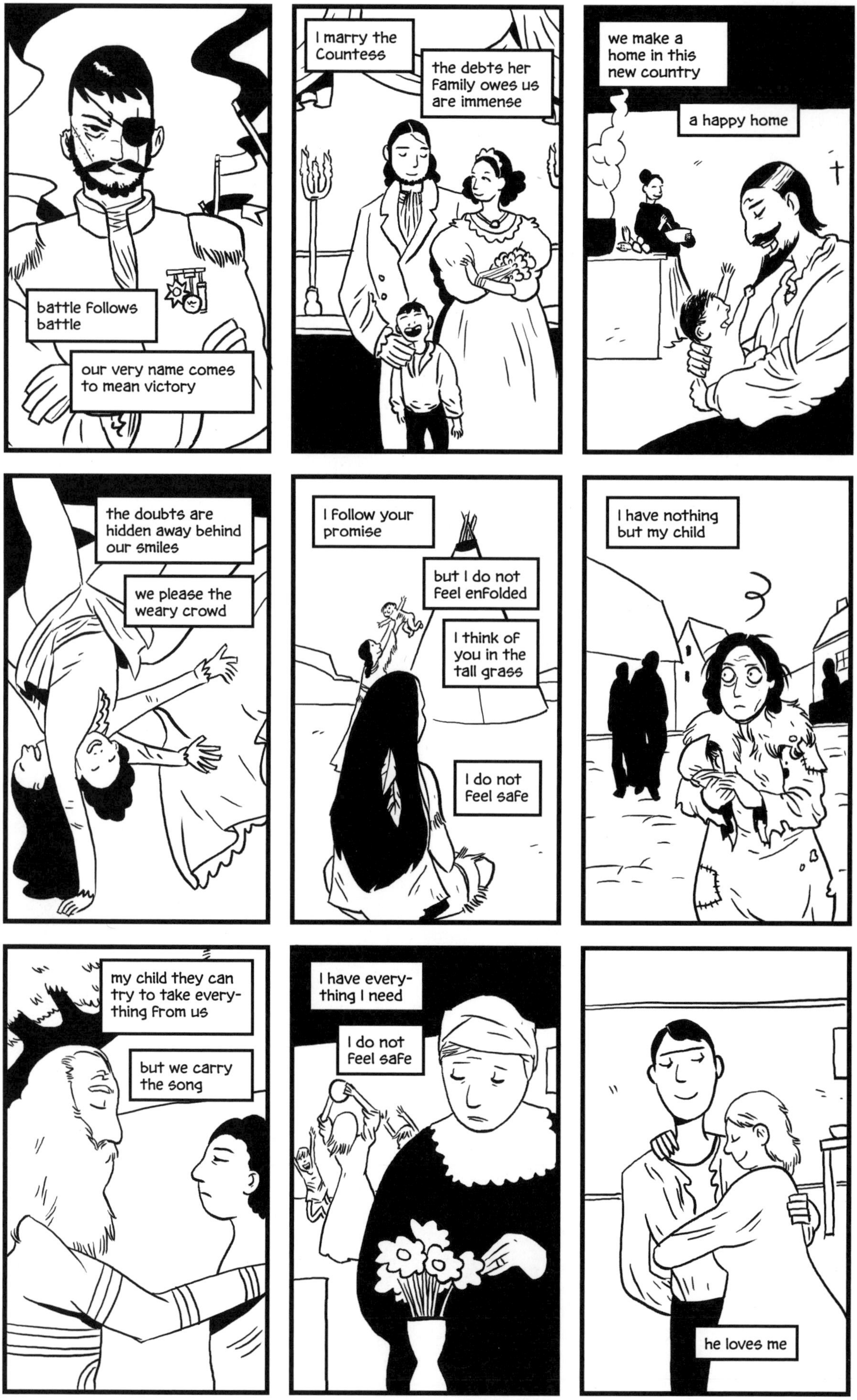
battle follows battle
our very name comes to mean victory
I marry the Countess
the debts her family owes us are immense
we make a home in this new country
a happy home
the doubts are hidden away behind our smiles
we please the weary crowd
I follow your promise
but I do not feel enfolded
I think of you in the tall grass
I do not feel safe
I have nothing but my child
my child they can try to take every-thing from us
but we carry the song
I have every-thing I need
I do not feel safe
he loves me

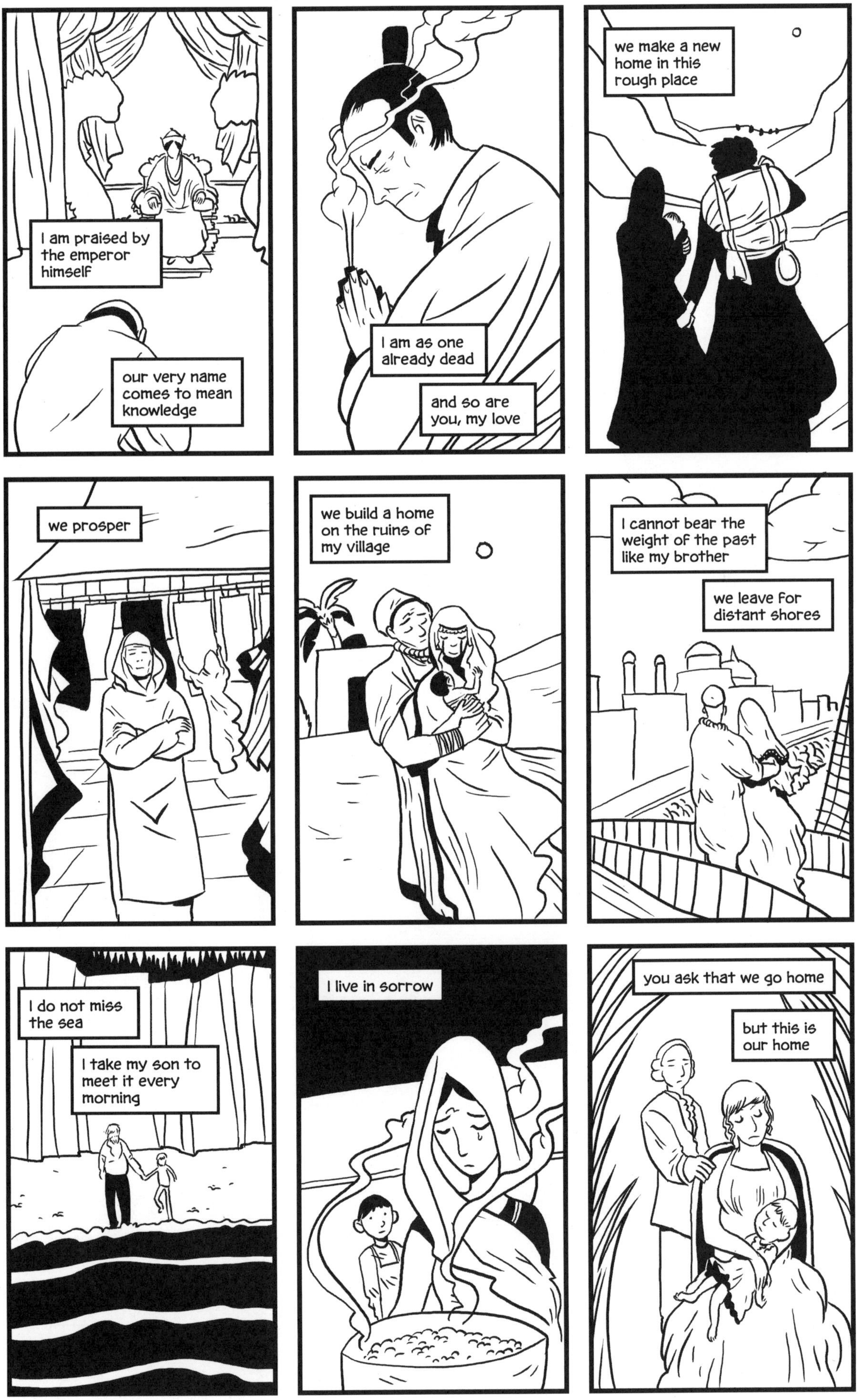
I am praised by the emperor himself
our very name comes to mean knowledge
I am as one already dead
and so are you, my love
we make a new home in this rough place
we prosper
we build a home on the ruins of my village
I cannot bear the weight of the past like my brother
we leave for distant shores
I do not miss the sea
I take my son to meet it every morning
I live in sorrow
you ask that we go home
but this is our home

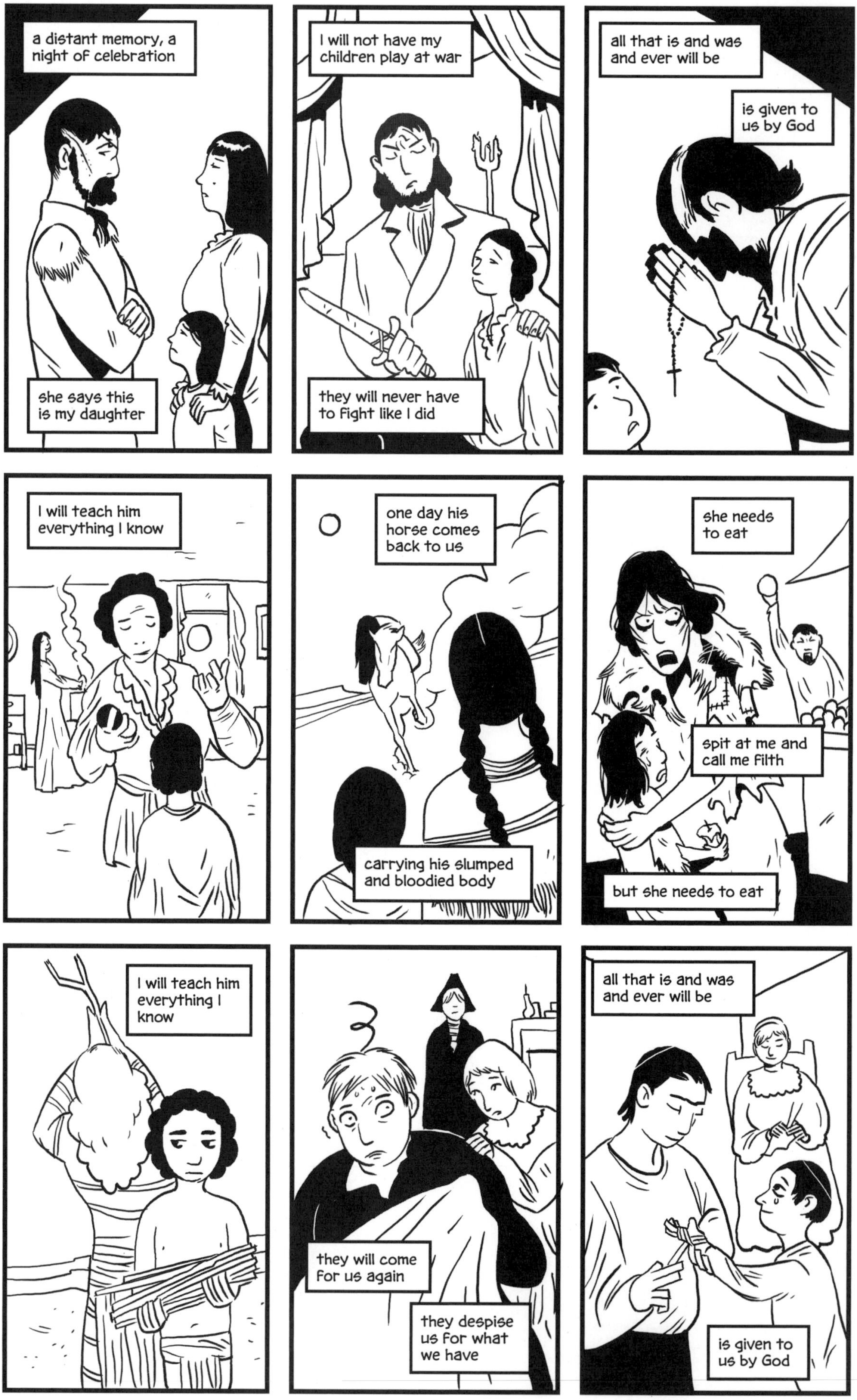
a distant memory, a night of celebration
she says this is my daughter
I will not have my children play at war
they will never have to fight like I did
all that is and was and ever will be
is given to us by God
I will teach him everything I know
one day his horse comes back to us
carrying his slumped and bloodied body
she needs to eat
spit at me and call me filth
but she needs to eat
I will teach him everything I know
they will come for us again
they despise us for what we have
all that is and was and ever will be
is given to us by God

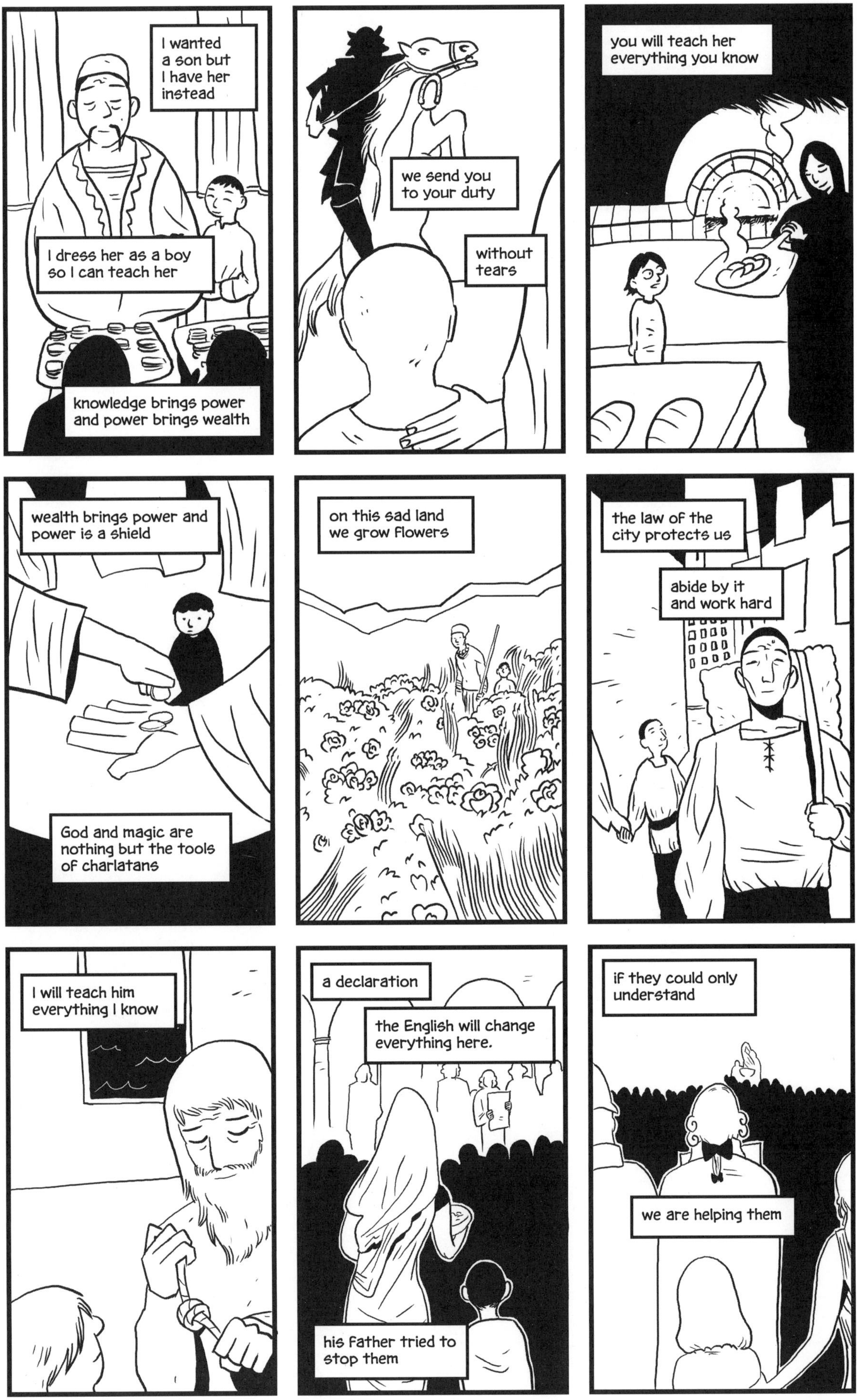
I wanted a son but I have her instead
I dress her as a boy so I can teach her
knowledge brings power and power brings wealth
we send you to your duty
without tears
you will teach her everything you know
wealth brings power and power is a shield
God and magic are nothing but the tools of charlatans
on this sad land we grow flowers
the law of the city protects us
abide by it and work hard
I will teach him everything I know
a declaration
the English will change everything here.
his father tried to stop them
if they could only understand
we are helping them

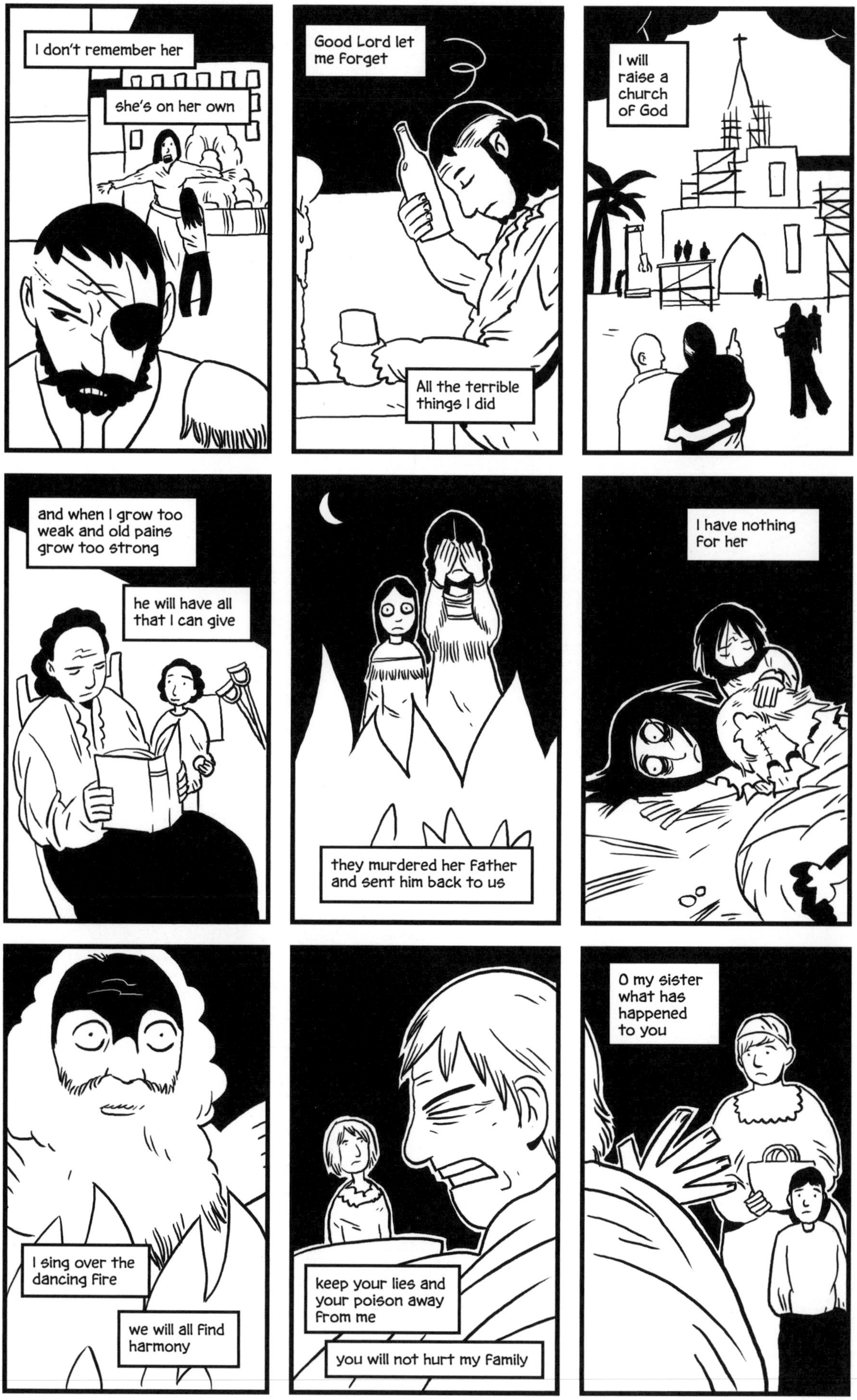
I don't remember her
she's on her own
Good Lord let me forget
All the terrible things I did
I will raise a church of God
and when I grow too weak and old pains grow too strong
he will have all that I can give
they murdered her father and sent him back to us
I have nothing for her
I sing over the dancing fire
we will all find harmony
keep your lies and your poison away from me
you will not hurt my family
O my sister what has happened to you

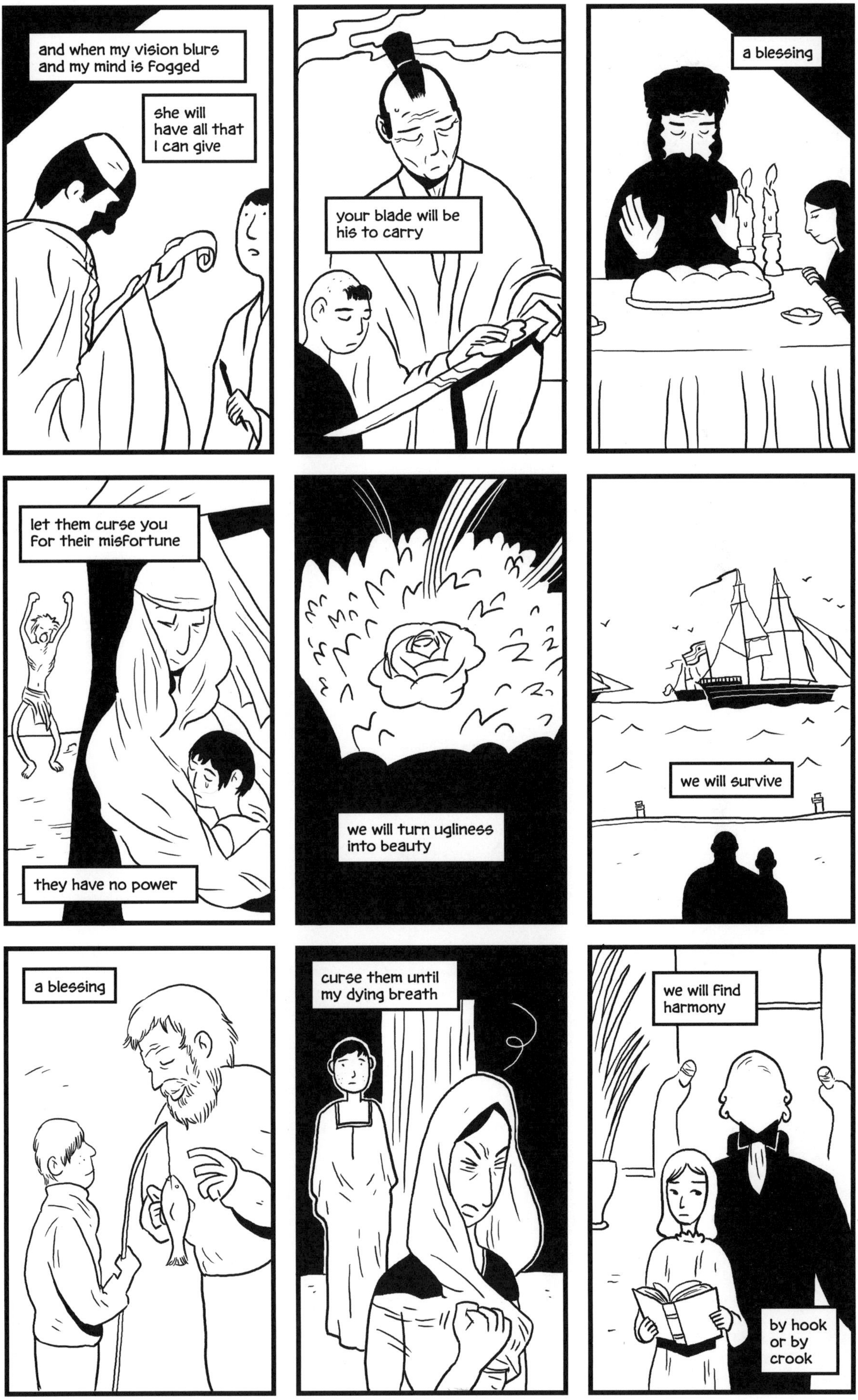
and when my vision blurs and my mind is fogged
she will have all that I can give
your blade will be his to carry
a blessing
let them curse you for their misfortune
they have no power
we will turn ugliness into beauty
we will survive
a blessing
curse them until my dying breath
we will find harmony
by hook or by crook

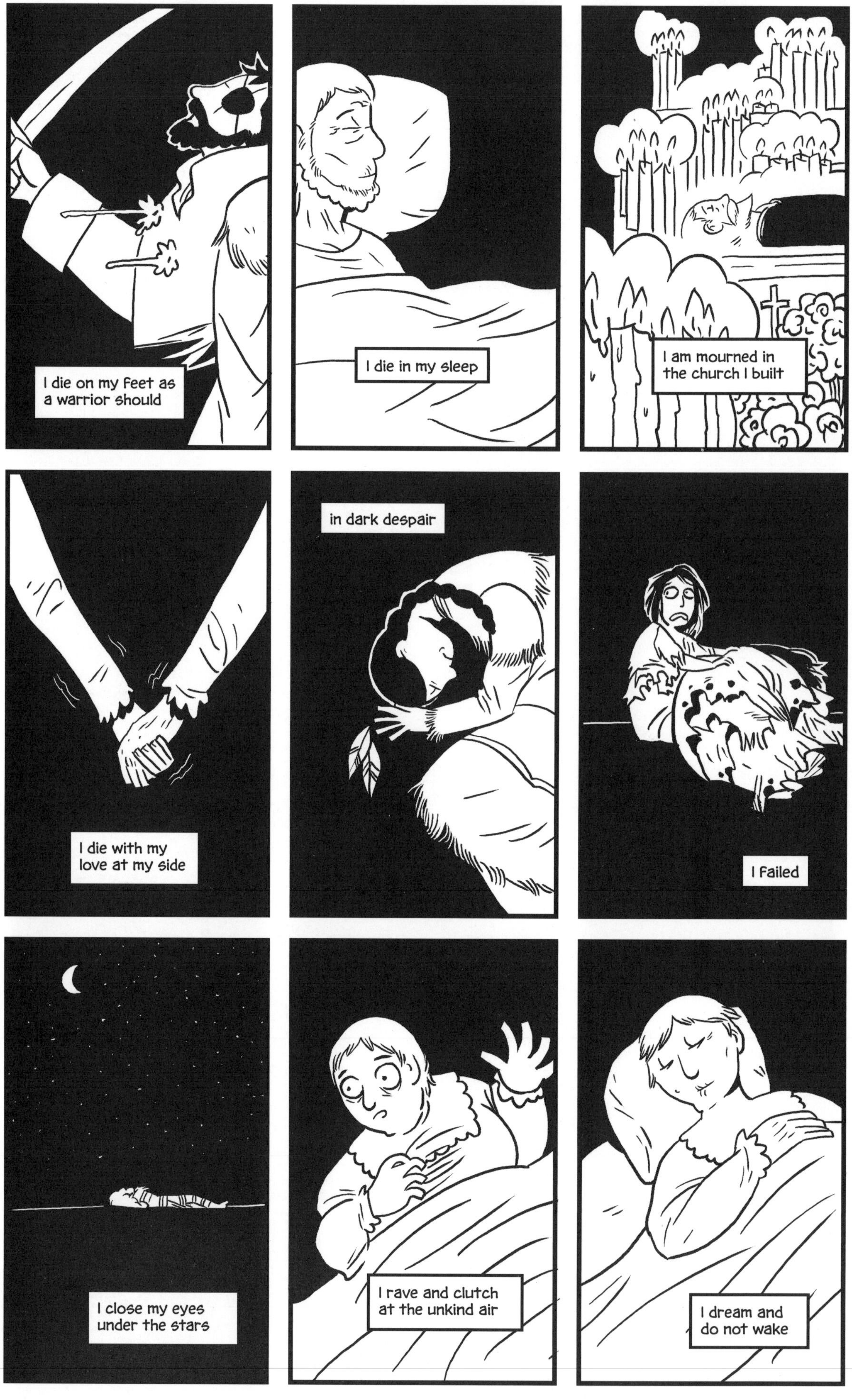
I die on my feet as a warrior should
I die in my sleep
I am mourned in the church I built
I die with my love at my side
in dark despair
I failed
I close my eyes under the stars
I rave and clutch at the unkind air
I dream and do not wake

I am mourned as befits my station

I meet my death with honor

I die in fever and pain

suddenly

my last wish was to see my brother

my brother is not here

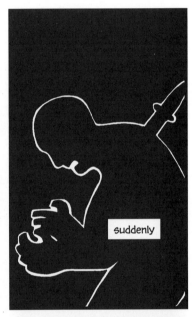

suddenly

one day the sea blackens and tilts

one day I stumble and cannot rise

I failed

PART TWO

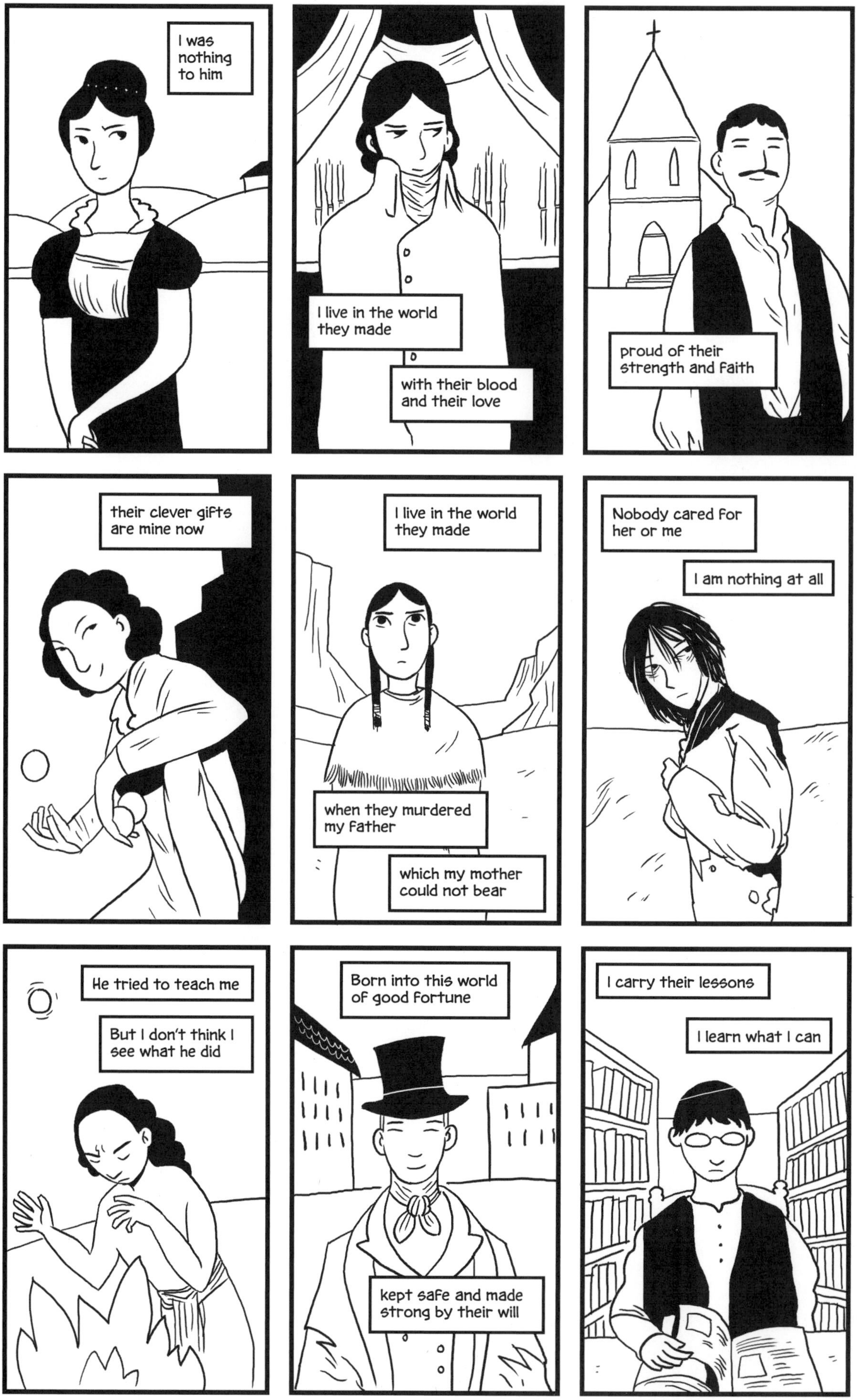
I was nothing to him
I live in the world they made
with their blood and their love
proud of their strength and faith
their clever gifts are mine now
I live in the world they made
when they murdered my father
which my mother could not bear
Nobody cared for her or me
I am nothing at all
He tried to teach me
But I don't think I see what he did
Born into this world of good fortune
kept safe and made strong by their will
I carry their lessons
I learn what I can

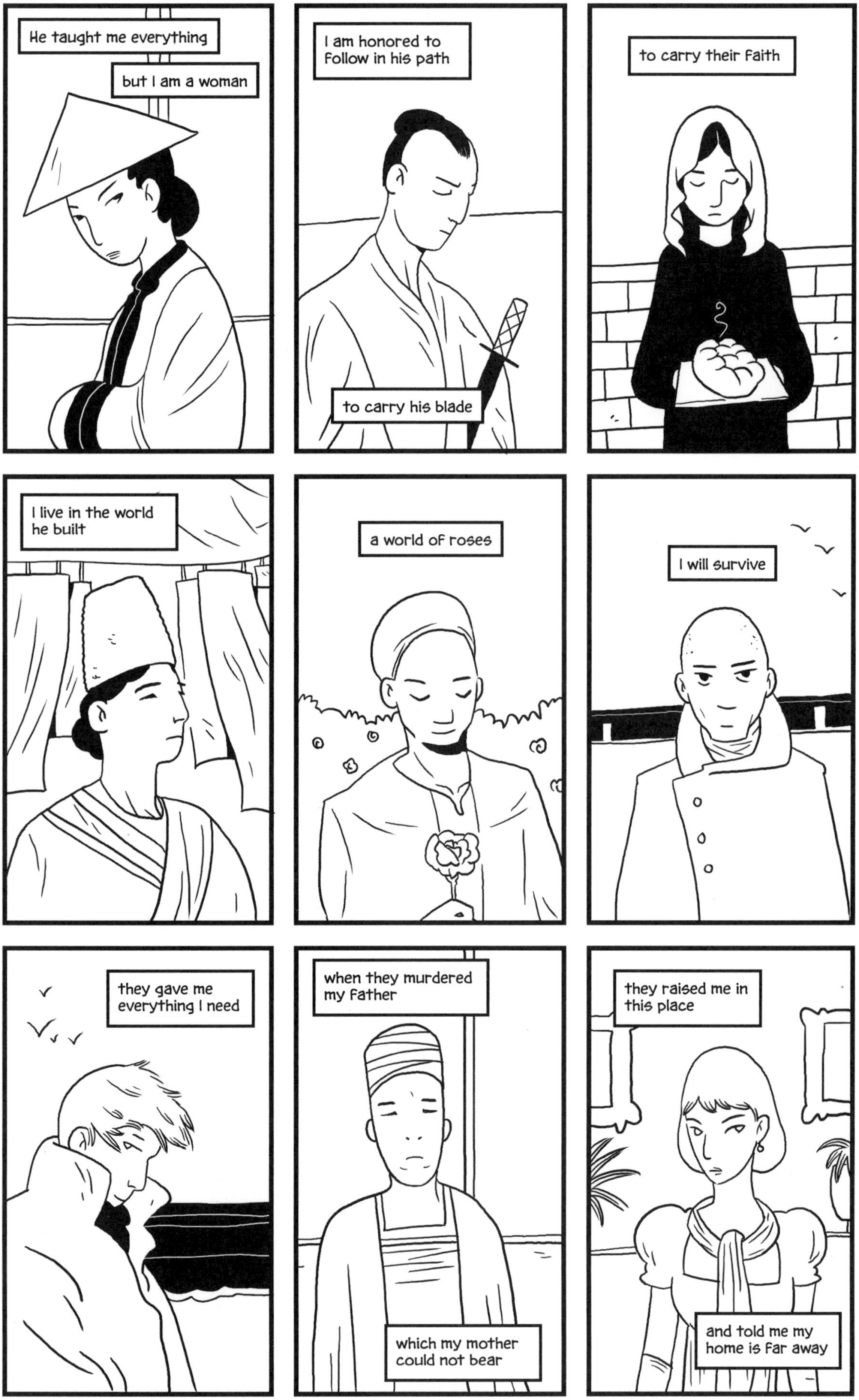
He taught me everything
but I am a woman
I am honored to follow in his path
to carry his blade
to carry their faith
I live in the world he built
a world of roses
I will survive
they gave me everything I need
when they murdered my father
which my mother could not bear
they raised me in this place
and told me my home is far away

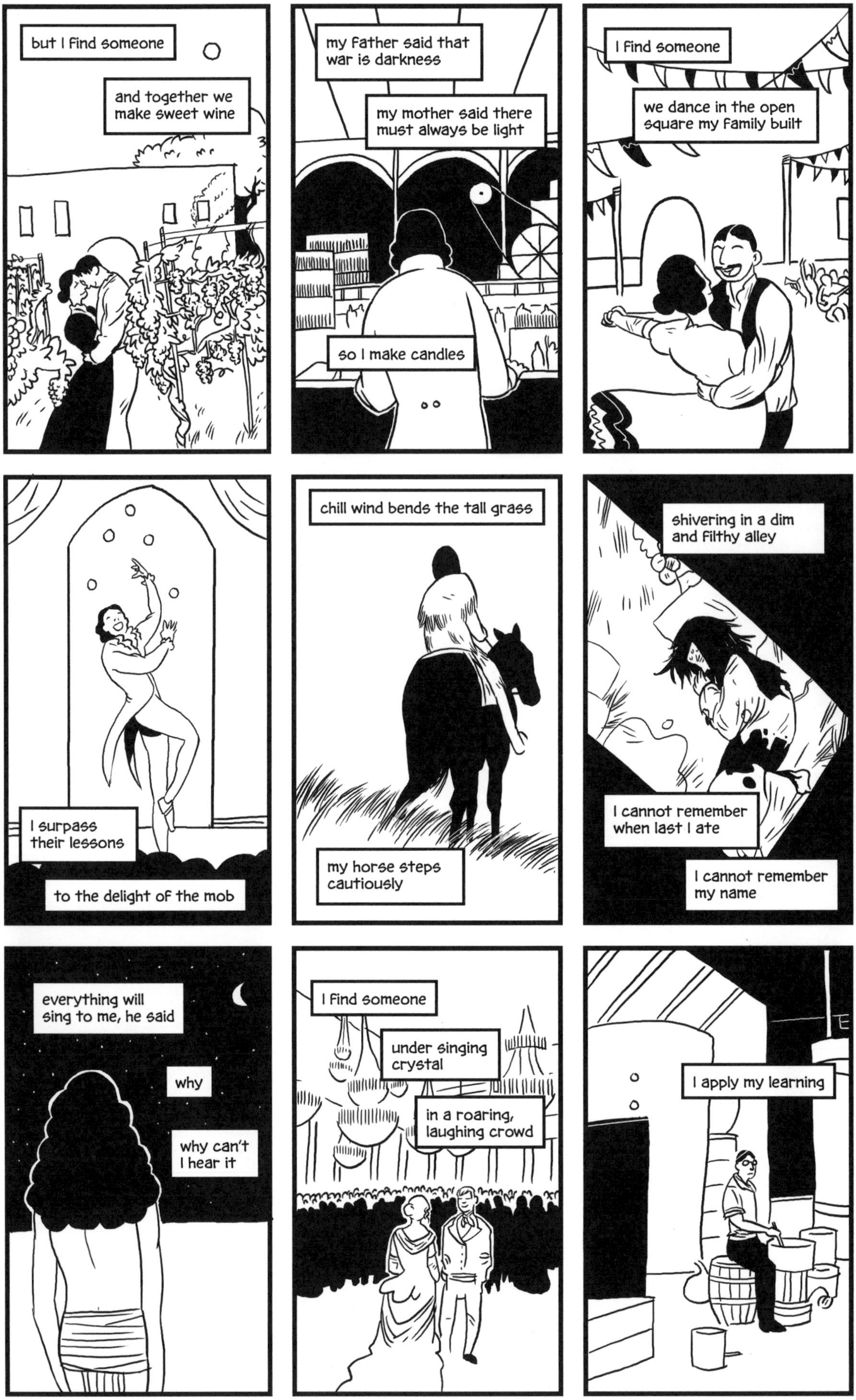
but I find someone
and together we make sweet wine
my father said that war is darkness
my mother said there must always be light
so I make candles
I find someone
we dance in the open square my family built
I surpass their lessons
to the delight of the mob
chill wind bends the tall grass
my horse steps cautiously
shivering in a dim and filthy alley
I cannot remember when last I ate
I cannot remember my name
everything will sing to me, he said
why
why can't I hear it
I find someone
under singing crystal
in a roaring, laughing crowd
I apply my learning

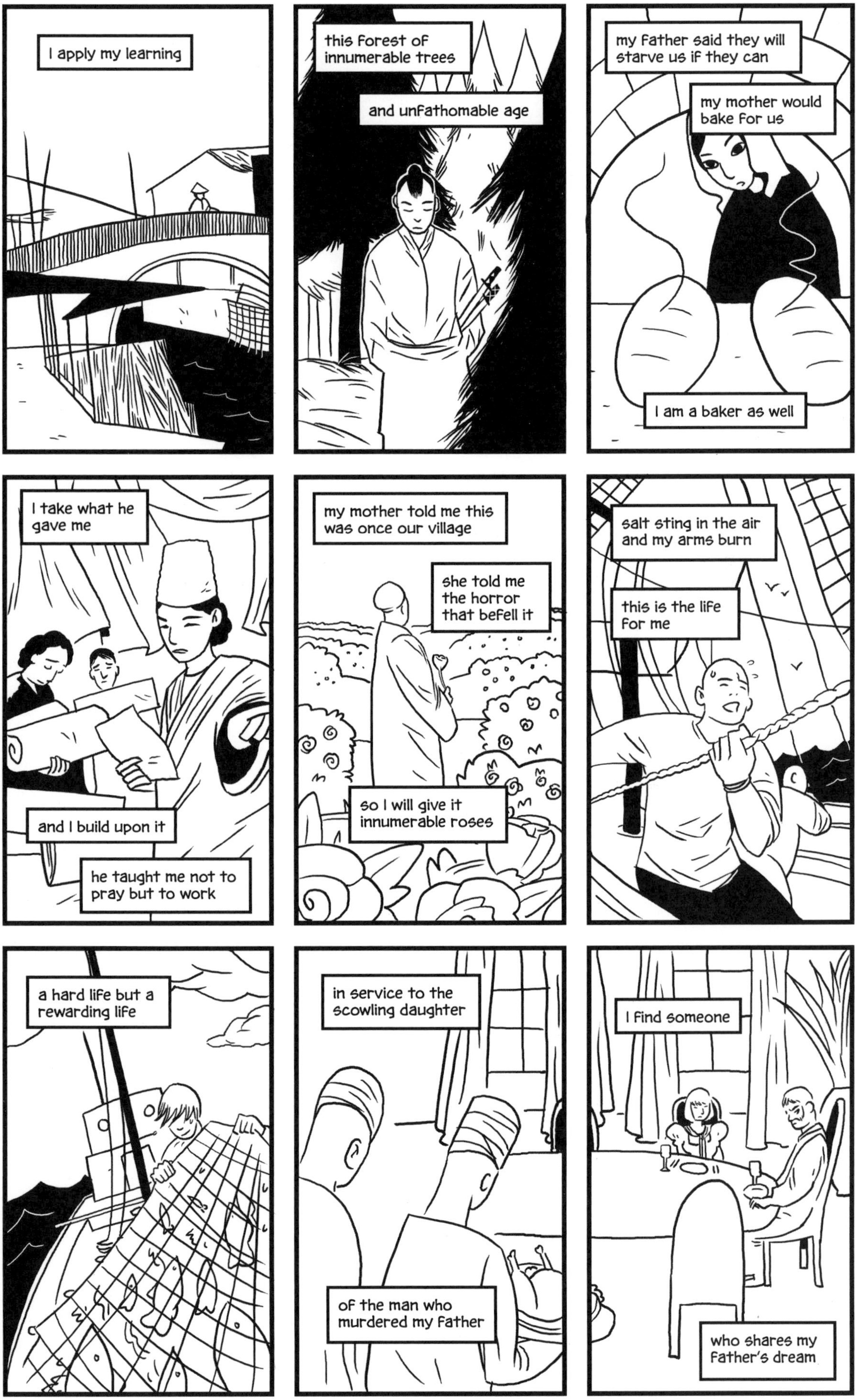
I apply my learning
this forest of innumerable trees
and unfathomable age
my father said they will starve us if they can
my mother would bake for us
I am a baker as well
I take what he gave me
and I build upon it
he taught me not to pray but to work
my mother told me this was once our village
she told me the horror that befell it
so I will give it innumerable roses
salt sting in the air and my arms burn
this is the life for me
a hard life but a rewarding life
in service to the scowling daughter
of the man who murdered my father
I find someone
who shares my father's dream

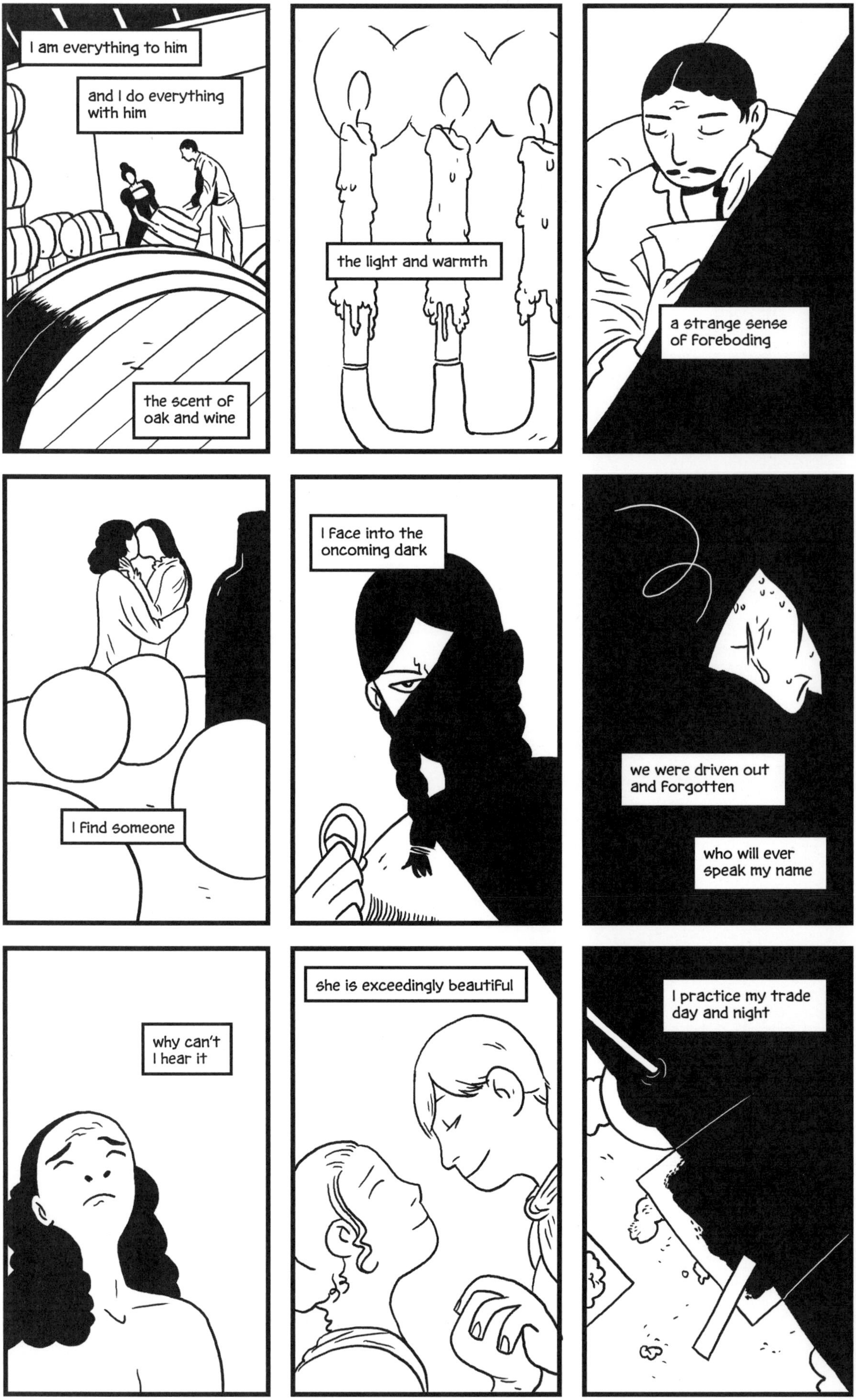
I am everything to him
and I do everything with him
the scent of oak and wine
the light and warmth
a strange sense of foreboding
I find someone
I face into the oncoming dark
we were driven out and forgotten
who will ever speak my name
why can't I hear it
she is exceedingly beautiful
I practice my trade day and night

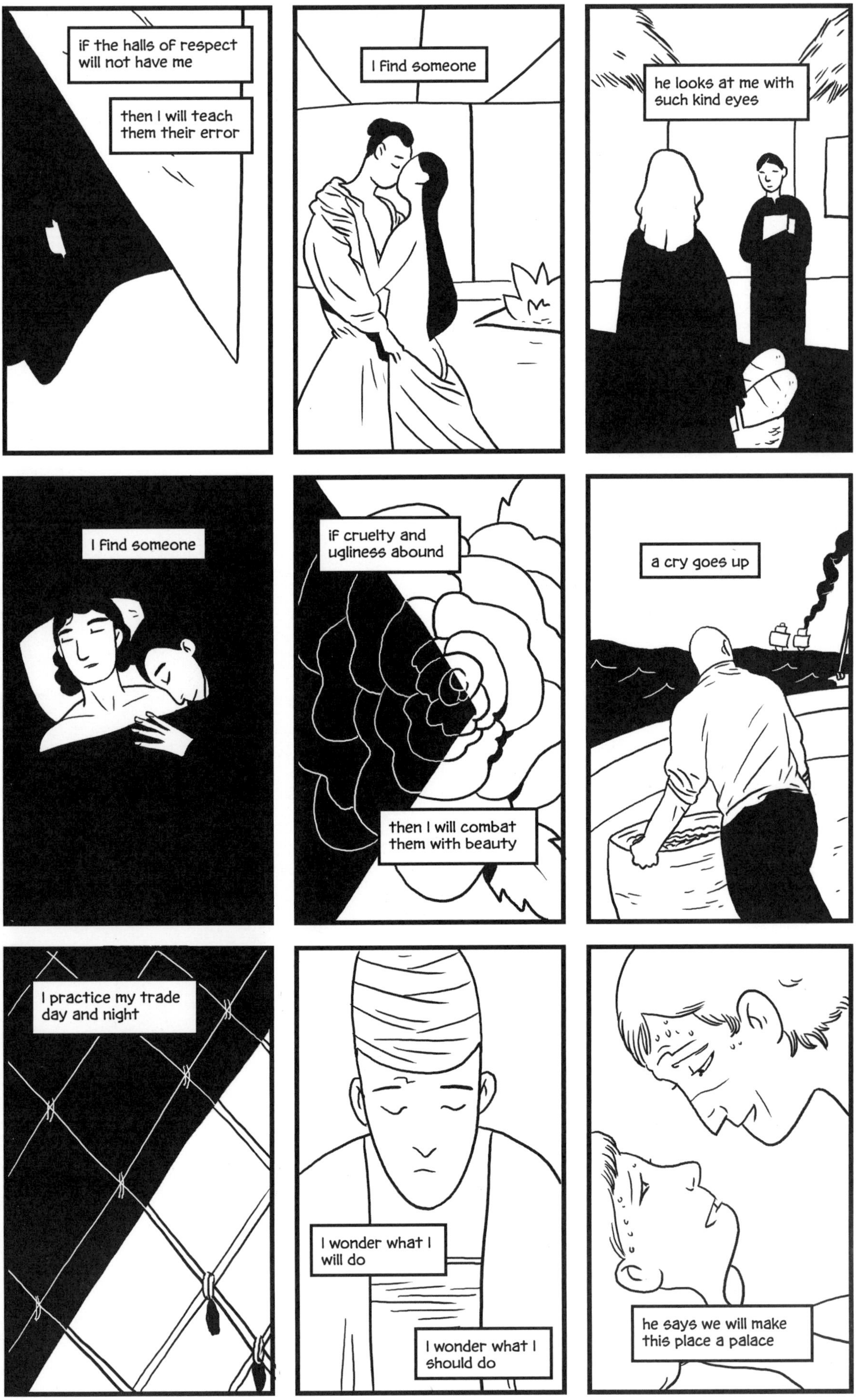
if the halls of respect will not have me
then I will teach them their error
I find someone
he looks at me with such kind eyes
I find someone
if cruelty and ugliness abound
then I will combat them with beauty
a cry goes up
I practice my trade day and night
I wonder what I will do
I wonder what I should do
he says we will make this place a palace

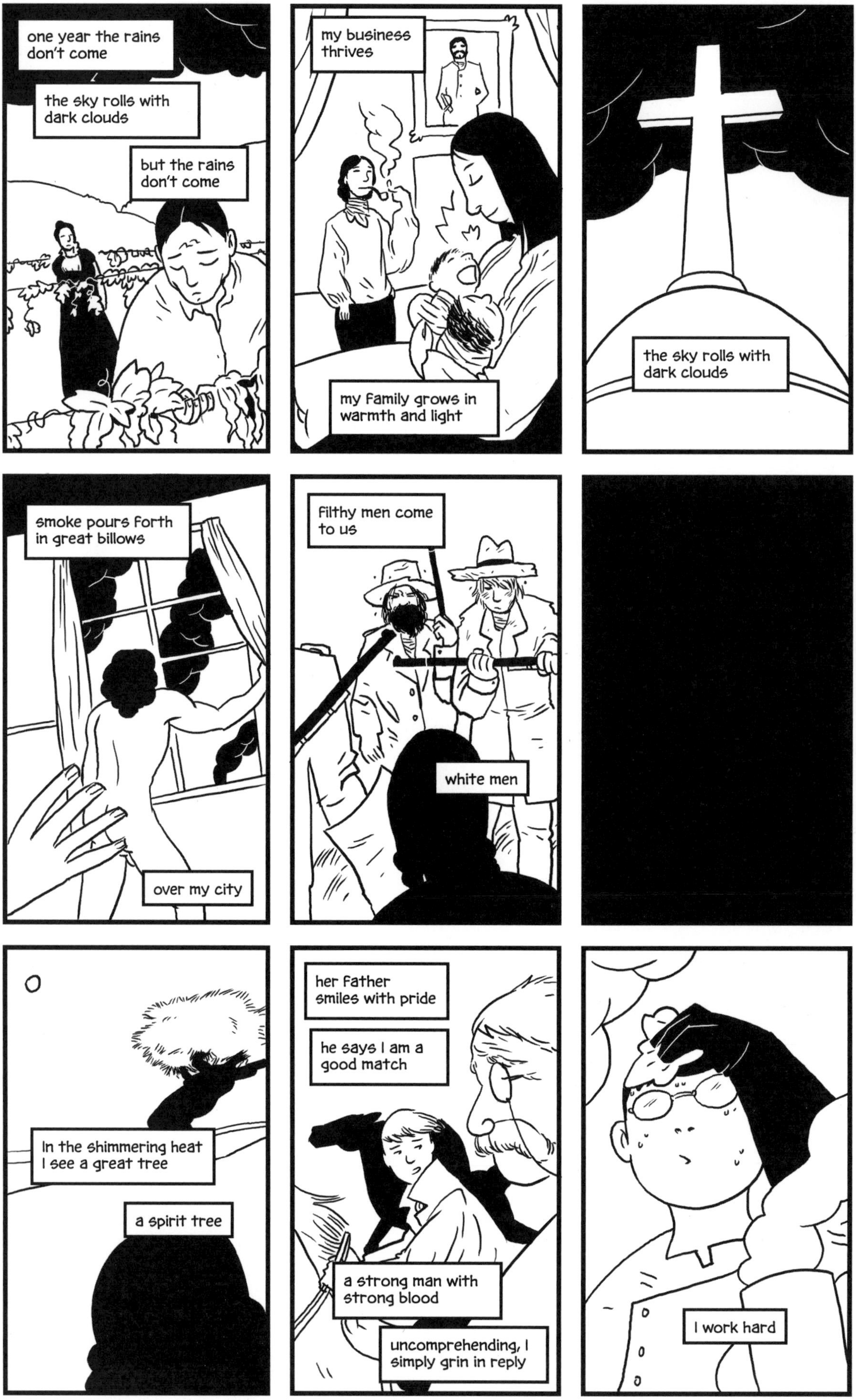
one year the rains don't come
the sky rolls with dark clouds
but the rains don't come
my business thrives
my family grows in warmth and light
the sky rolls with dark clouds
smoke pours forth in great billows
over my city
filthy men come to us
white men
In the shimmering heat I see a great tree
a spirit tree
her father smiles with pride
he says I am a good match
a strong man with strong blood
uncomprehending, I simply grin in reply
I work hard

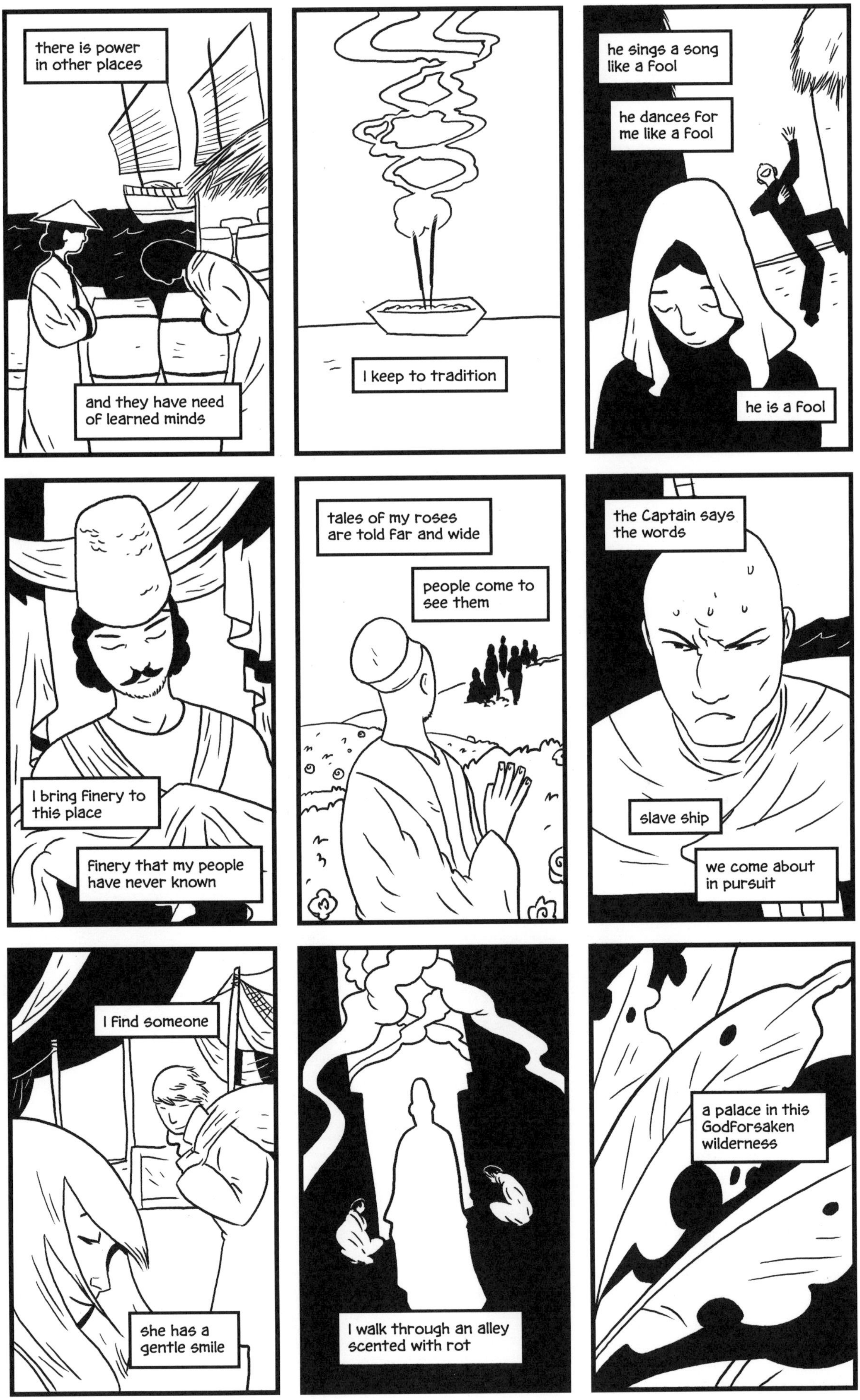
there is power in other places
and they have need of learned minds
I keep to tradition
he sings a song like a fool
he dances for me like a fool
he is a fool
I bring finery to this place
finery that my people have never known
tales of my roses are told far and wide
people come to see them
the Captain says the words
slave ship
we come about in pursuit
I find someone
she has a gentle smile
I walk through an alley scented with rot
a palace in this Godforsaken wilderness

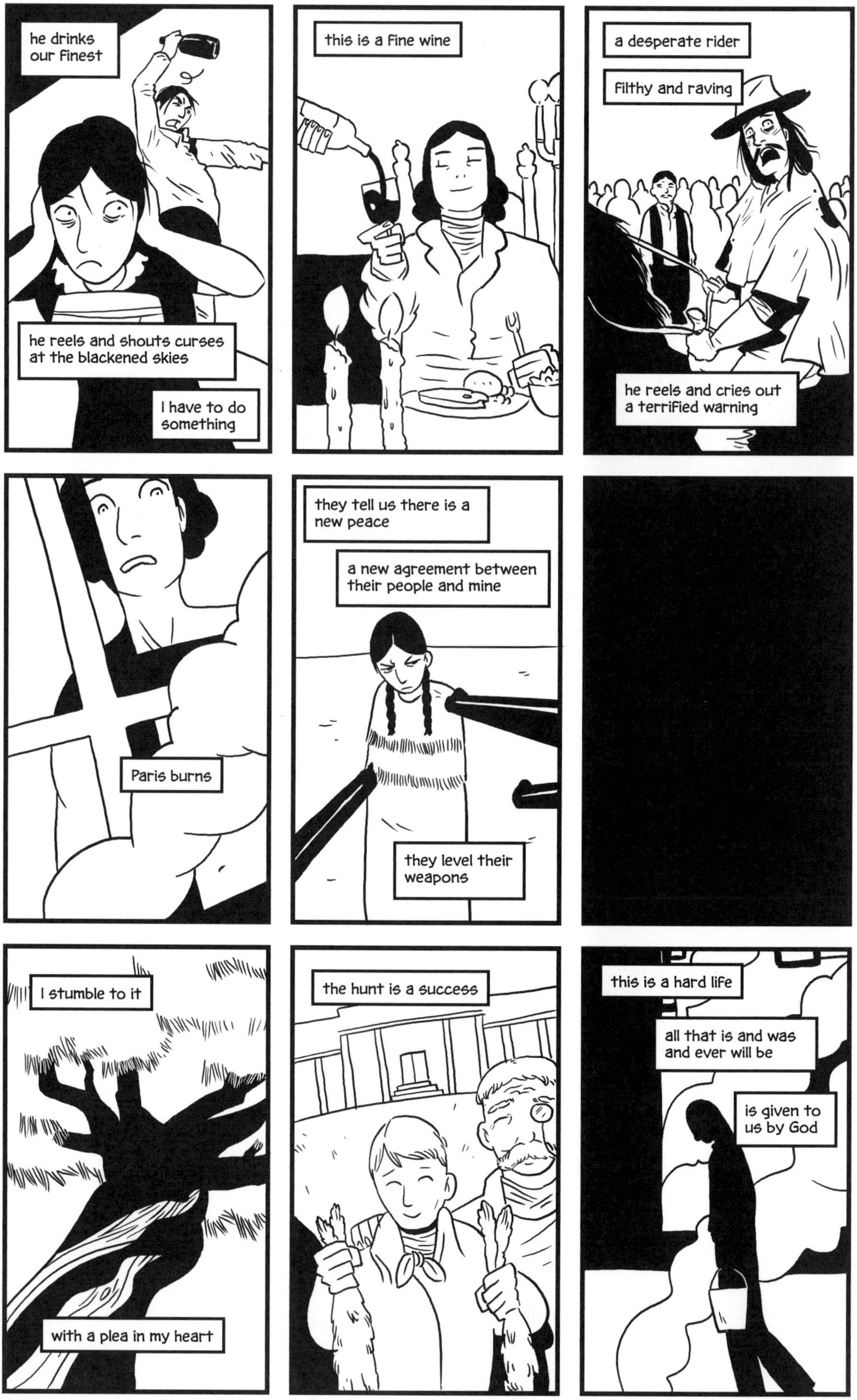
he drinks our finest
he reels and shouts curses at the blackened skies
I have to do something
this is a fine wine
a desperate rider
filthy and raving
he reels and cries out a terrified warning
Paris burns
they tell us there is a new peace
a new agreement between their people and mine
they level their weapons
I stumble to it
with a plea in my heart
the hunt is a success
this is a hard life
all that is and was and ever will be
is given to us by God

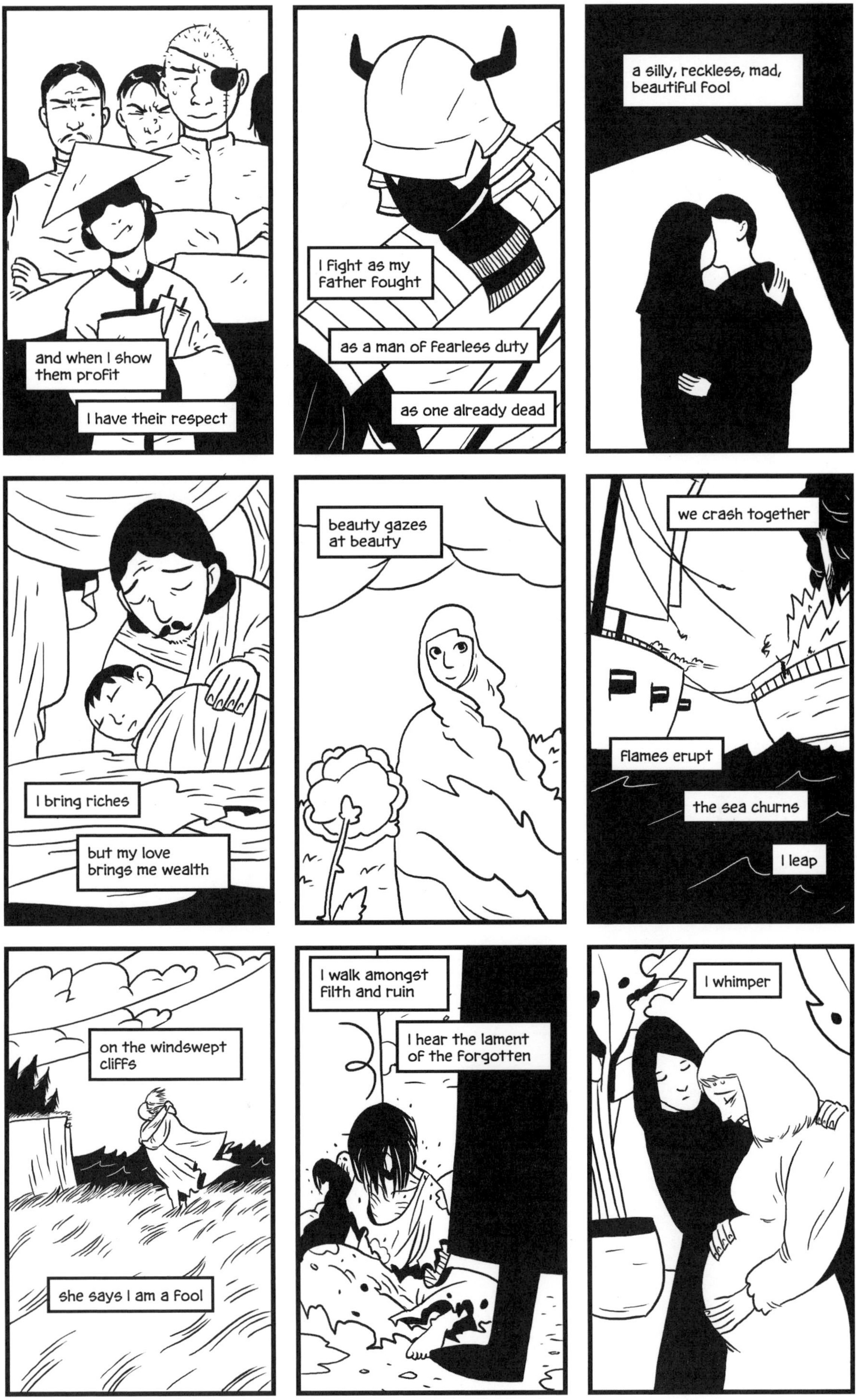

and when I show them profit
I have their respect
I fight as my father fought
as a man of fearless duty
as one already dead
a silly, reckless, mad, beautiful fool
I bring riches
but my love brings me wealth
beauty gazes at beauty
we crash together
flames erupt
the sea churns
I leap
on the windswept cliffs
she says I am a fool
I walk amongst filth and ruin
I hear the lament of the forgotten
I whimper

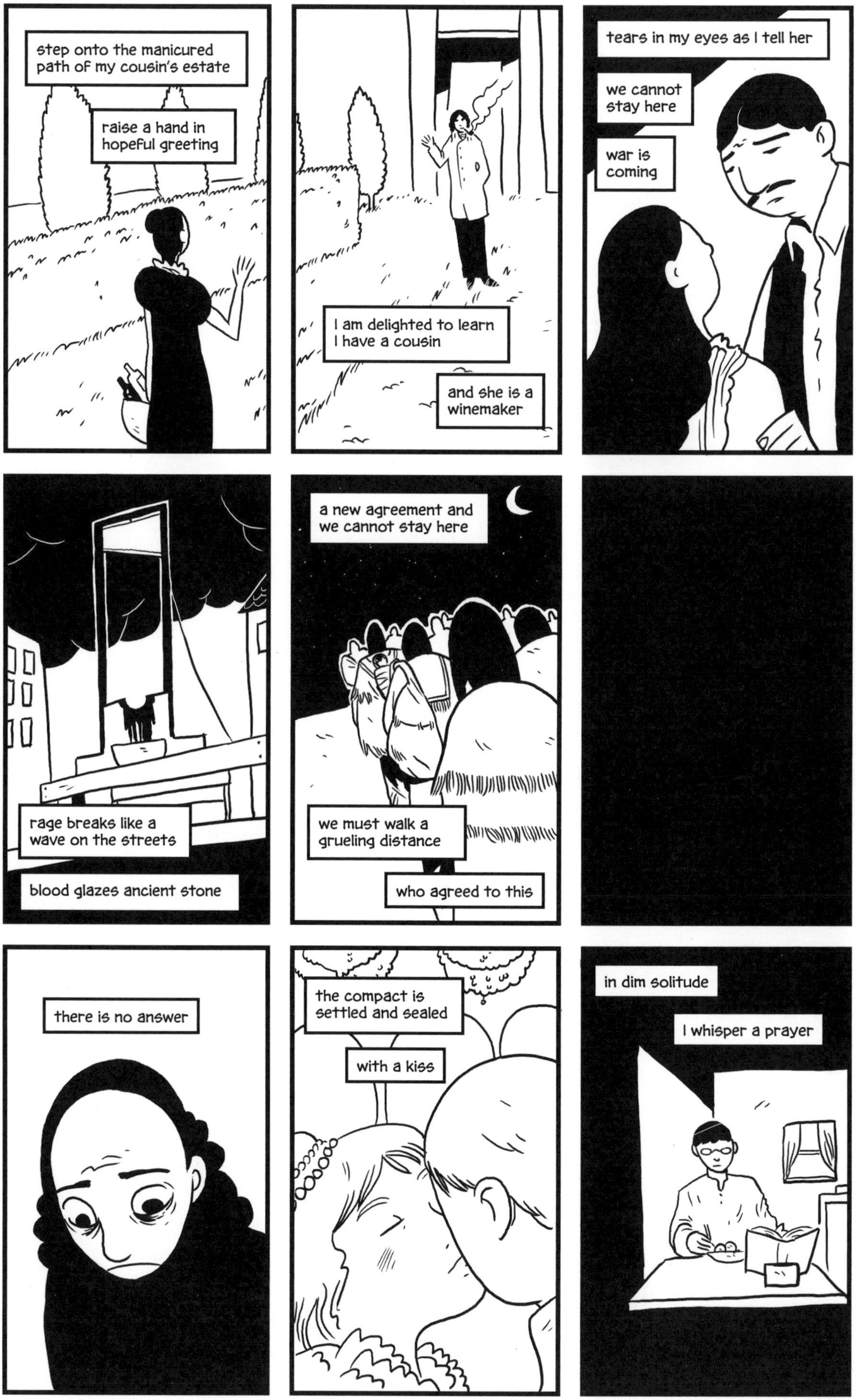
step onto the manicured path of my cousin's estate
raise a hand in hopeful greeting
I am delighted to learn I have a cousin
and she is a winemaker
tears in my eyes as I tell her
we cannot stay here
war is coming
rage breaks like a wave on the streets
blood glazes ancient stone
a new agreement and we cannot stay here
we must walk a grueling distance
who agreed to this
there is no answer
the compact is settled and sealed
with a kiss
in dim solitude
I whisper a prayer

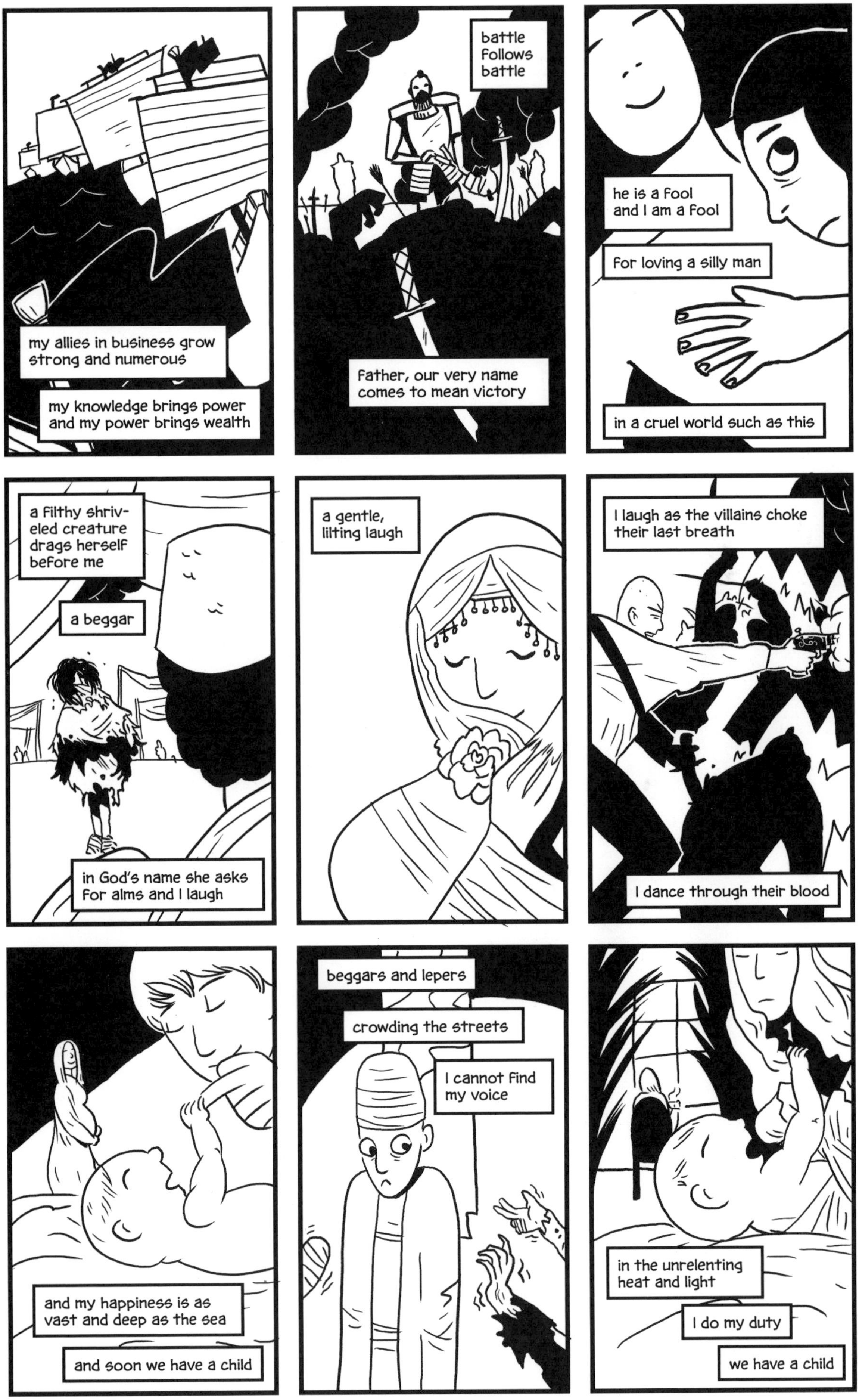
my allies in business grow strong and numerous
my knowledge brings power and my power brings wealth
battle follows battle
Father, our very name comes to mean victory
he is a fool and I am a fool
for loving a silly man
in a cruel world such as this
a filthy shriveled creature drags herself before me
a beggar
in God's name she asks for alms and I laugh
a gentle, lilting laugh
I laugh as the villains choke their last breath
I dance through their blood
and my happiness is as vast and deep as the sea
and soon we have a child
beggars and lepers
crowding the streets
I cannot find my voice
in the unrelenting heat and light
I do my duty
we have a child

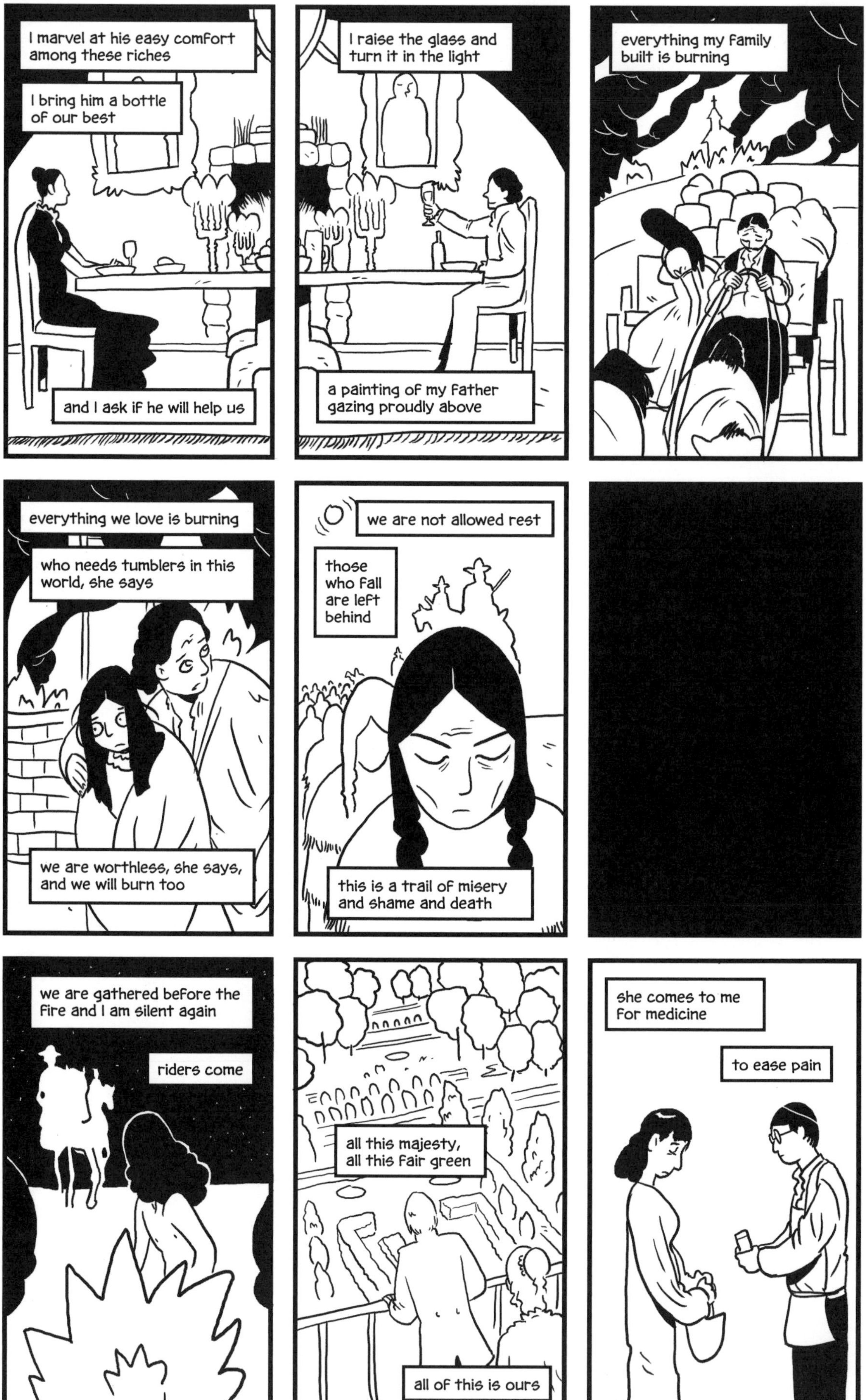
I marvel at his easy comfort among these riches
I bring him a bottle of our best
and I ask if he will help us
I raise the glass and turn it in the light
a painting of my father gazing proudly above
everything my family built is burning
everything we love is burning
who needs tumblers in this world, she says
we are worthless, she says, and we will burn too
we are not allowed rest
those who fall are left behind
this is a trail of misery and shame and death
we are gathered before the fire and I am silent again
riders come
all this majesty, all this fair green
all of this is ours
she comes to me for medicine
to ease pain

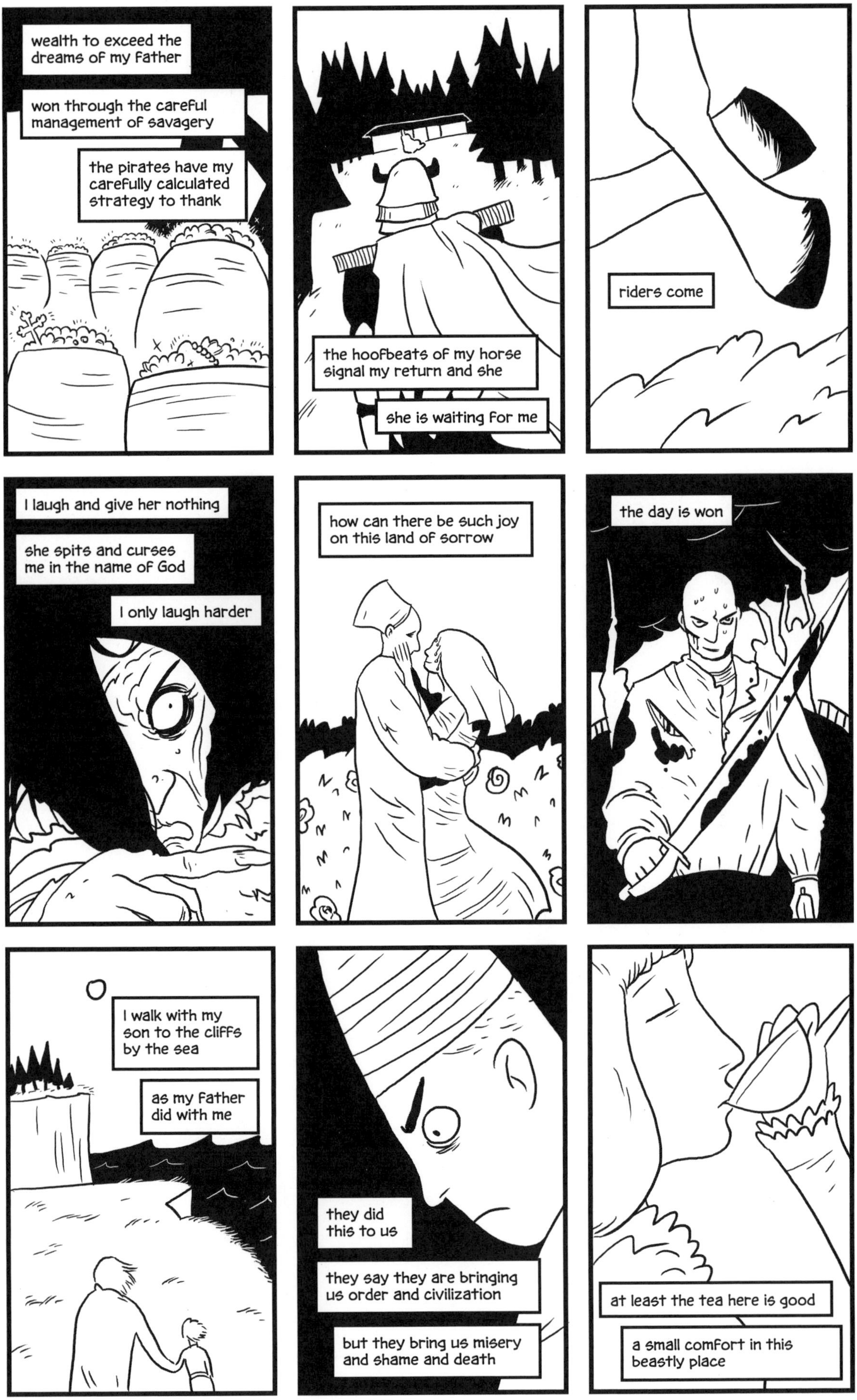
wealth to exceed the dreams of my father
won through the careful management of savagery
the pirates have my carefully calculated strategy to thank
the hoofbeats of my horse signal my return and she
she is waiting for me
riders come
I laugh and give her nothing
she spits and curses me in the name of God
I only laugh harder
how can there be such joy on this land of sorrow
the day is won
I walk with my son to the cliffs by the sea
as my father did with me
they did this to us
they say they are bringing us order and civilization
but they bring us misery and shame and death
at least the tea here is good
a small comfort in this beastly place

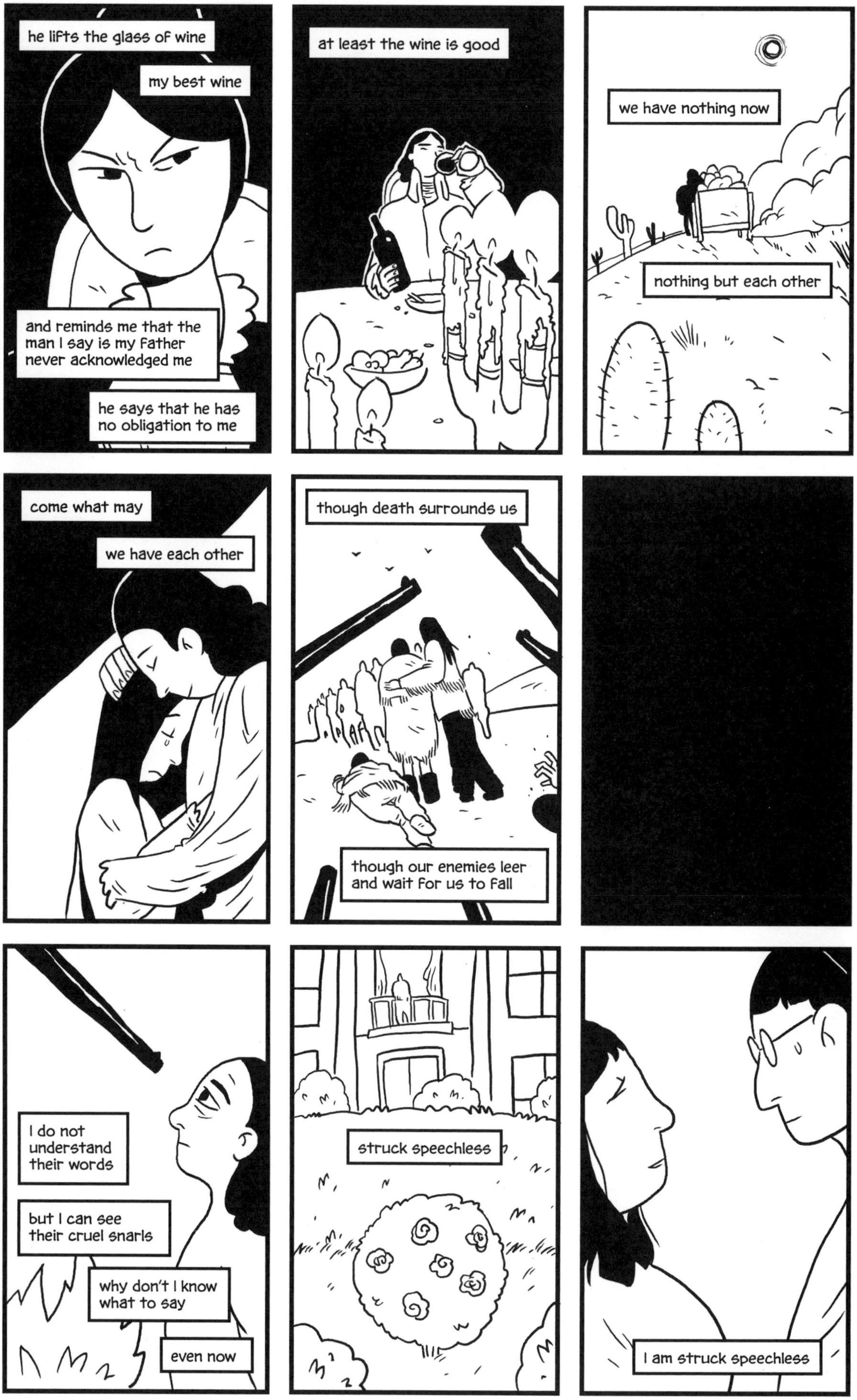
he lifts the glass of wine
my best wine
and reminds me that the man I say is my father never acknowledged me
he says that he has no obligation to me
at least the wine is good
we have nothing now
nothing but each other
come what may
we have each other
though death surrounds us
though our enemies leer and wait for us to fall
I do not understand their words
but I can see their cruel snarls
why don't I know what to say
even now
struck speechless
I am struck speechless

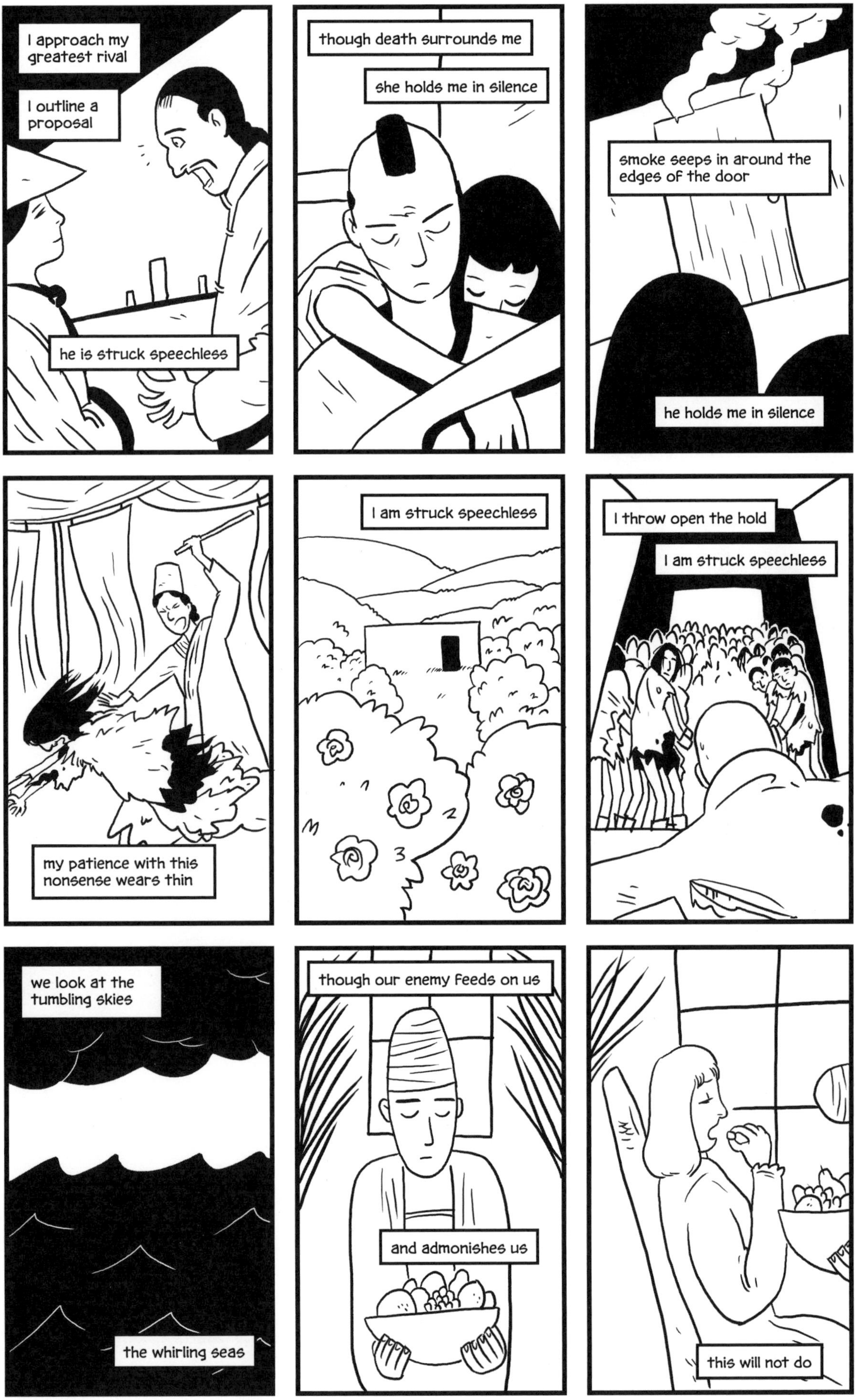
I approach my greatest rival
I outline a proposal
he is struck speechless
though death surrounds me
she holds me in silence
smoke seeps in around the edges of the door
he holds me in silence
my patience with this nonsense wears thin
I am struck speechless
I throw open the hold
I am struck speechless
we look at the tumbling skies
the whirling seas
though our enemy feeds on us
and admonishes us
this will not do

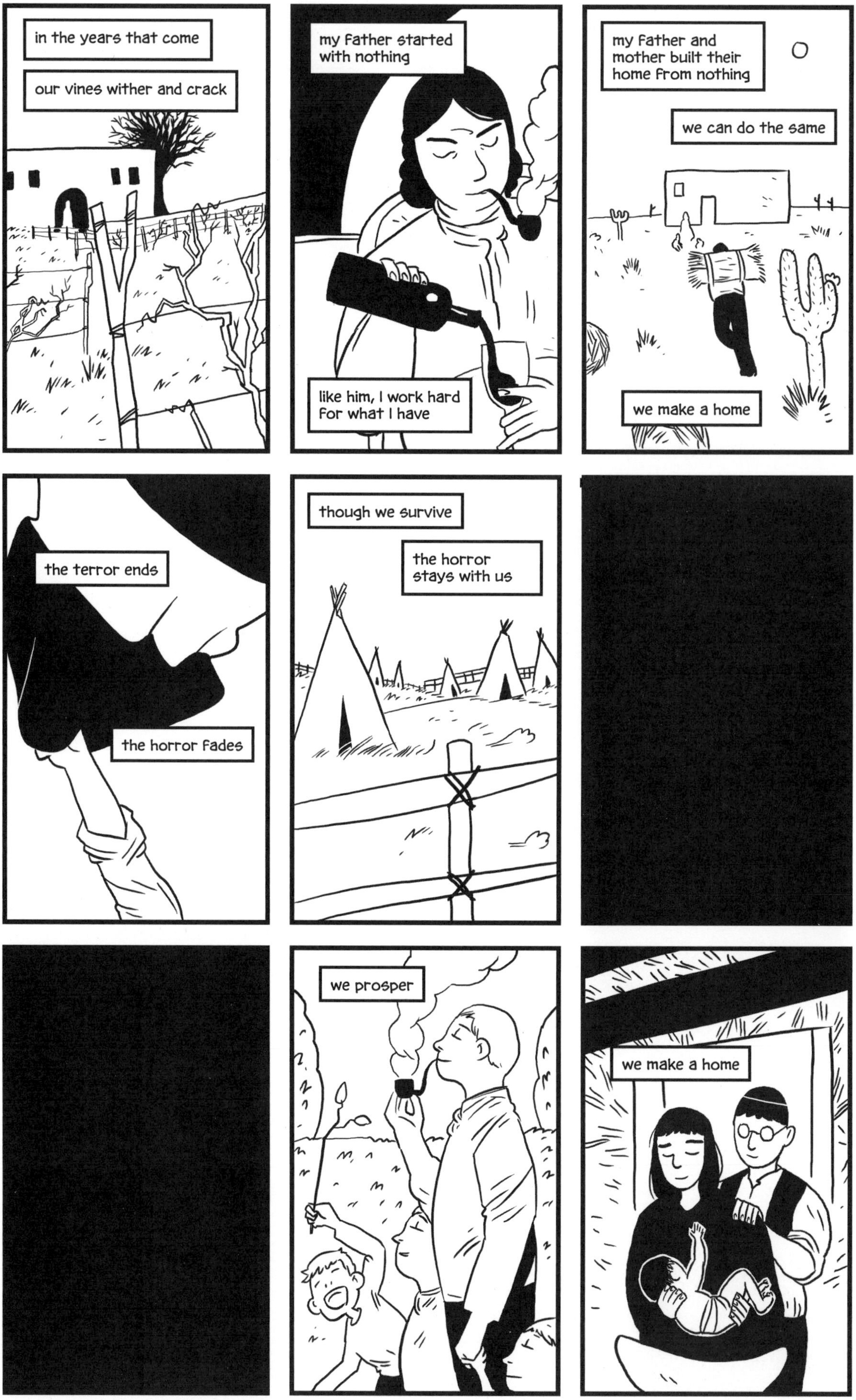
in the years that come
our vines wither and crack
my father started with nothing
like him, I work hard for what I have
my father and mother built their home from nothing
we can do the same
we make a home
the terror ends
the horror fades
though we survive
the horror stays with us
we prosper
we make a home

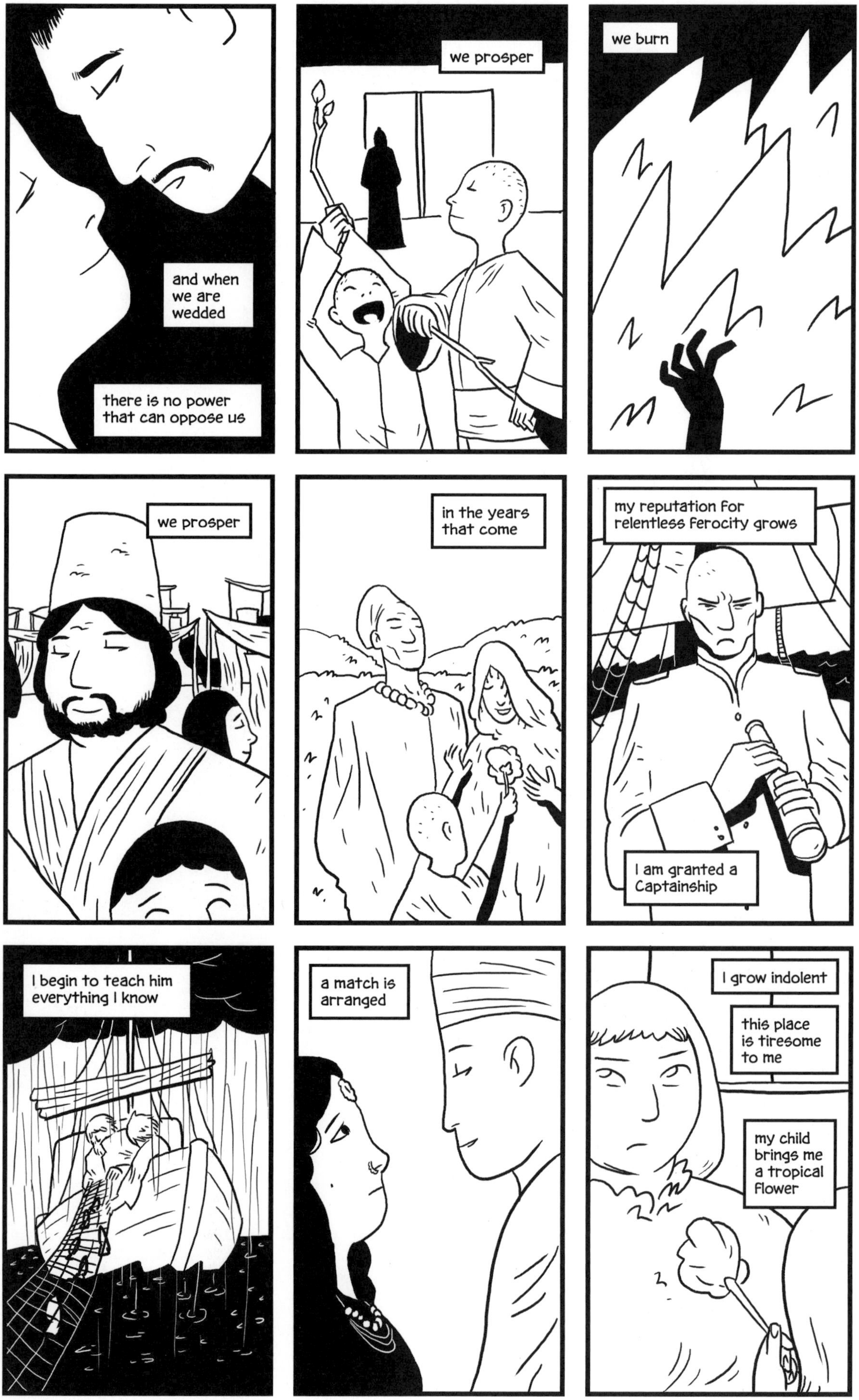
and when we are wedded
there is no power that can oppose us
we prosper
we burn
we prosper
in the years that come
my reputation for relentless ferocity grows
I am granted a Captainship
I begin to teach him everything I know
a match is arranged
I grow indolent
this place is tiresome to me
my child brings me a tropical flower

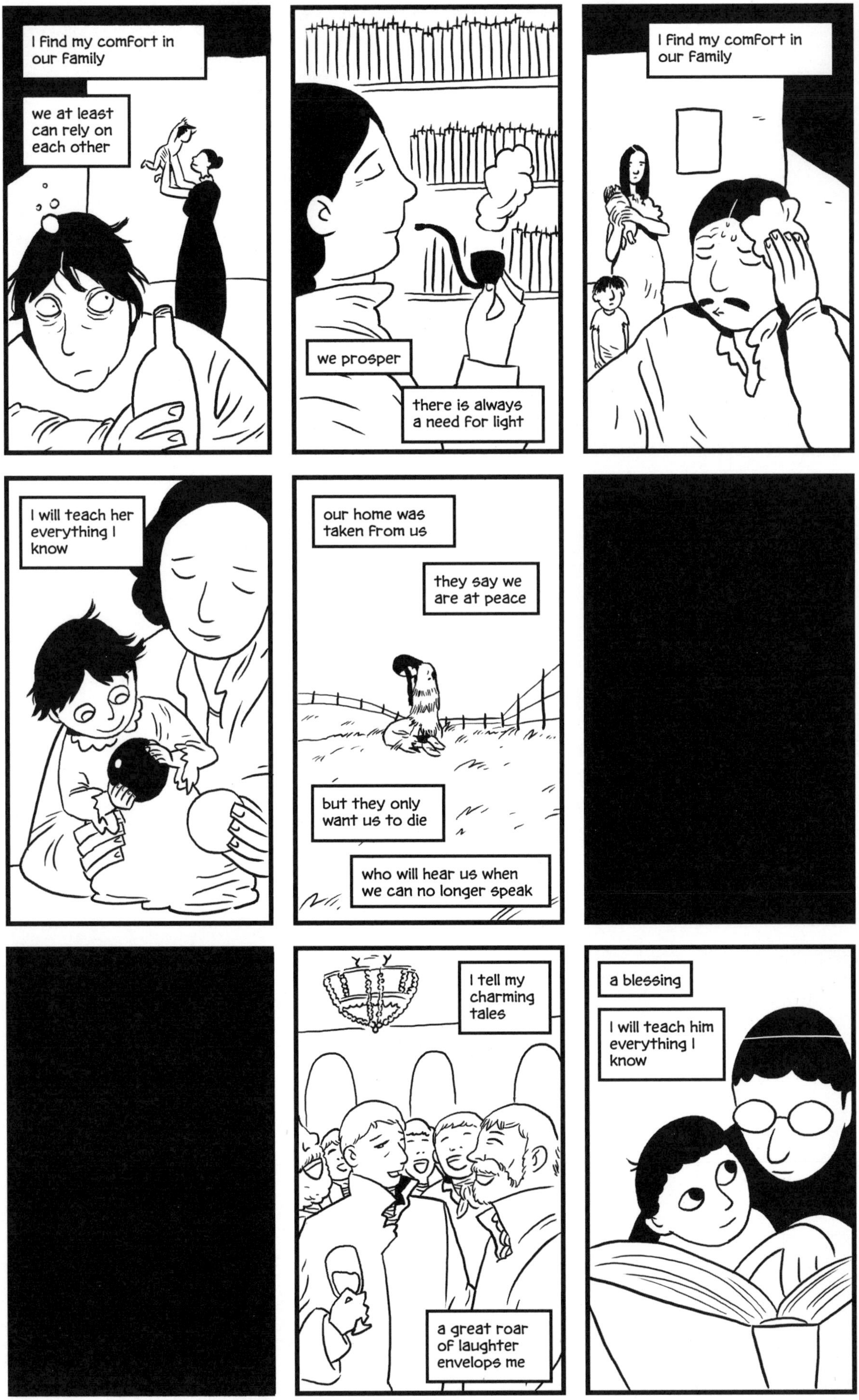
I find my comfort in our family
we at least can rely on each other
we prosper
there is always a need for light
I find my comfort in our family
I will teach her everything I know
our home was taken from us
they say we are at peace
but they only want us to die
who will hear us when we can no longer speak
I tell my charming tales
a great roar of laughter envelops me
a blessing
I will teach him everything I know

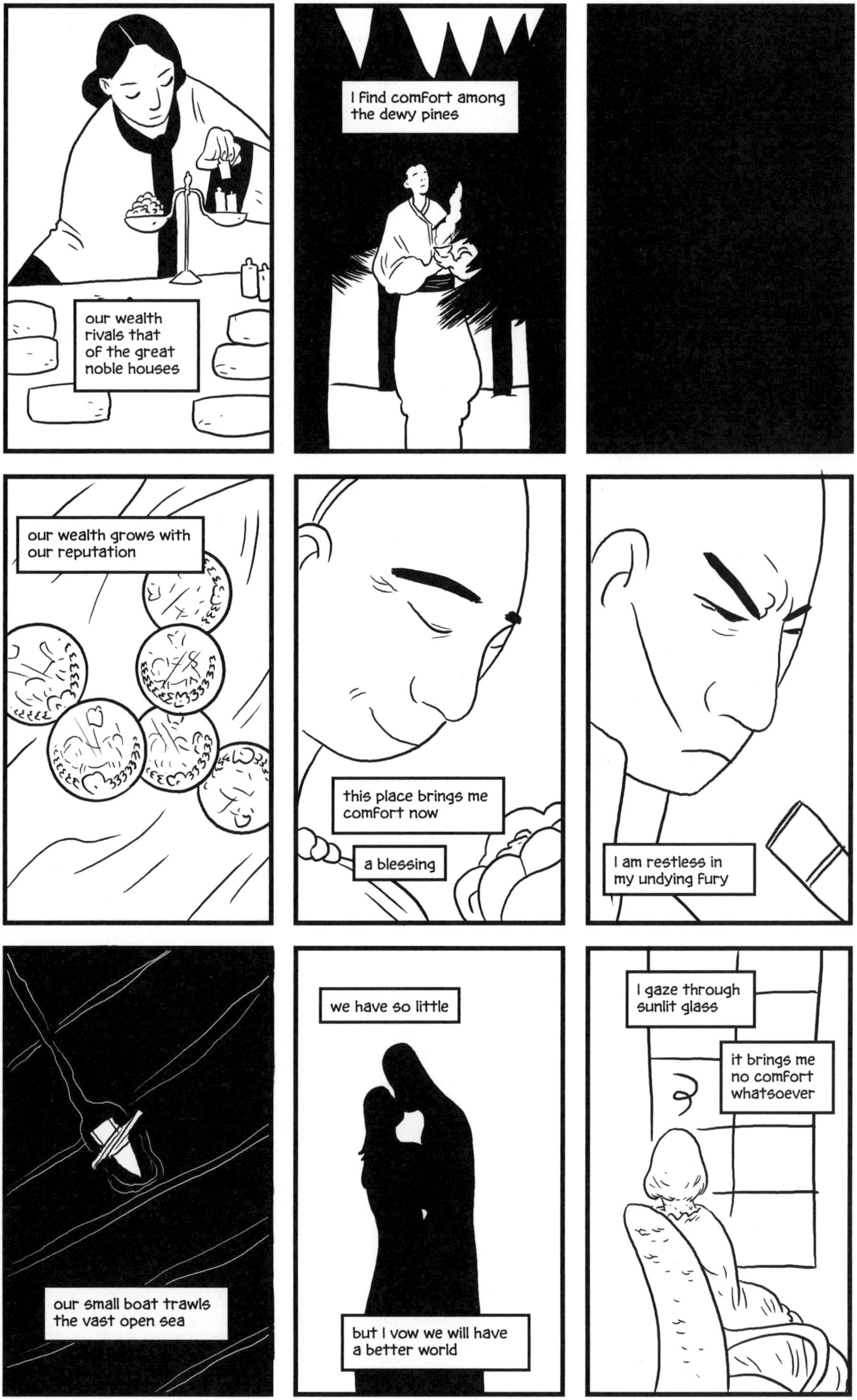
our wealth rivals that of the great noble houses
I find comfort among the dewy pines
our wealth grows with our reputation
this place brings me comfort now
a blessing
I am restless in my undying fury
our small boat trawls the vast open sea
we have so little
but I vow we will have a better world
I gaze through sunlit glass
it brings me no comfort whatsoever

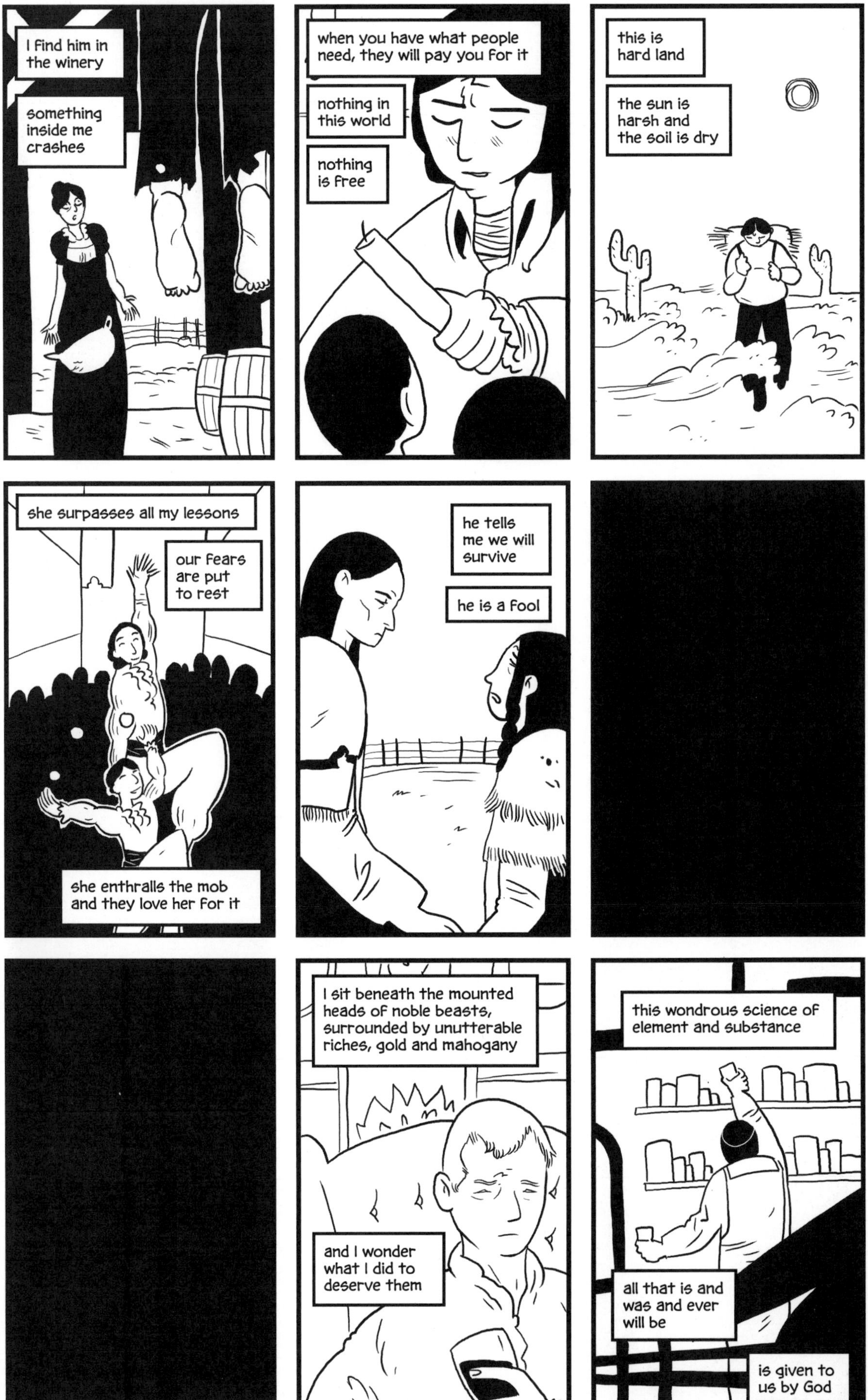
I find him in the winery
something inside me crashes
when you have what people need, they will pay you for it
nothing in this world
nothing is free
this is hard land
the sun is harsh and the soil is dry
she surpasses all my lessons
our fears are put to rest
she enthralls the mob and they love her for it
he tells me we will survive
he is a fool
I sit beneath the mounted heads of noble beasts, surrounded by unutterable riches, gold and mahogany
and I wonder what I did to deserve them
this wondrous science of element and substance
all that is and was and ever will be
is given to us by God

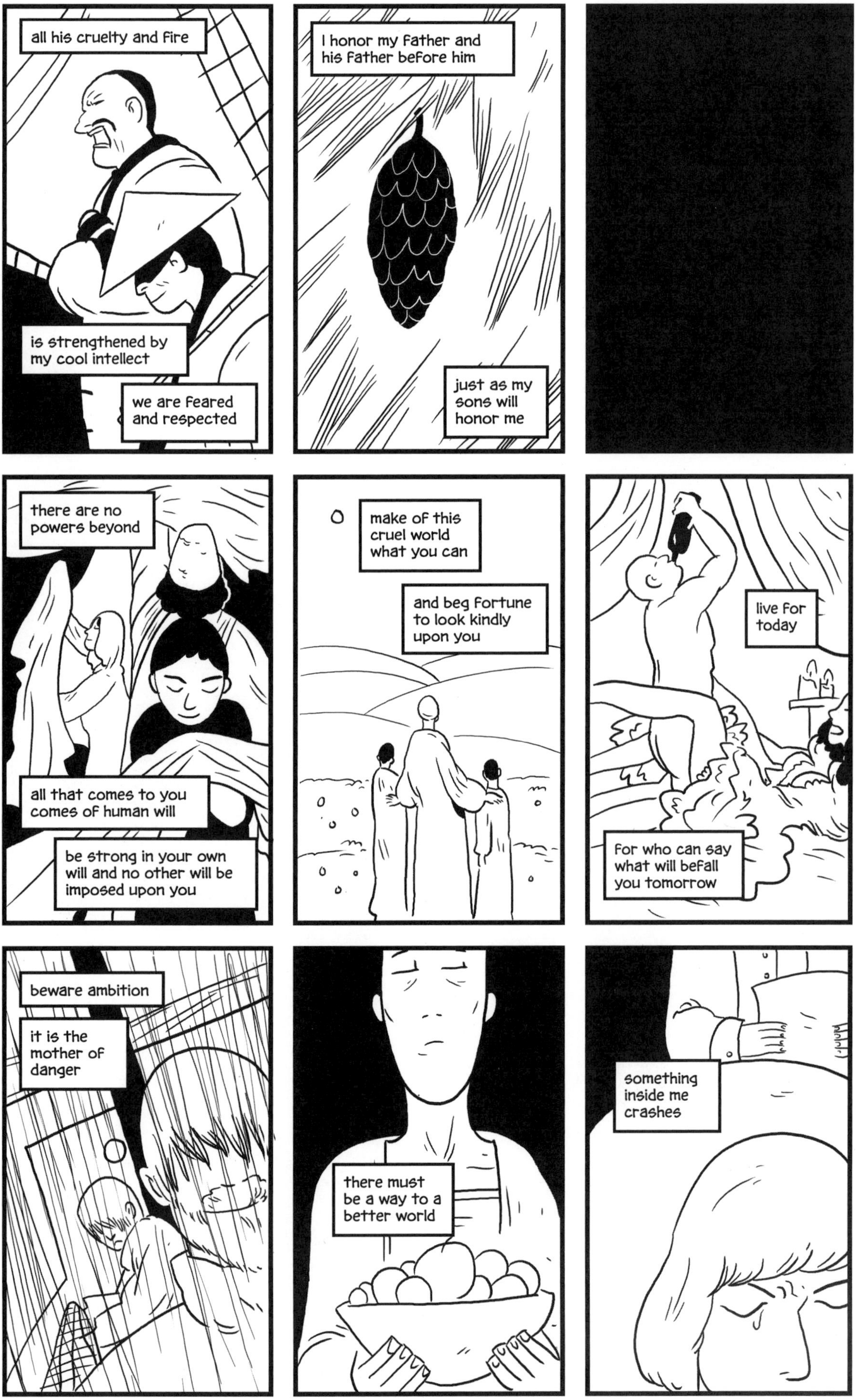
all his cruelty and fire
is strengthened by my cool intellect
we are feared and respected
I honor my father and his father before him
just as my sons will honor me
there are no powers beyond
all that comes to you comes of human will
be strong in your own will and no other will be imposed upon you
make of this cruel world what you can
and beg fortune to look kindly upon you
live for today
for who can say what will befall you tomorrow
beware ambition
it is the mother of danger
there must be a way to a better world
something inside me crashes

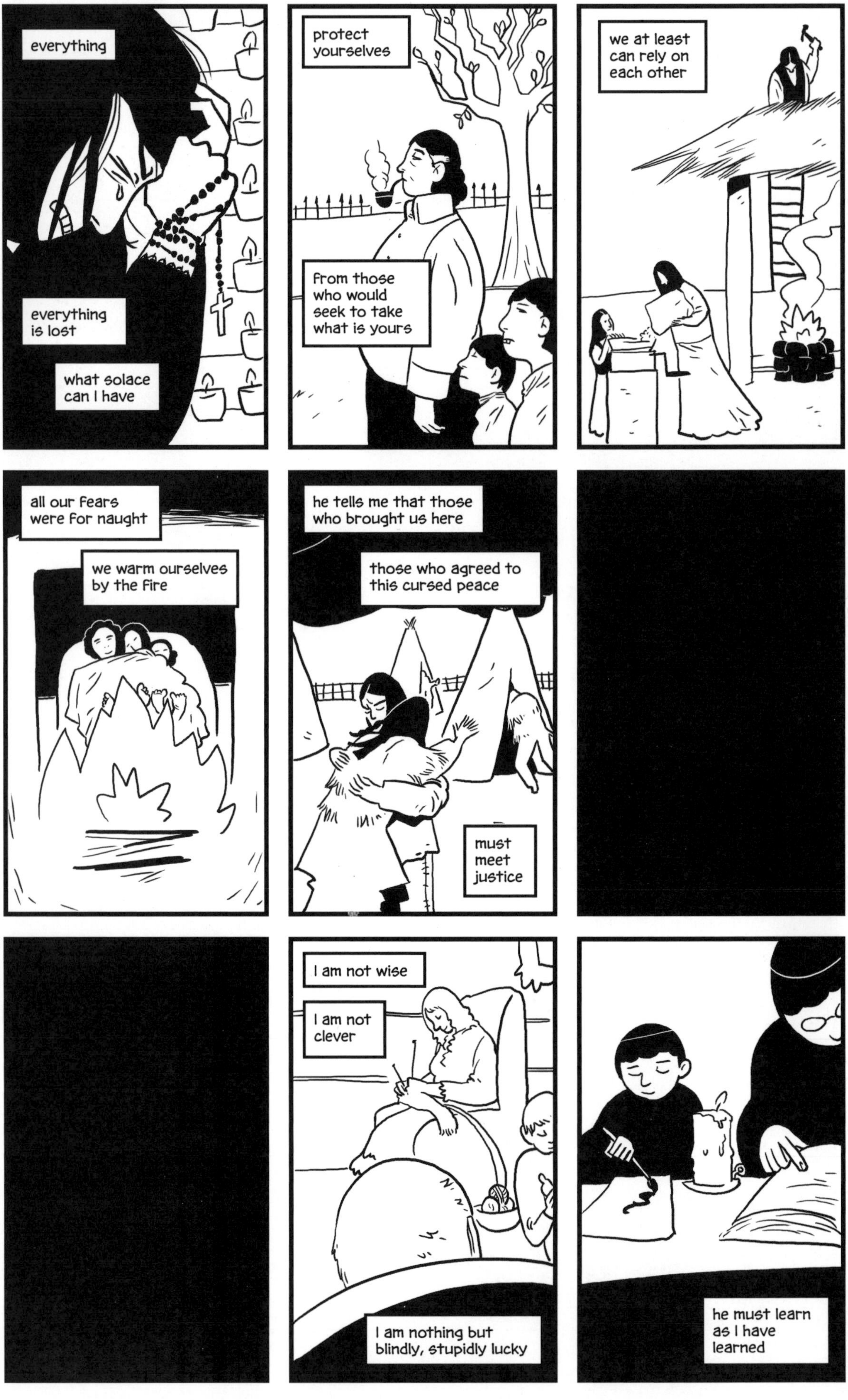
everything
everything is lost
what solace can I have
protect yourselves
from those who would seek to take what is yours
we at least can rely on each other
all our fears were for naught
we warm ourselves by the fire
he tells me that those who brought us here
those who agreed to this cursed peace
must meet justice
I am not wise
I am not clever
I am nothing but blindly, stupidly lucky
he must learn as I have learned

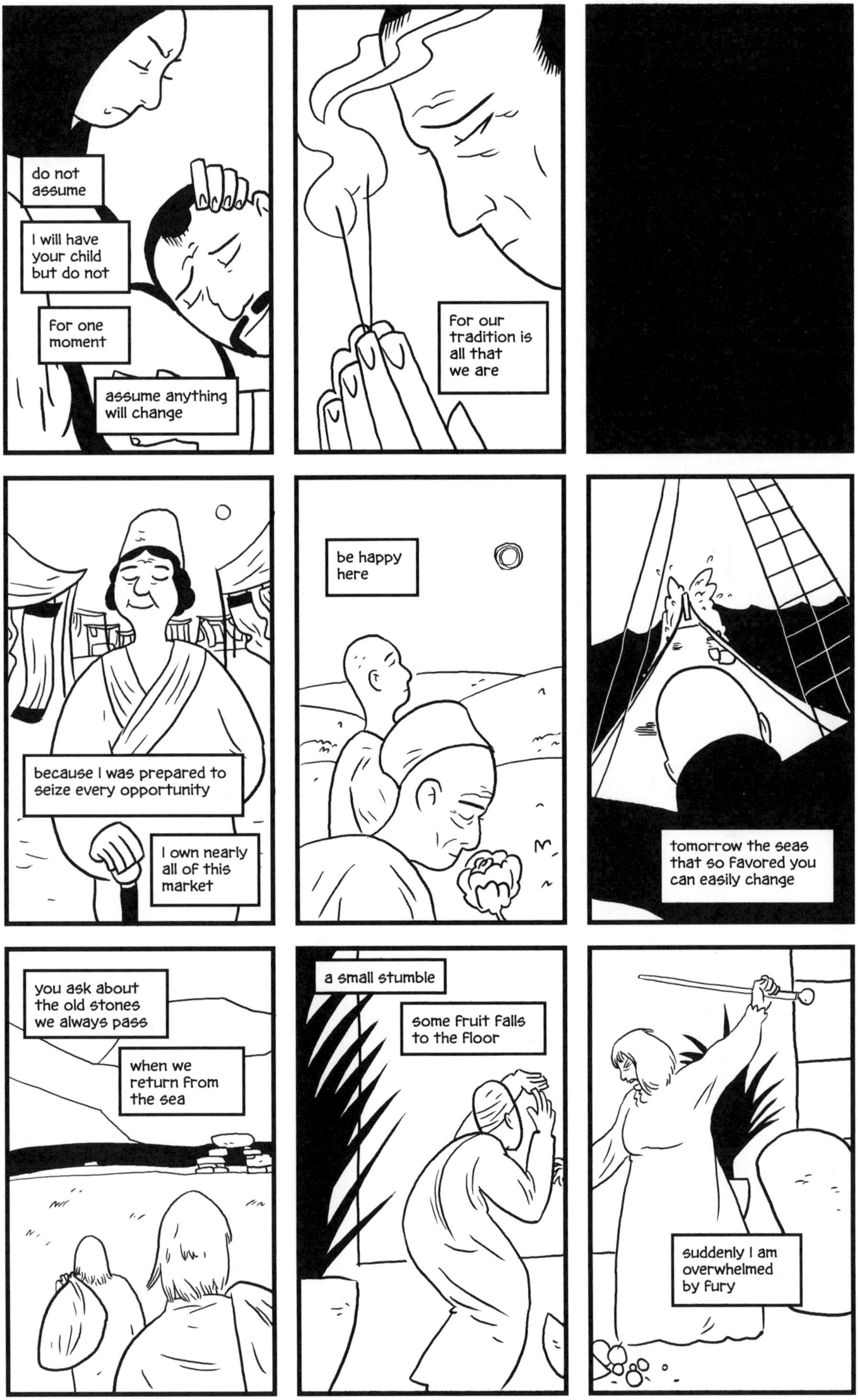
do not assume
I will have your child but do not
for one moment
assume anything will change
for our tradition is all that we are
because I was prepared to seize every opportunity
I own nearly all of this market
be happy here
tomorrow the seas that so favored you can easily change
you ask about the old stones we always pass
when we return from the sea
a small stumble
some fruit falls to the floor
suddenly I am overwhelmed by fury

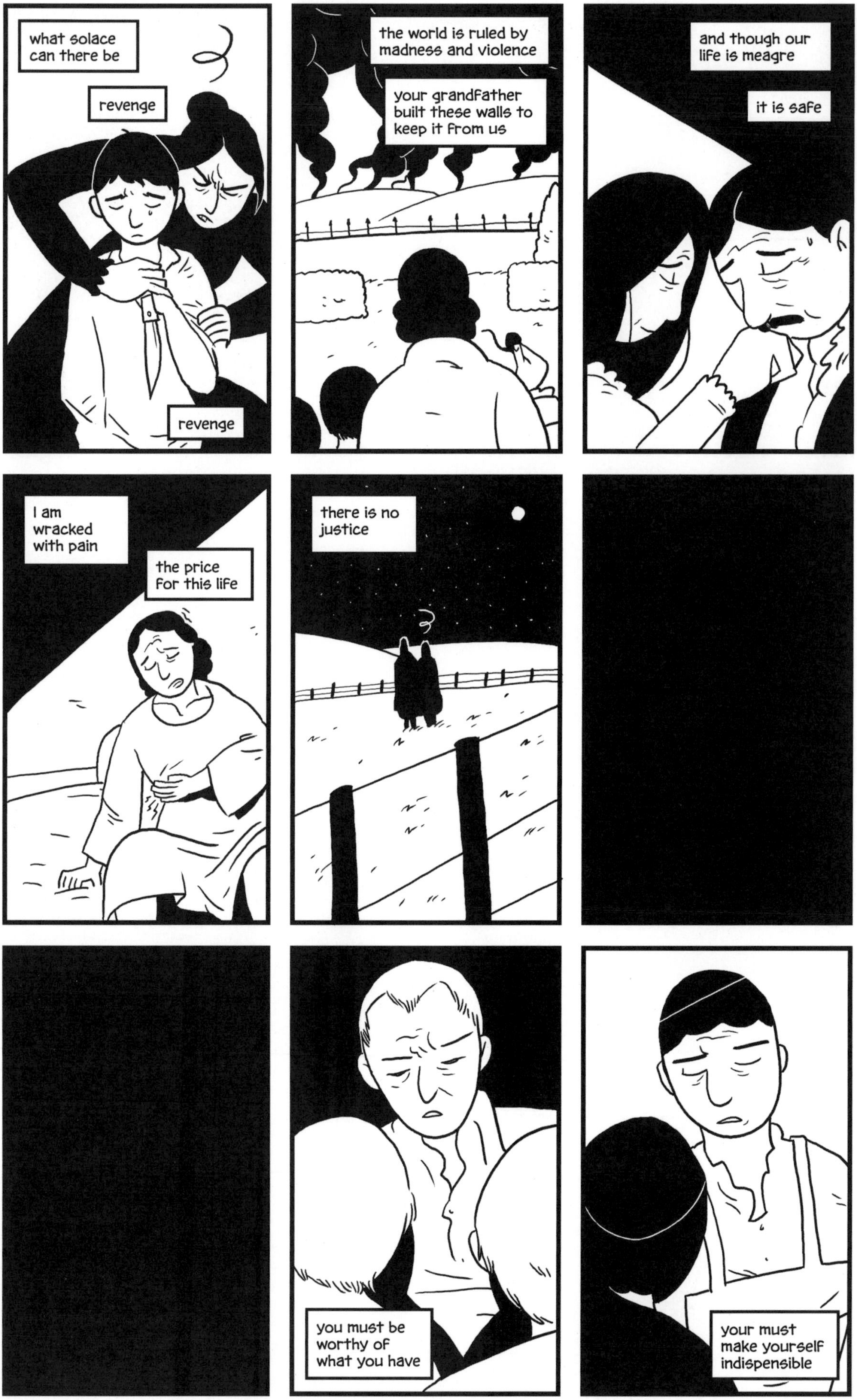
what solace can there be
revenge
revenge
the world is ruled by madness and violence
your grandfather built these walls to keep it from us
and though our life is meagre
it is safe
I am wracked with pain
the price for this life
there is no justice
you must be worthy of what you have
your must make yourself indispensible

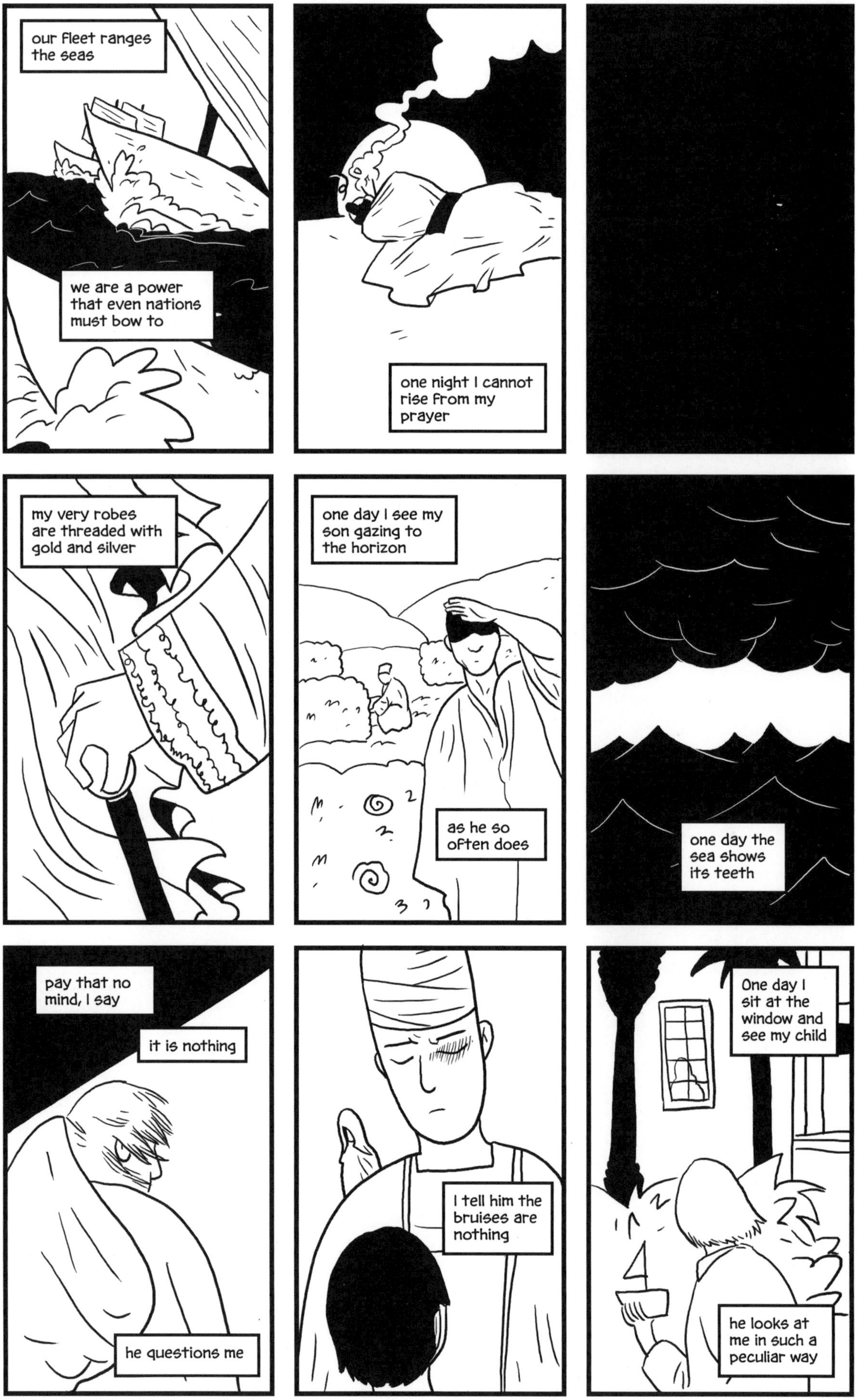
our fleet ranges the seas
we are a power that even nations must bow to
one night I cannot rise from my prayer
my very robes are threaded with gold and silver
one day I see my son gazing to the horizon
as he so often does
one day the sea shows its teeth
pay that no mind, I say
it is nothing
he questions me
I tell him the bruises are nothing
One day I sit at the window and see my child
he looks at me in such a peculiar way

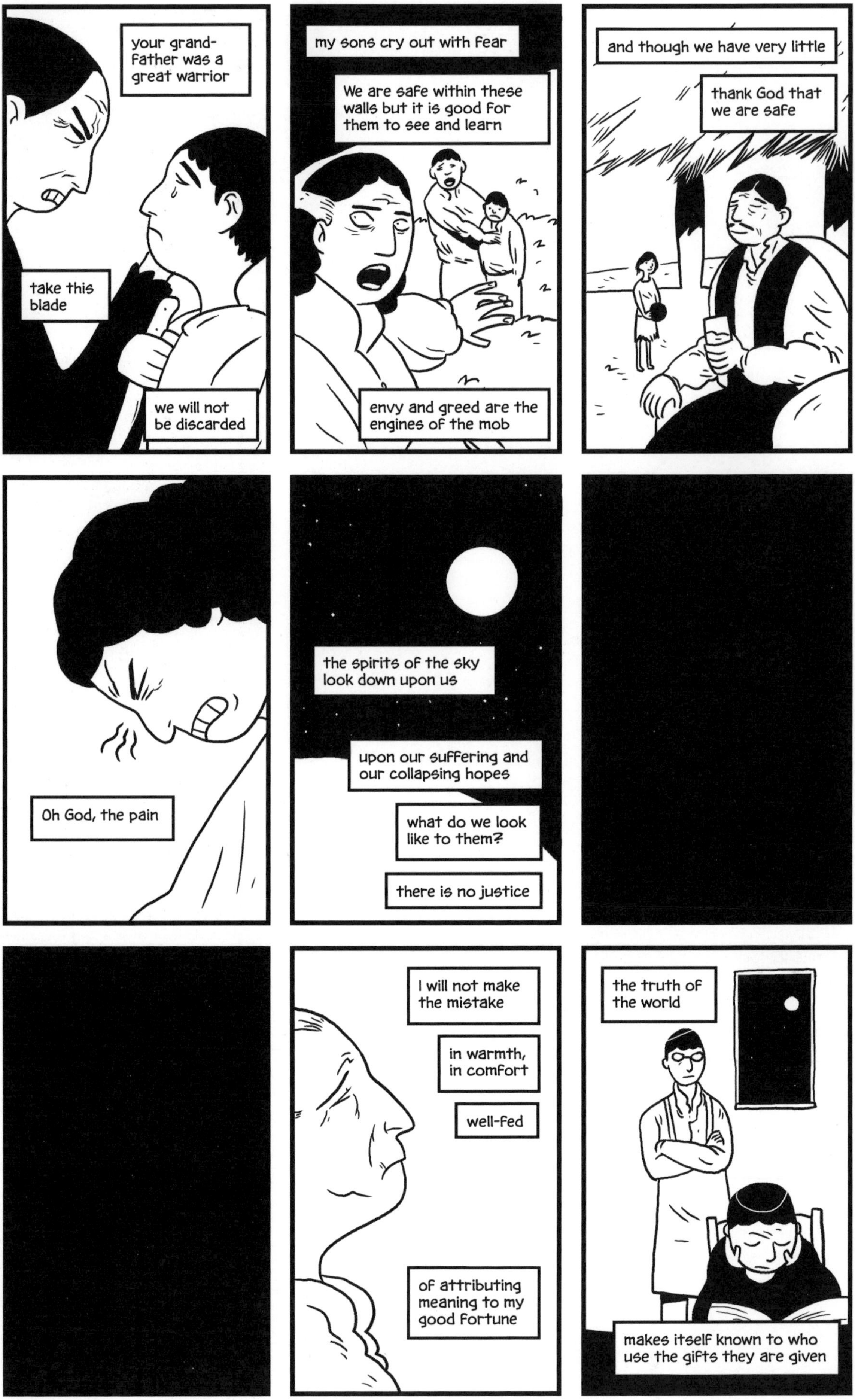
your grand-father was a great warrior
take this blade
we will not be discarded
my sons cry out with fear
We are safe within these walls but it is good for them to see and learn
envy and greed are the engines of the mob
and though we have very little
thank God that we are safe
Oh God, the pain
the spirits of the sky look down upon us
upon our suffering and our collapsing hopes
what do we look like to them?
there is no justice
I will not make the mistake
in warmth, in comfort
well-fed
of attributing meaning to my good fortune
the truth of the world
makes itself known to who use the gifts they are given

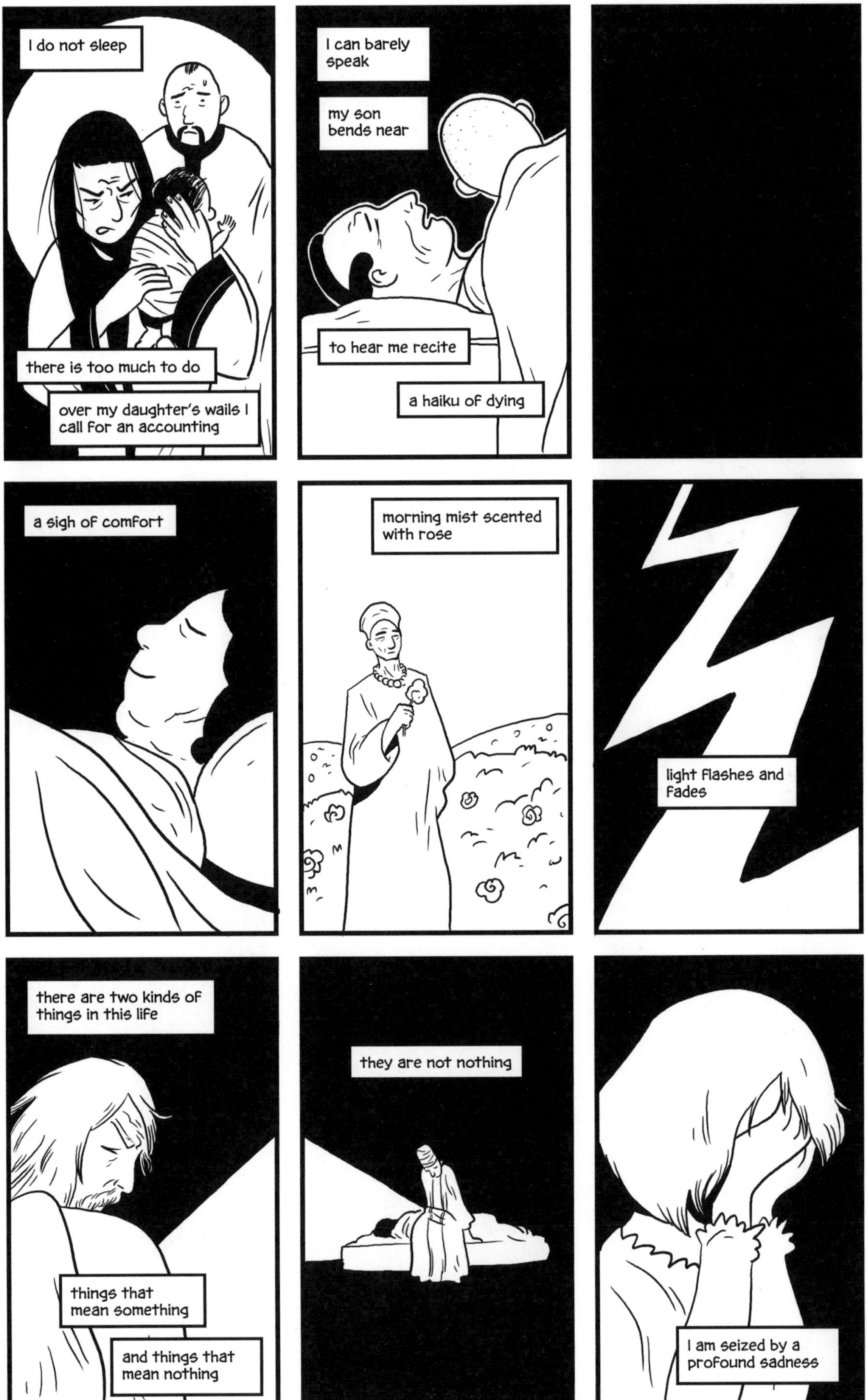
I do not sleep
there is too much to do
over my daughter's wails I call for an accounting
I can barely speak
my son bends near
to hear me recite
a haiku of dying
a sigh of comfort
morning mist scented with rose
light flashes and fades
there are two kinds of things in this life
things that mean something
and things that mean nothing
they are not nothing
I am seized by a profound sadness

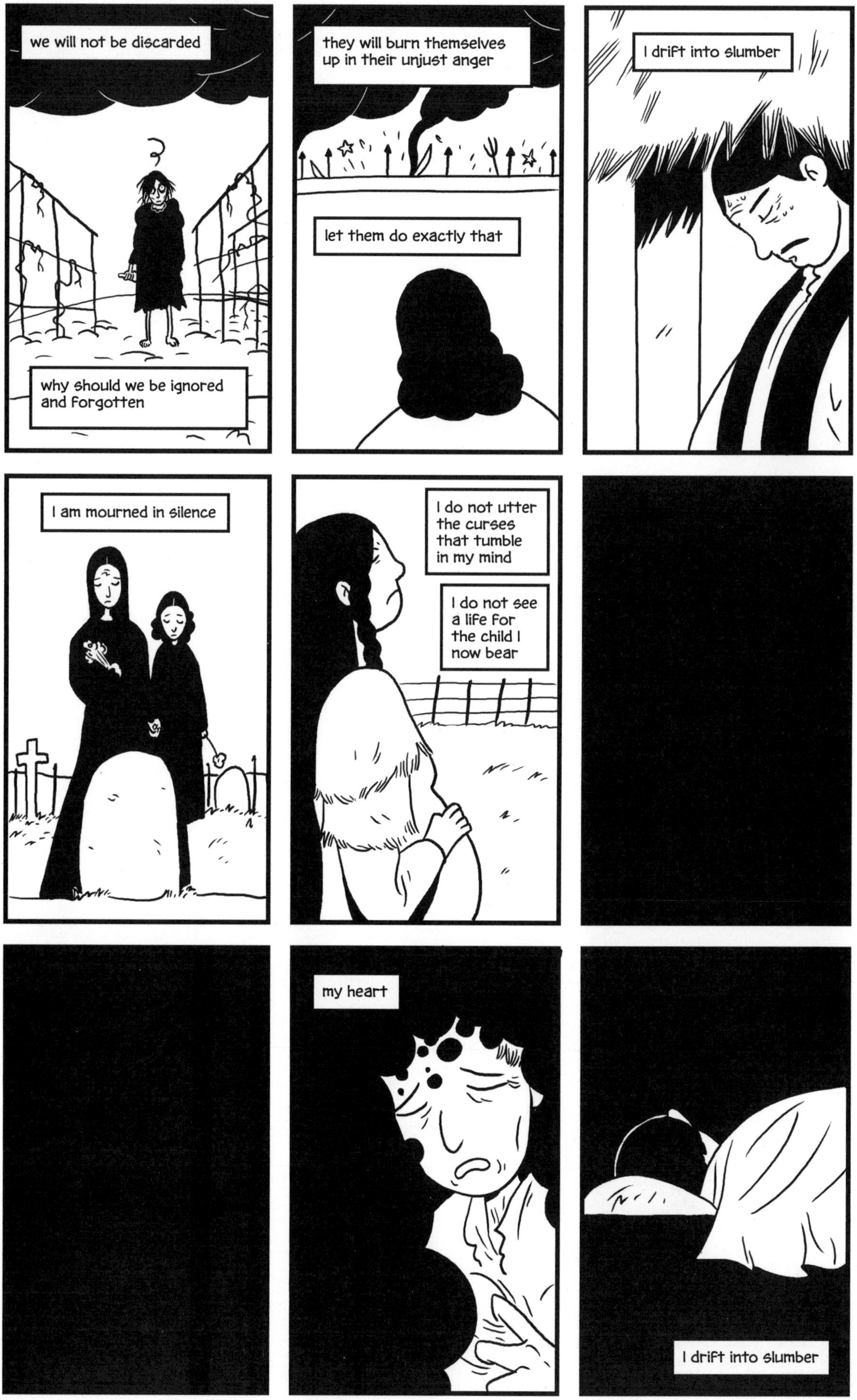
we will not be discarded
why should we be ignored and forgotten
they will burn themselves up in their unjust anger
let them do exactly that
I drift into slumber
I am mourned in silence
I do not utter the curses that tumble in my mind
I do not see a life for the child I now bear
my heart
I drift into slumber

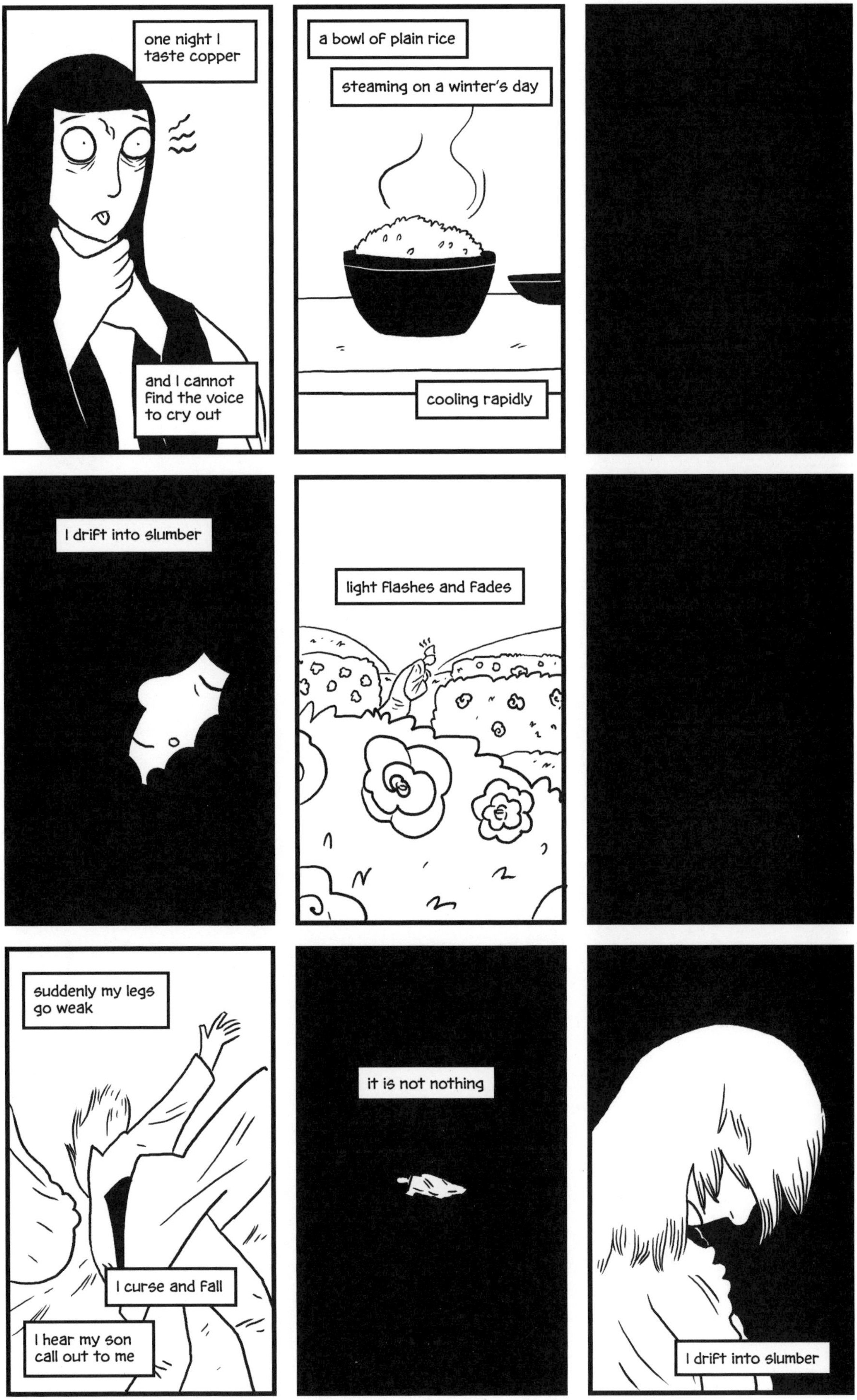
one night I taste copper
and I cannot find the voice to cry out
a bowl of plain rice
steaming on a winter's day
cooling rapidly
I drift into slumber
light flashes and fades
suddenly my legs go weak
I curse and fall
I hear my son call out to me
it is not nothing
I drift into slumber

PART THREE

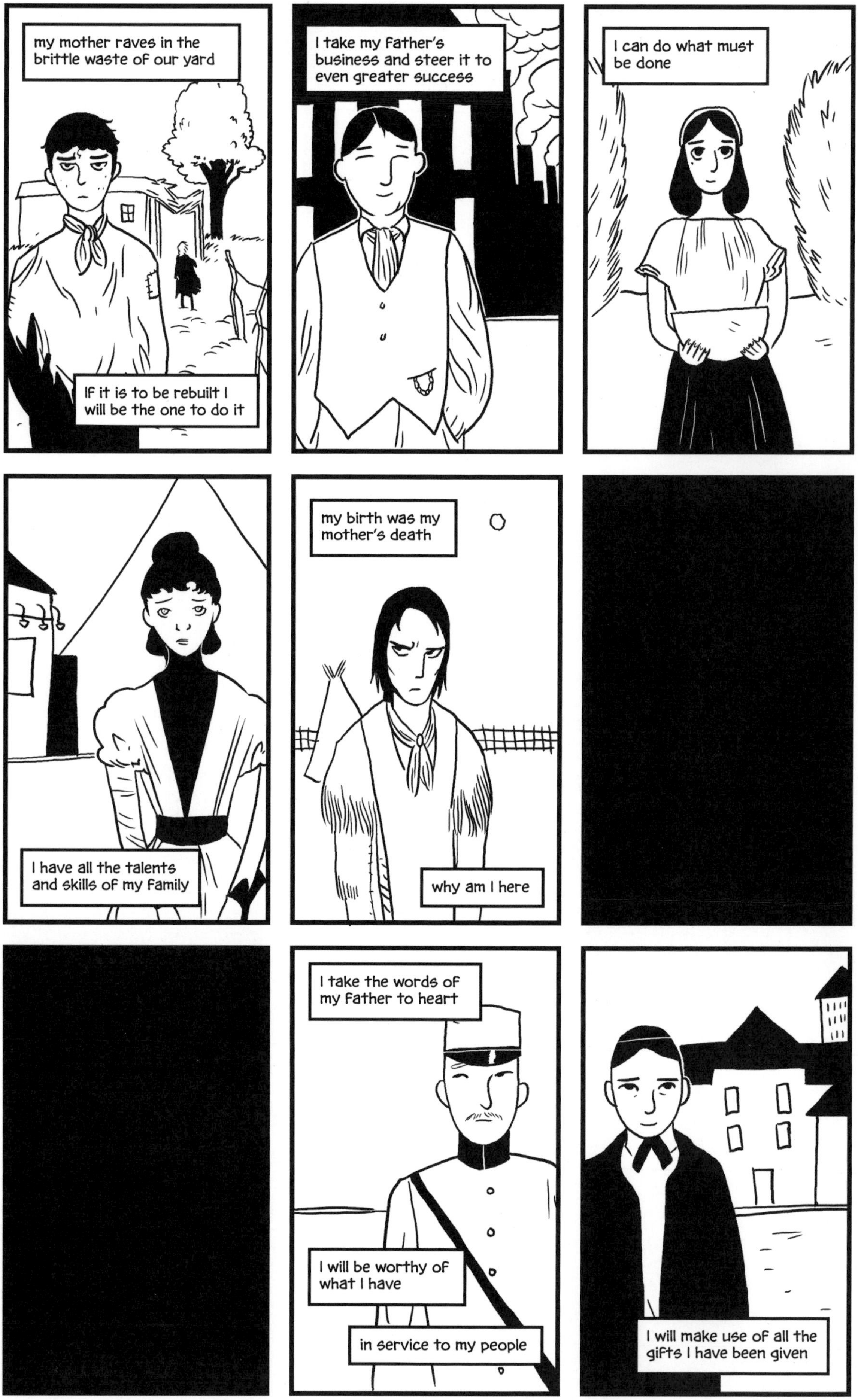
my mother raves in the brittle waste of our yard
If it is to be rebuilt I will be the one to do it
I take my father's business and steer it to even greater success
I can do what must be done
I have all the talents and skills of my family
my birth was my mother's death
why am I here
I take the words of my father to heart
I will be worthy of what I have
in service to my people
I will make use of all the gifts I have been given

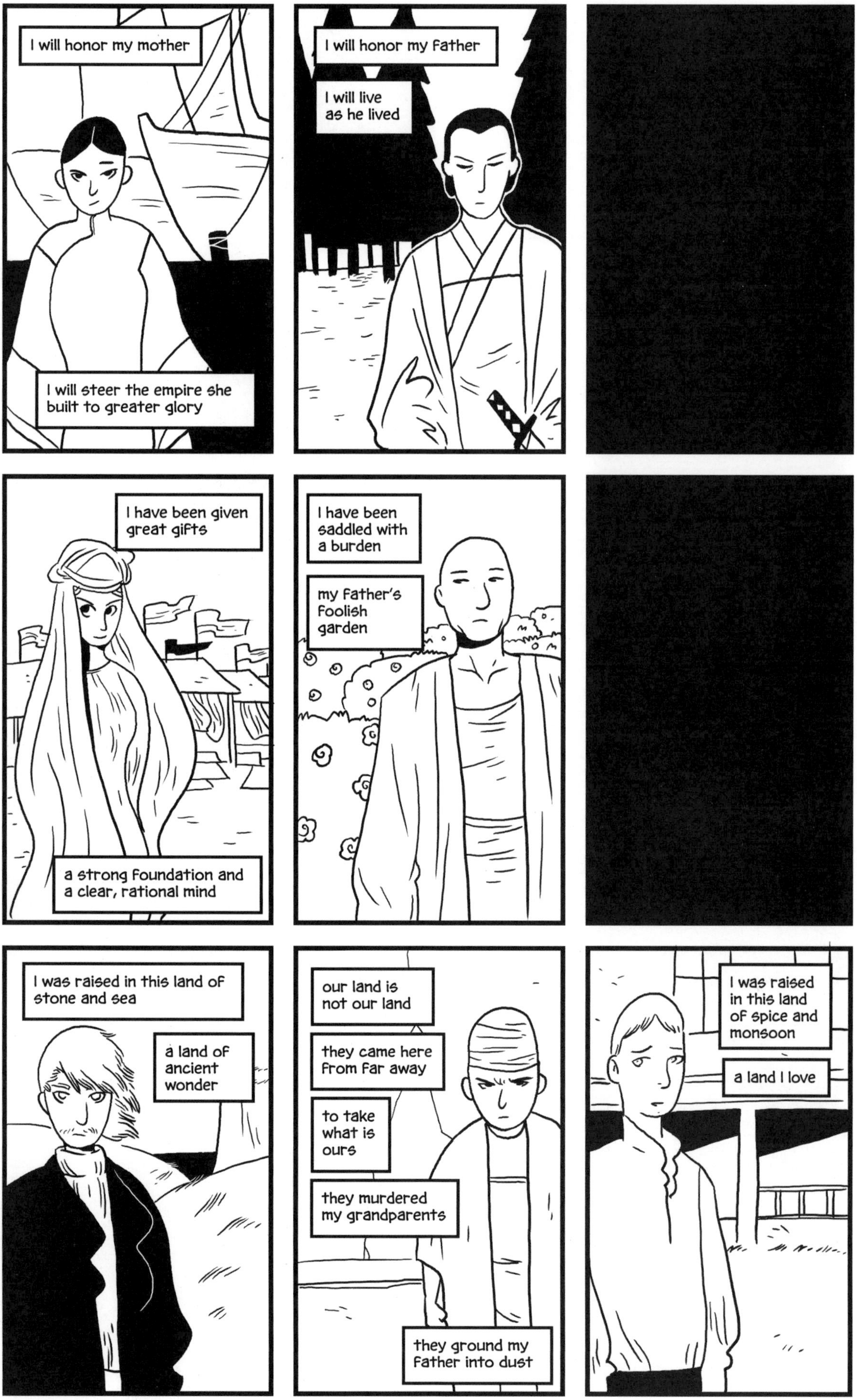
I will honor my mother
I will steer the empire she built to greater glory
I will honor my father
I will live as he lived
I have been given great gifts
a strong foundation and a clear, rational mind
I have been saddled with a burden
my father's foolish garden
I was raised in this land of stone and sea
a land of ancient wonder
our land is not our land
they came here from far away
to take what is ours
they murdered my grandparents
they ground my father into dust
I was raised in this land of spice and monsoon
a land I love

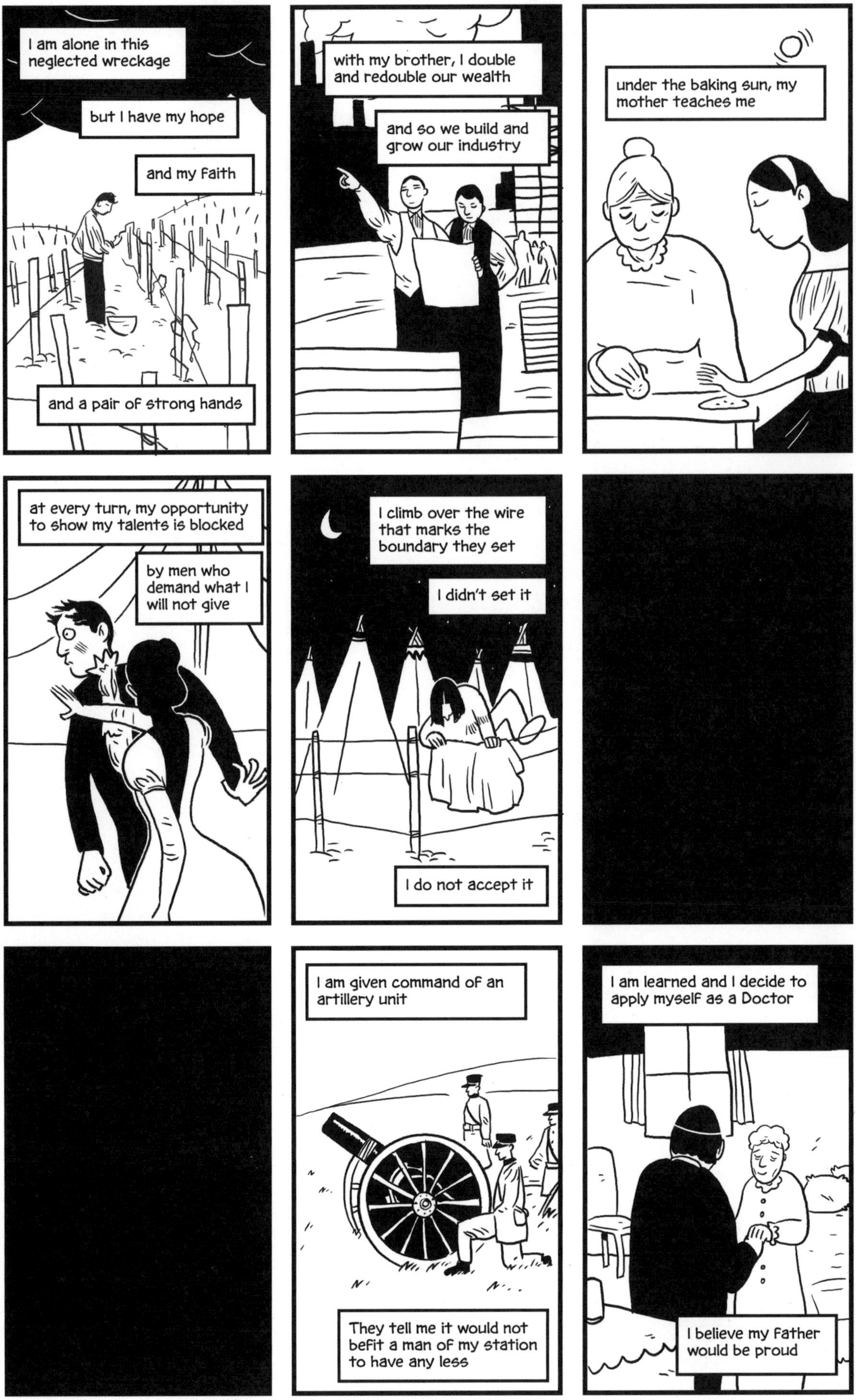
I am alone in this neglected wreckage
but I have my hope
and my faith
and a pair of strong hands
with my brother, I double and redouble our wealth
and so we build and grow our industry
under the baking sun, my mother teaches me
at every turn, my opportunity to show my talents is blocked
by men who demand what I will not give
I climb over the wire that marks the boundary they set
I didn't set it
I do not accept it
I am given command of an artillery unit
They tell me it would not befit a man of my station to have any less
I am learned and I decide to apply myself as a Doctor
I believe my Father would be proud

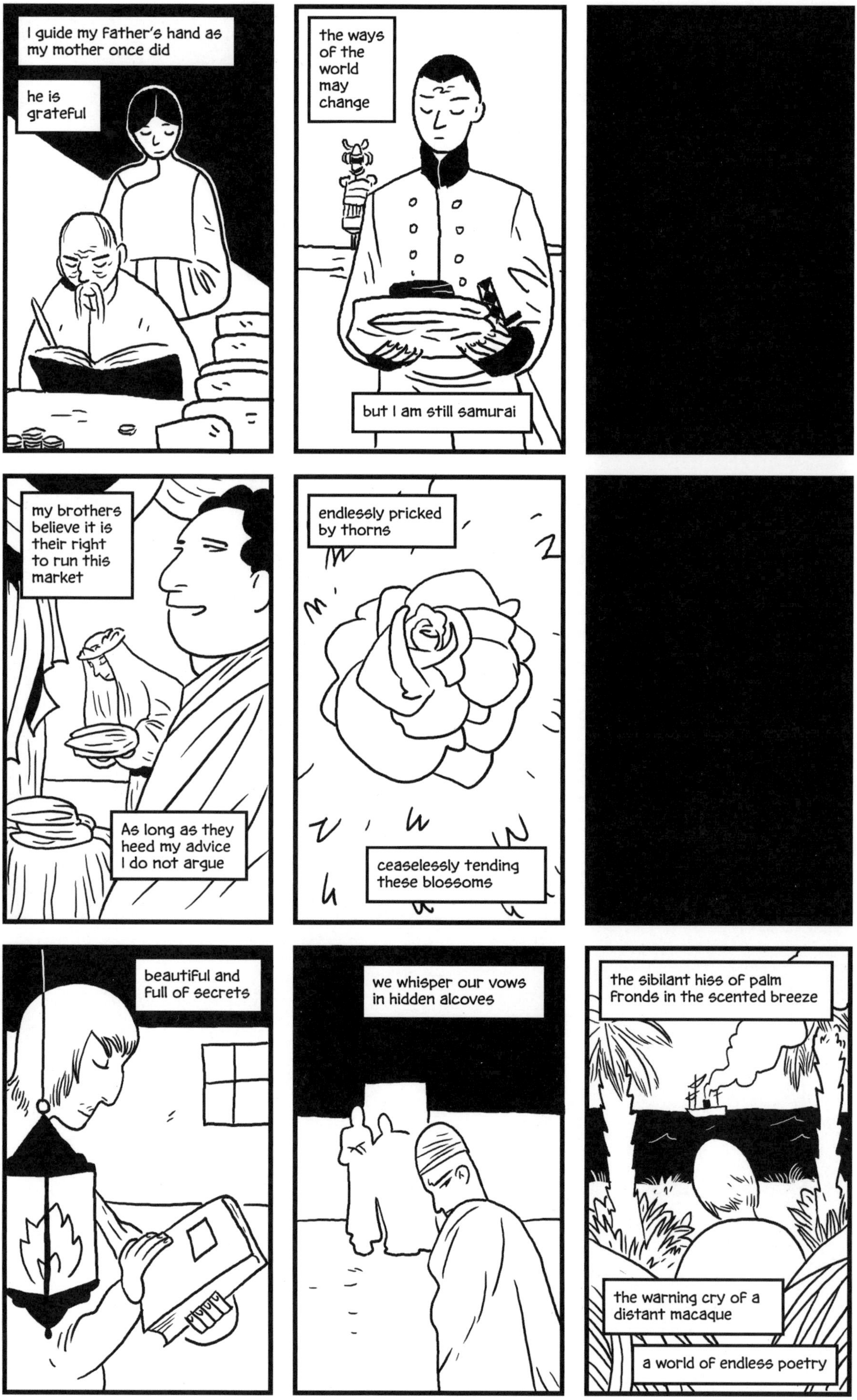
I guide my father's hand as my mother once did
he is grateful
the ways of the world may change
but I am still samurai
my brothers believe it is their right to run this market
As long as they heed my advice I do not argue
endlessly pricked by thorns
ceaselessly tending these blossoms
beautiful and full of secrets
we whisper our vows in hidden alcoves
the sibilant hiss of palm fronds in the scented breeze
the warning cry of a distant macaque
a world of endless poetry

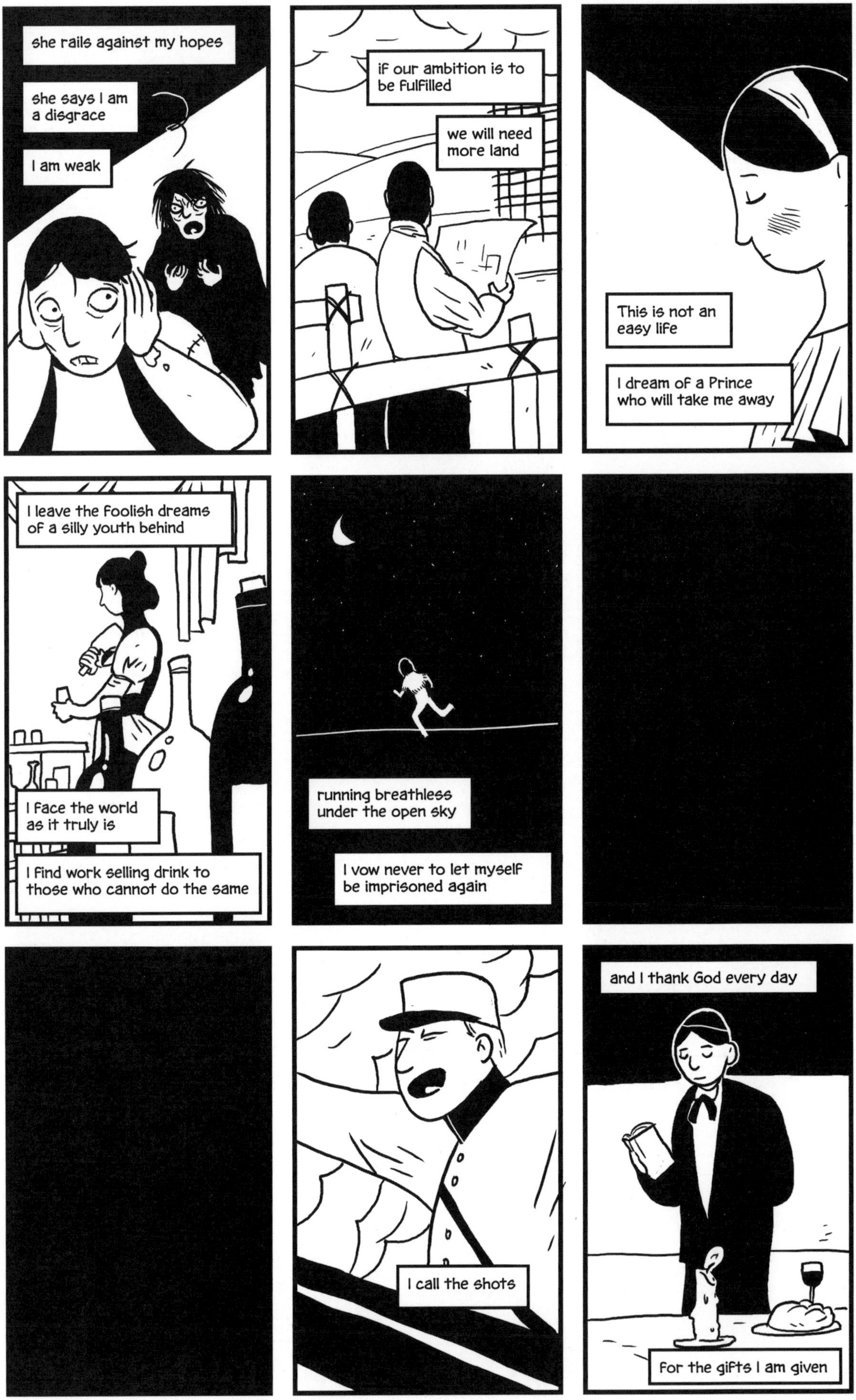
she rails against my hopes
she says I am a disgrace
I am weak
if our ambition is to be fulfilled
we will need more land
This is not an easy life
I dream of a Prince who will take me away
I leave the foolish dreams of a silly youth behind
I face the world as it truly is
I find work selling drink to those who cannot do the same
running breathless under the open sky
I vow never to let myself be imprisoned again
I call the shots
and I thank God every day
for the gifts I am given

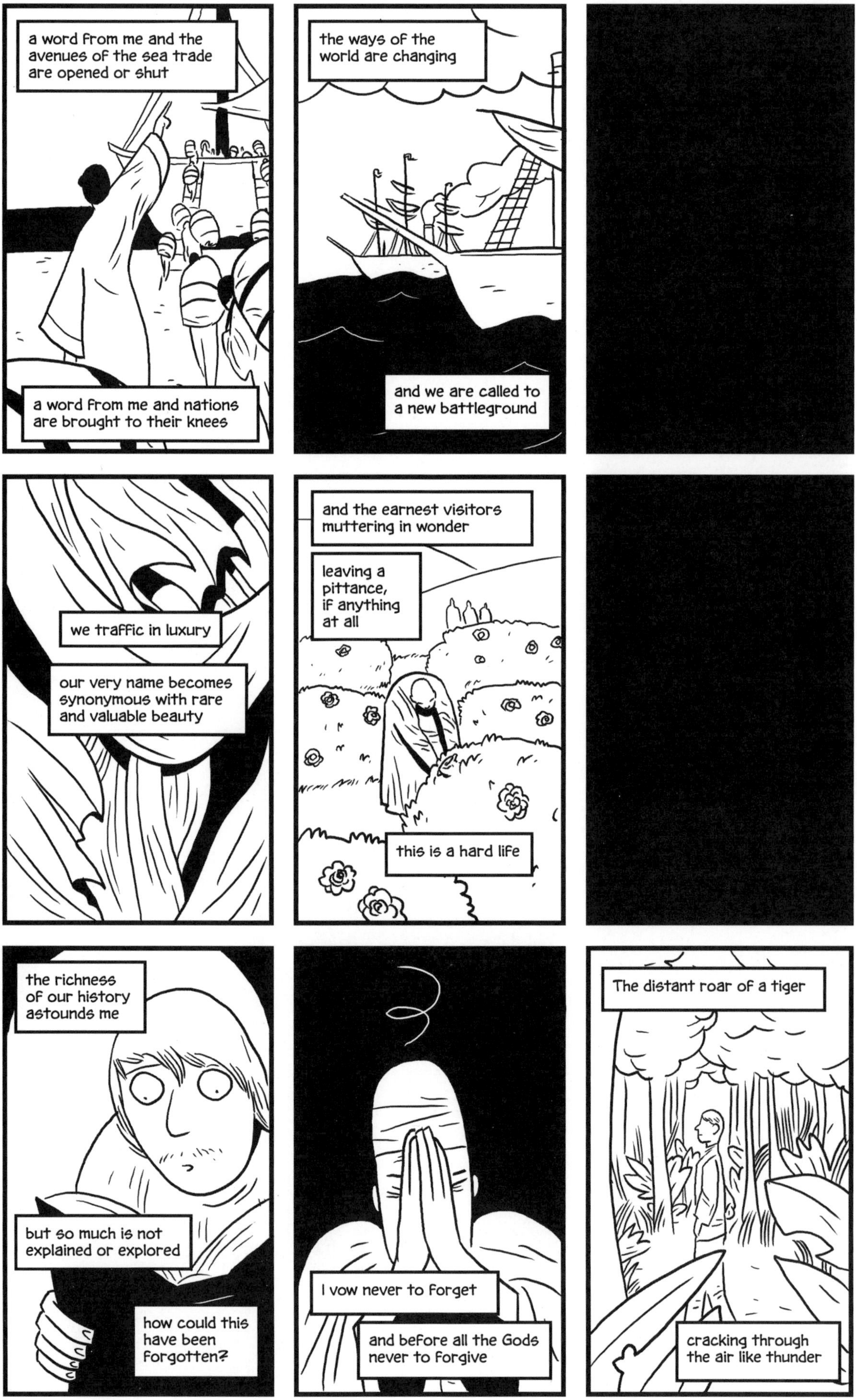
a word from me and the avenues of the sea trade are opened or shut
a word from me and nations are brought to their knees
the ways of the world are changing
and we are called to a new battleground
we traffic in luxury
our very name becomes synonymous with rare and valuable beauty
and the earnest visitors muttering in wonder
leaving a pittance, if anything at all
this is a hard life
the richness of our history astounds me
but so much is not explained or explored
how could this have been forgotten?
I vow never to forget
and before all the Gods never to forgive
The distant roar of a tiger
cracking through the air like thunder

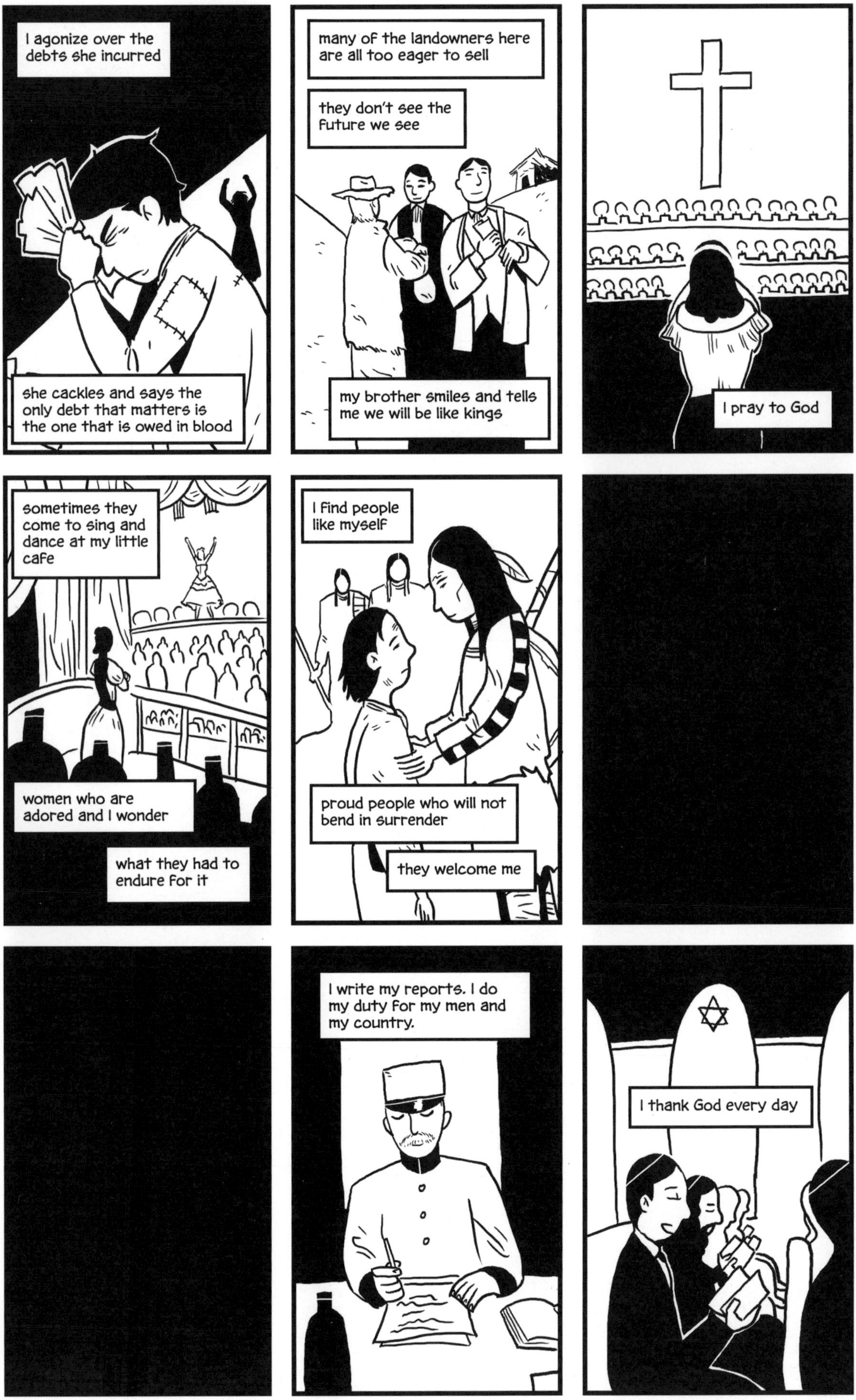
I agonize over the debts she incurred
she cackles and says the only debt that matters is the one that is owed in blood
many of the landowners here are all too eager to sell
they don't see the future we see
my brother smiles and tells me we will be like kings
I pray to God
sometimes they come to sing and dance at my little cafe
women who are adored and I wonder
what they had to endure for it
I find people like myself
proud people who will not bend in surrender
they welcome me
I write my reports. I do my duty for my men and my country.
I thank God every day

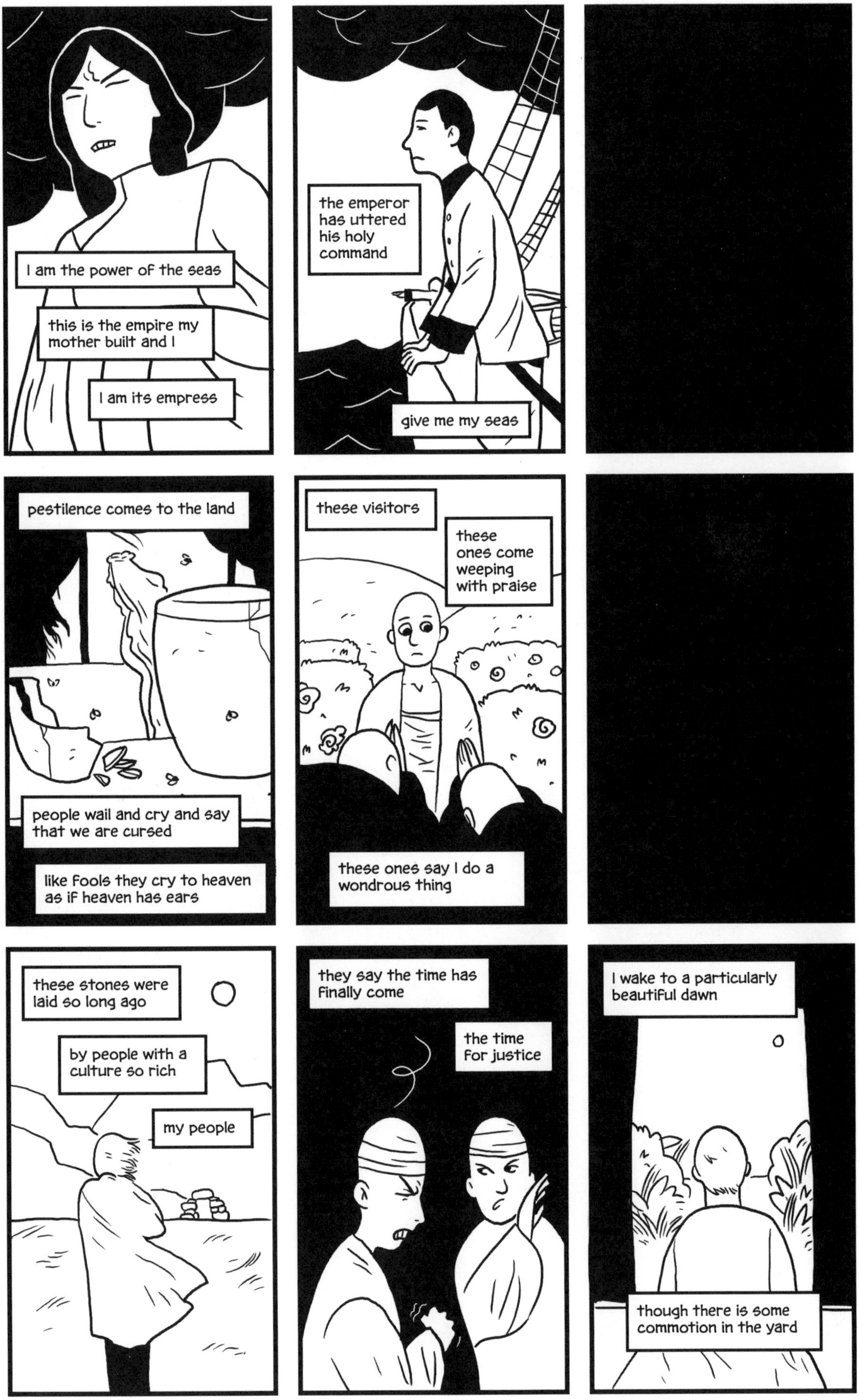

I am the power of the seas
this is the empire my mother built and I
I am its empress
the emperor has uttered his holy command
give me my seas
pestilence comes to the land
people wail and cry and say that we are cursed
like fools they cry to heaven as if heaven has ears
these visitors
these ones come weeping with praise
these ones say I do a wondrous thing
these stones were laid so long ago
by people with a culture so rich
my people
they say the time has finally come
the time for justice
I wake to a particularly beautiful dawn
though there is some commotion in the yard

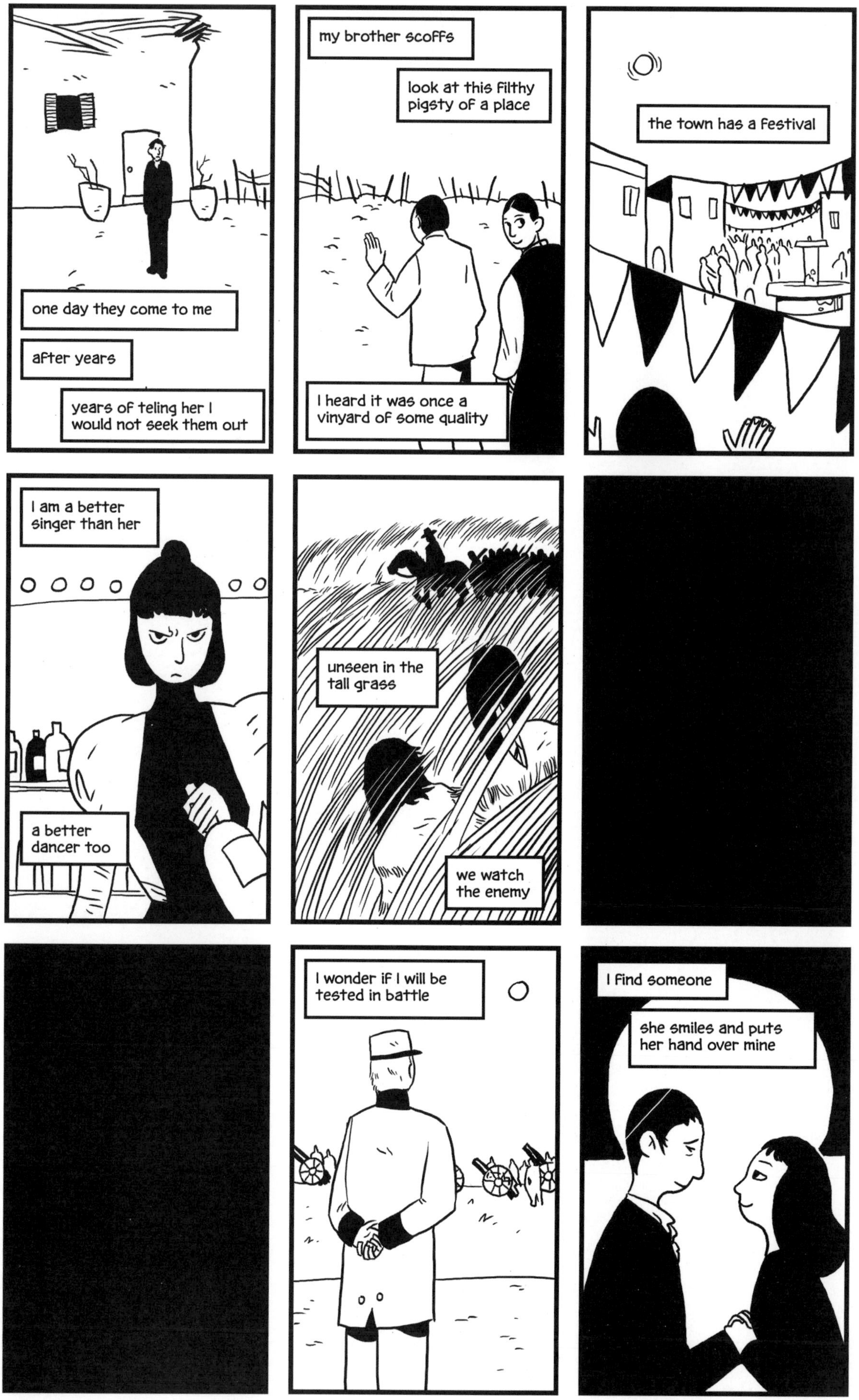
one day they come to me
after years
years of teling her I would not seek them out
my brother scoffs
look at this filthy pigsty of a place
I heard it was once a vinyard of some quality
the town has a festival
I am a better singer than her
a better dancer too
unseen in the tall grass
we watch the enemy
I wonder if I will be tested in battle
I find someone
she smiles and puts her hand over mine

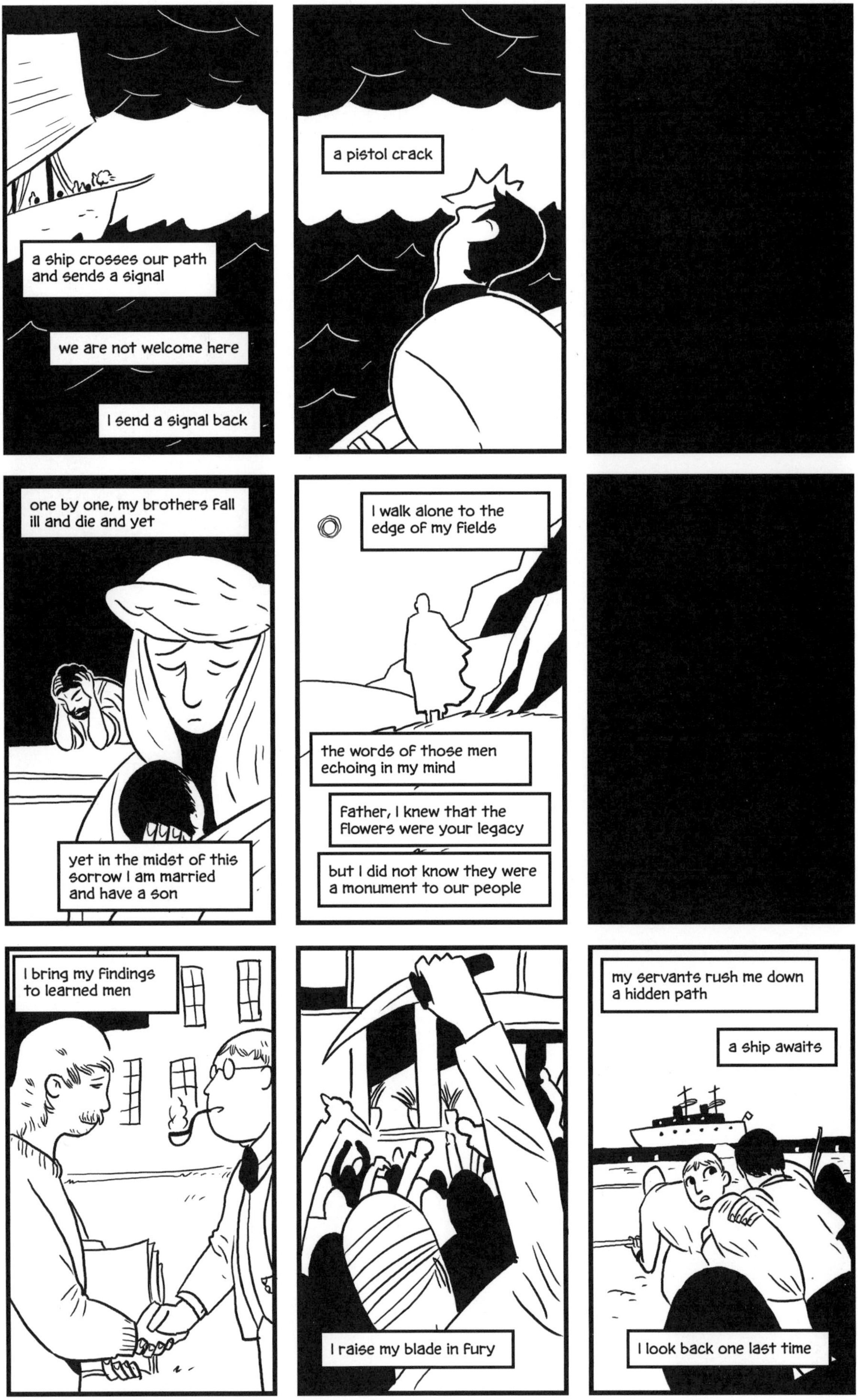
a ship crosses our path and sends a signal
we are not welcome here
I send a signal back
a pistol crack
one by one, my brothers fall ill and die and yet
yet in the midst of this sorrow I am married and have a son
I walk alone to the edge of my fields
the words of those men echoing in my mind
Father, I knew that the flowers were your legacy
but I did not know they were a monument to our people
I bring my findings to learned men
I raise my blade in fury
my servants rush me down a hidden path
a ship awaits
I look back one last time

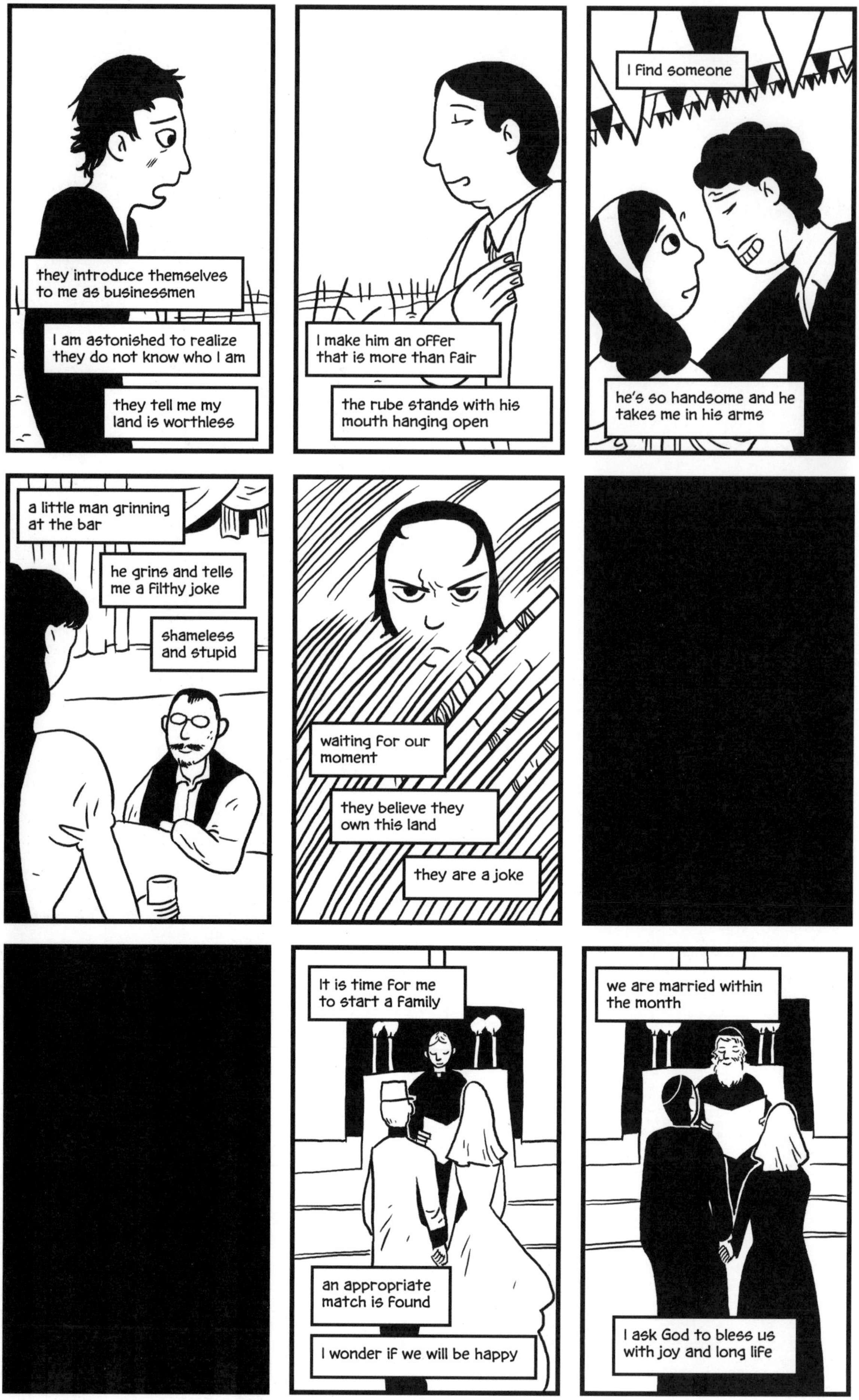
they introduce themselves to me as businessmen
I am astonished to realize they do not know who I am
they tell me my land is worthless
I make him an offer that is more than fair
the rube stands with his mouth hanging open
I find someone
he's so handsome and he takes me in his arms
a little man grinning at the bar
he grins and tells me a filthy joke
shameless and stupid
waiting for our moment
they believe they own this land
they are a joke
It is time for me to start a family
an appropriate match is found
I wonder if we will be happy
we are married within the month
I ask God to bless us with joy and long life

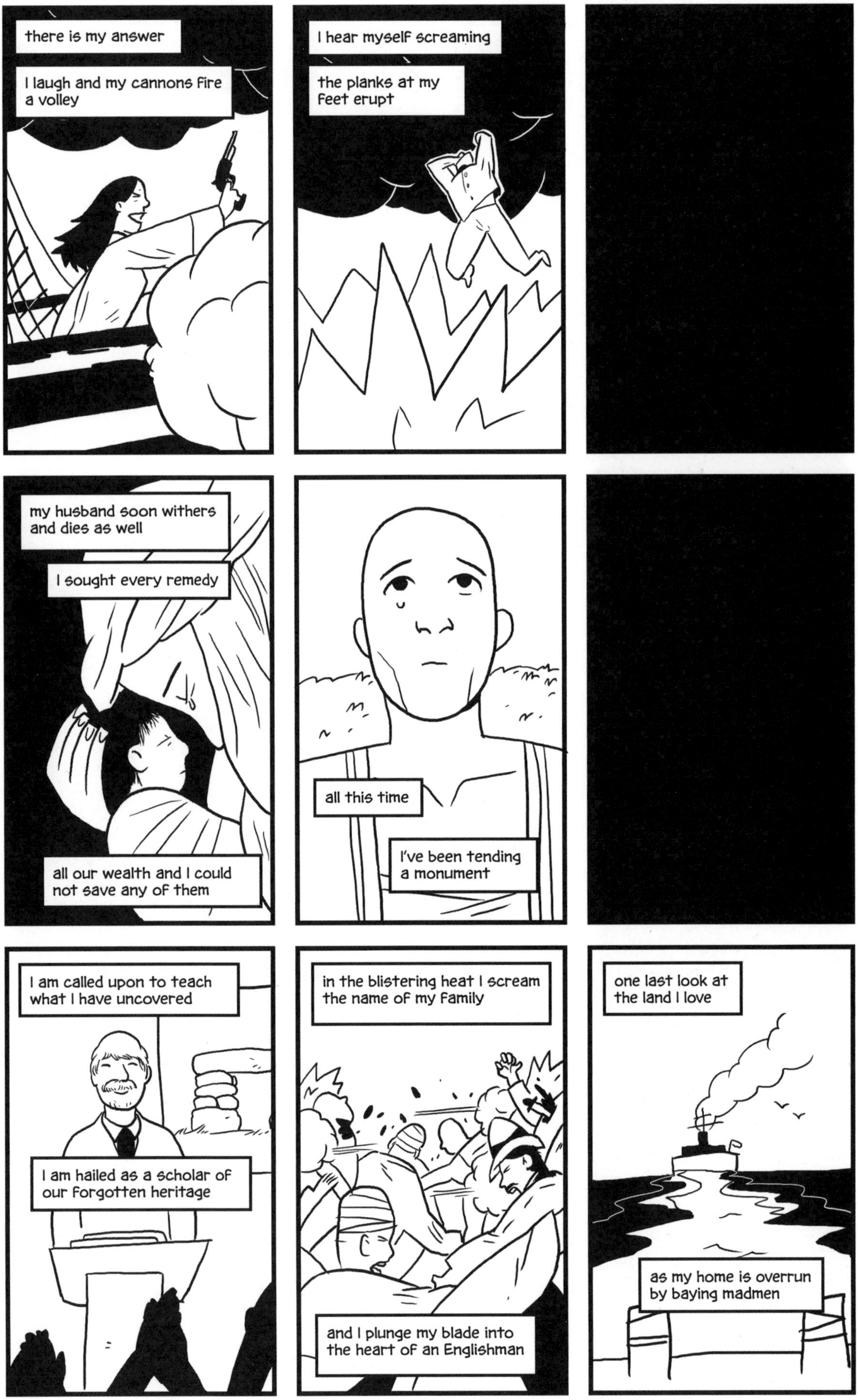
there is my answer
I laugh and my cannons fire a volley
I hear myself screaming
the planks at my feet erupt
my husband soon withers and dies as well
I sought every remedy
all our wealth and I could not save any of them
all this time
I've been tending a monument
I am called upon to teach what I have uncovered
I am hailed as a scholar of our forgotten heritage
in the blistering heat I scream the name of my family
and I plunge my blade into the heart of an Englishman
one last look at the land I love
as my home is overrun by baying madmen

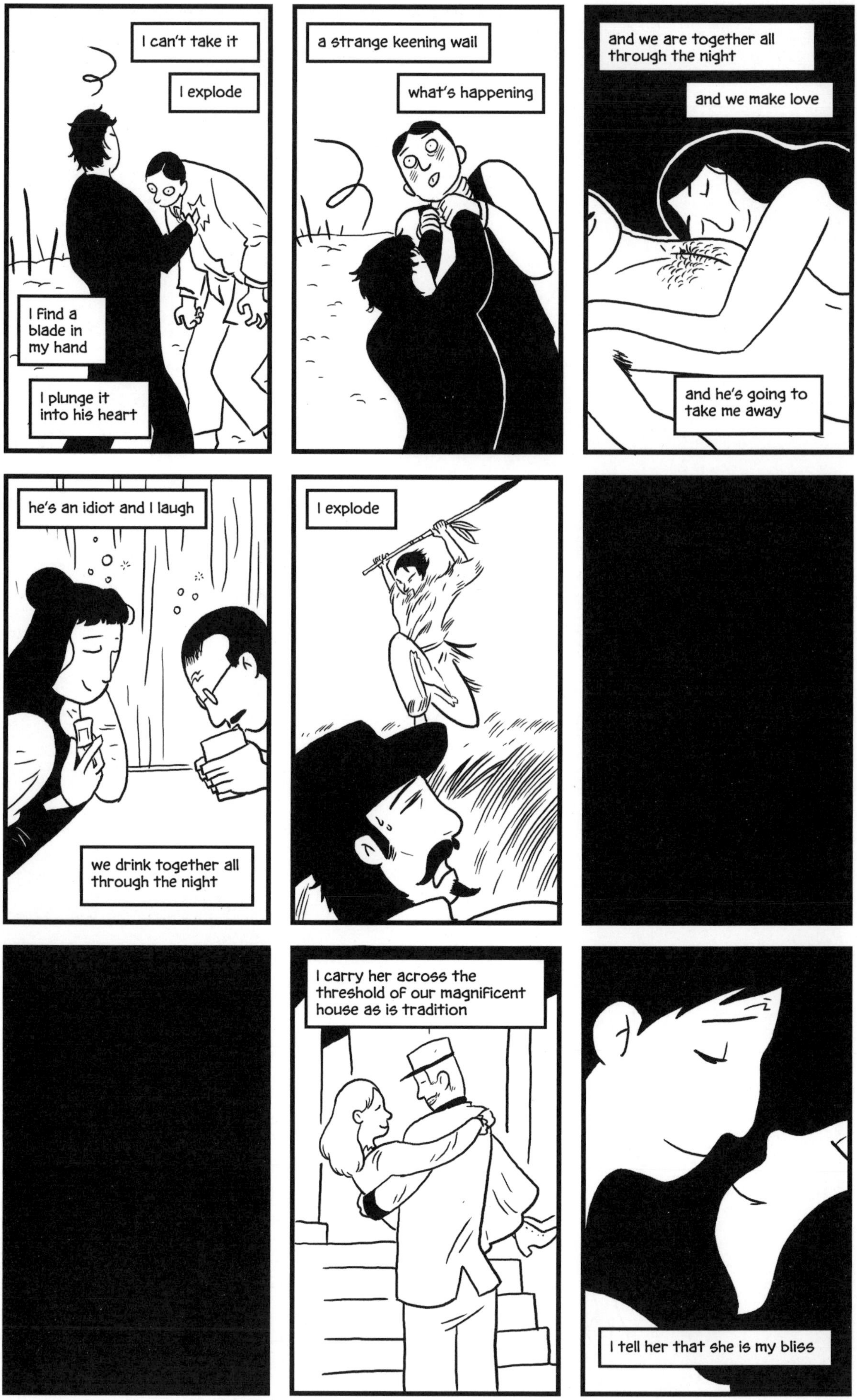
I can't take it
I explode
I find a blade in my hand
I plunge it into his heart
a strange keening wail
what's happening
and we are together all through the night
and we make love
and he's going to take me away
he's an idiot and I laugh
we drink together all through the night
I explode
I carry her across the threshold of our magnificent house as is tradition
I tell her that she is my bliss

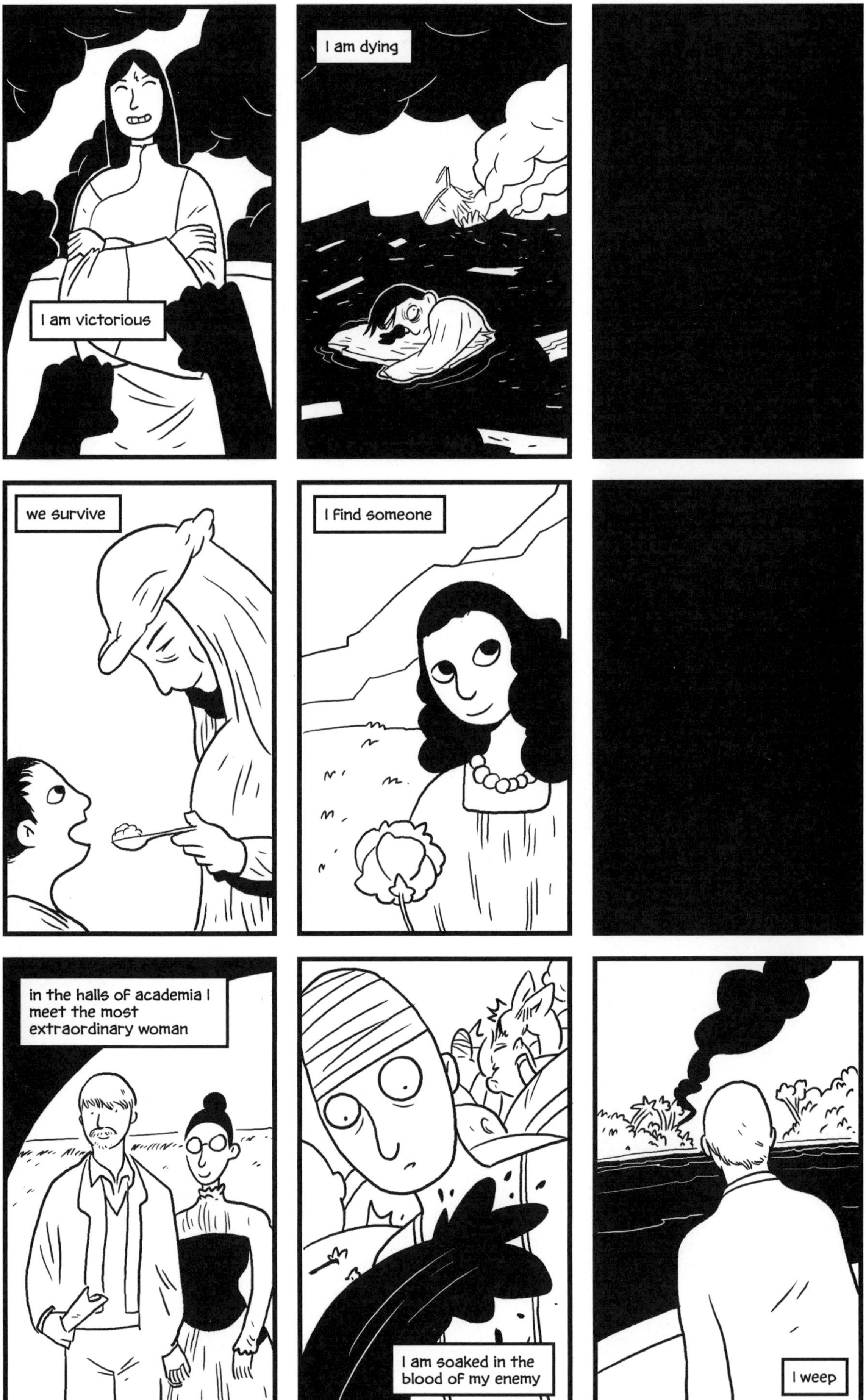
I am victorious
I am dying
we survive
I find someone
in the halls of academia I meet the most extraordinary woman
I am soaked in the blood of my enemy
I weep

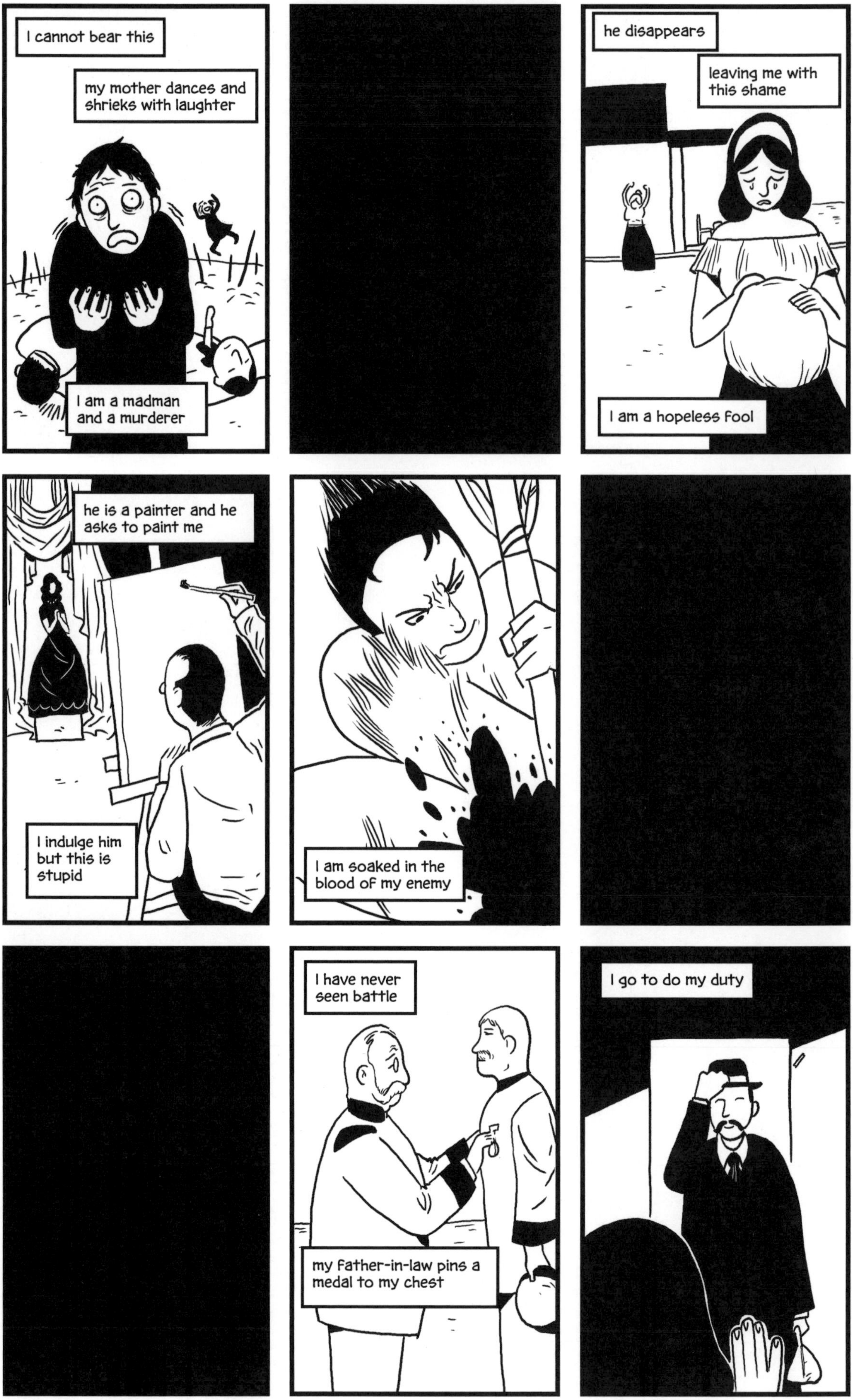
I cannot bear this
my mother dances and shrieks with laughter
I am a madman and a murderer
he disappears
leaving me with this shame
I am a hopeless fool
he is a painter and he asks to paint me
I indulge him but this is stupid
I am soaked in the blood of my enemy
I have never seen battle
my father-in-law pins a medal to my chest
I go to do my duty

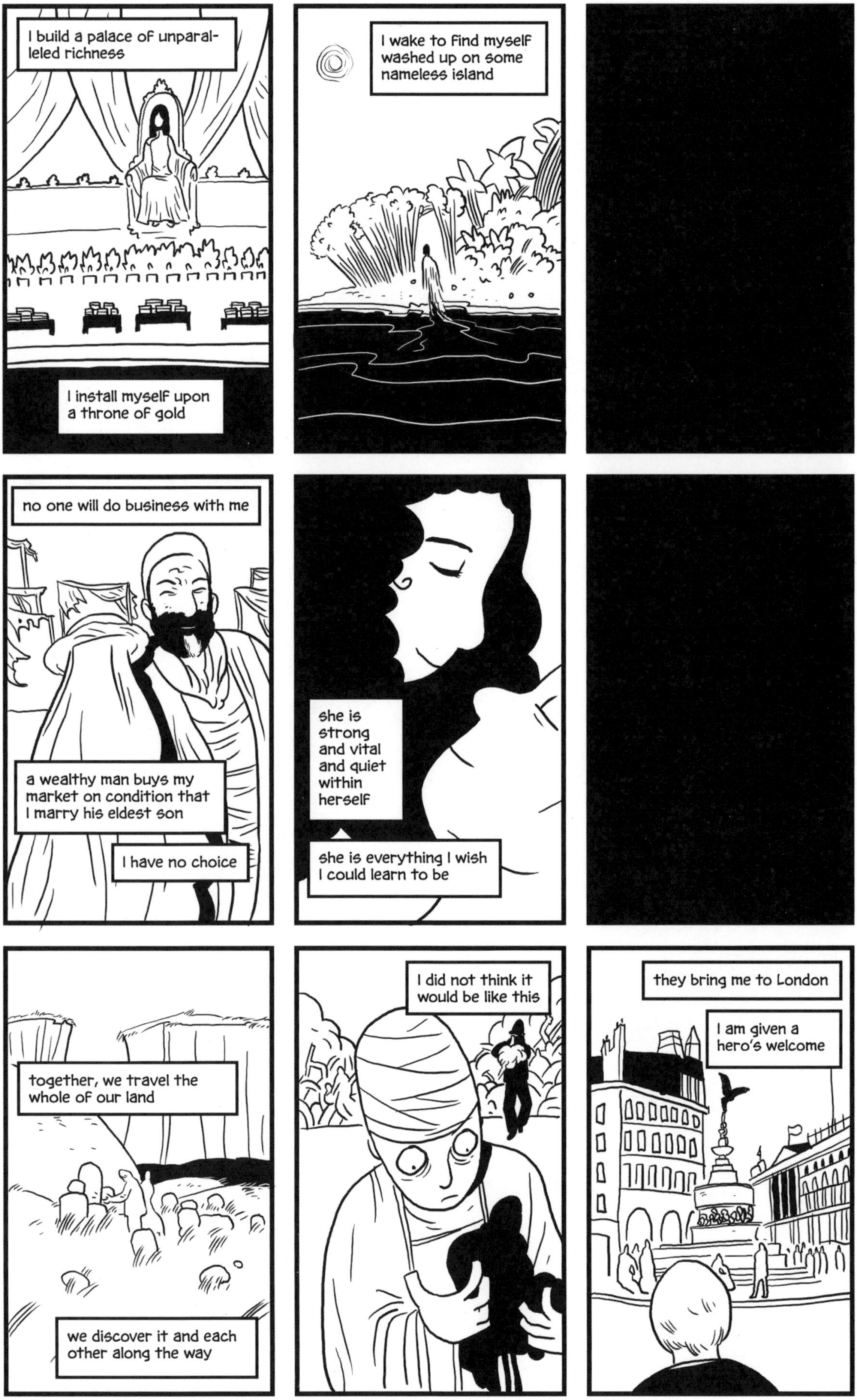
I build a palace of unparal-
leled richness
I install myself upon
a throne of gold
I wake to find myself
washed up on some
nameless island
no one will do business with me
a wealthy man buys my
market on condition that
I marry his eldest son
I have no choice
she is
strong
and vital
and quiet
within
herself
she is everything I wish
I could learn to be
together, we travel the
whole of our land
we discover it and each
other along the way
I did not think it
would be like this
they bring me to London
I am given a
hero's welcome

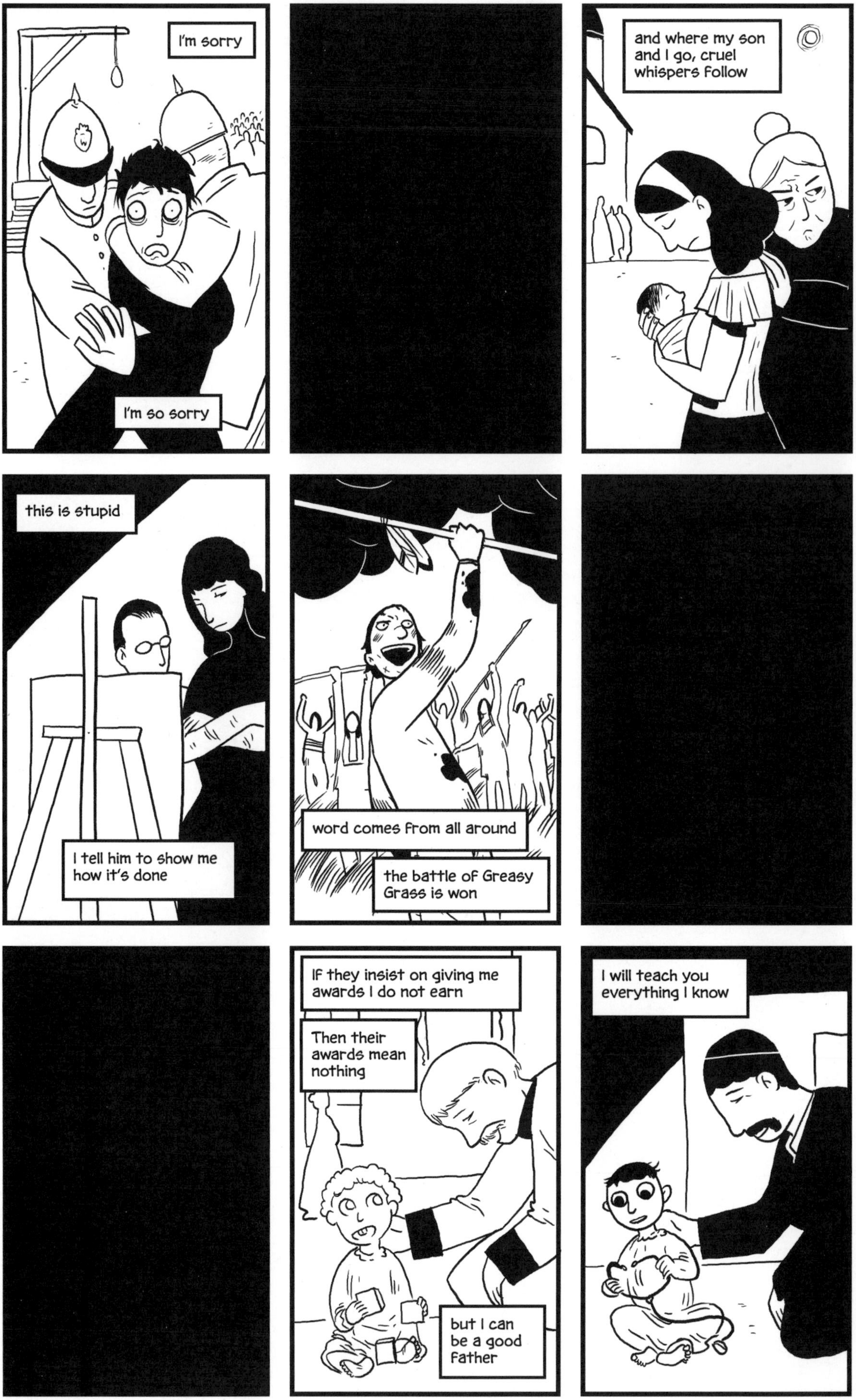
I'm sorry
I'm so sorry
and where my son and I go, cruel whispers follow
this is stupid
I tell him to show me how it's done
word comes from all around
the battle of Greasy Grass is won
If they insist on giving me awards I do not earn
Then their awards mean nothing
but I can be a good father
I will teach you everything I know

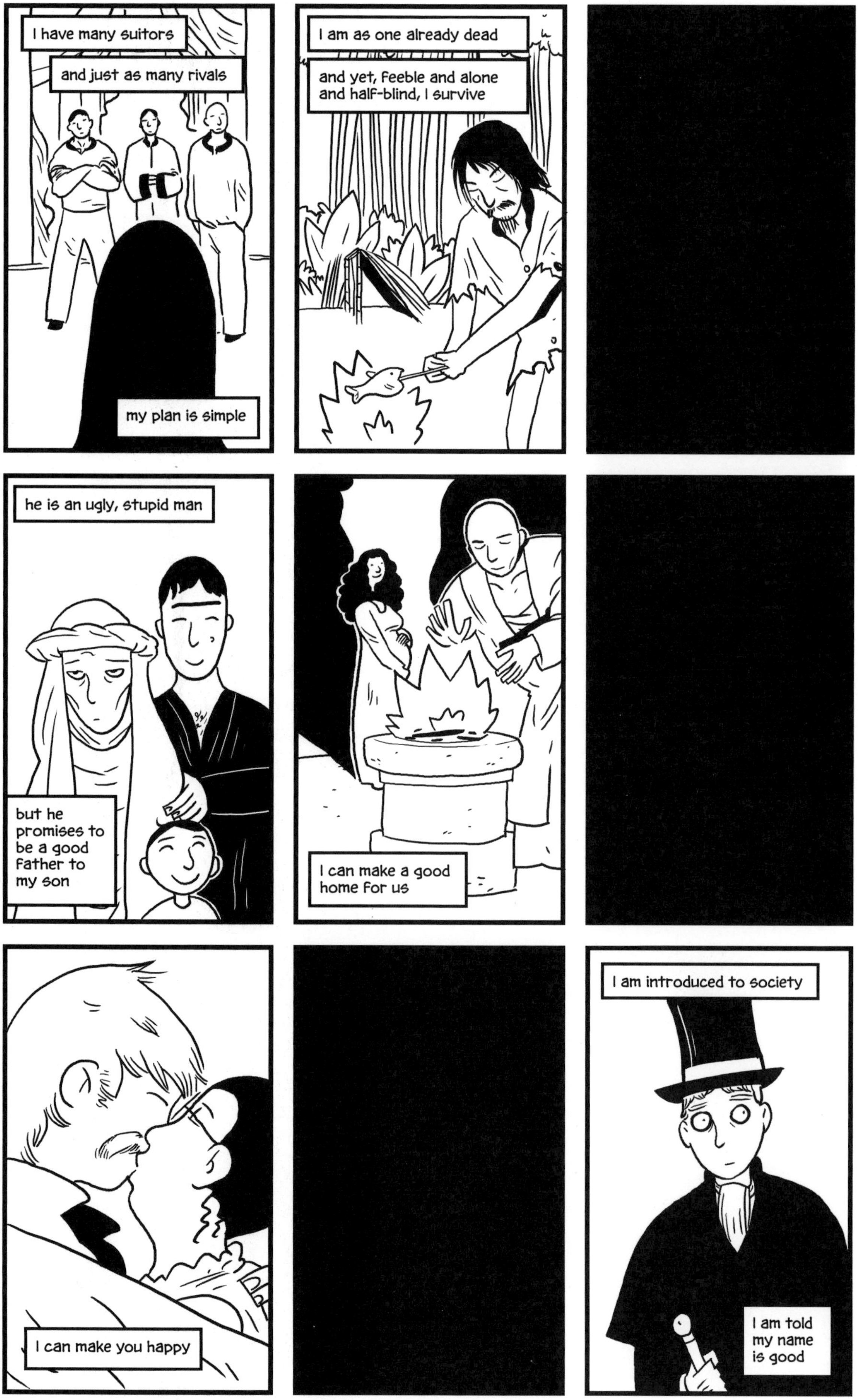
I have many suitors
and just as many rivals
my plan is simple
I am as one already dead
and yet, feeble and alone
and half-blind, I survive
he is an ugly, stupid man
but he promises to be a good father to my son
I can make a good home for us
I can make you happy
I am introduced to society
I am told my name is good

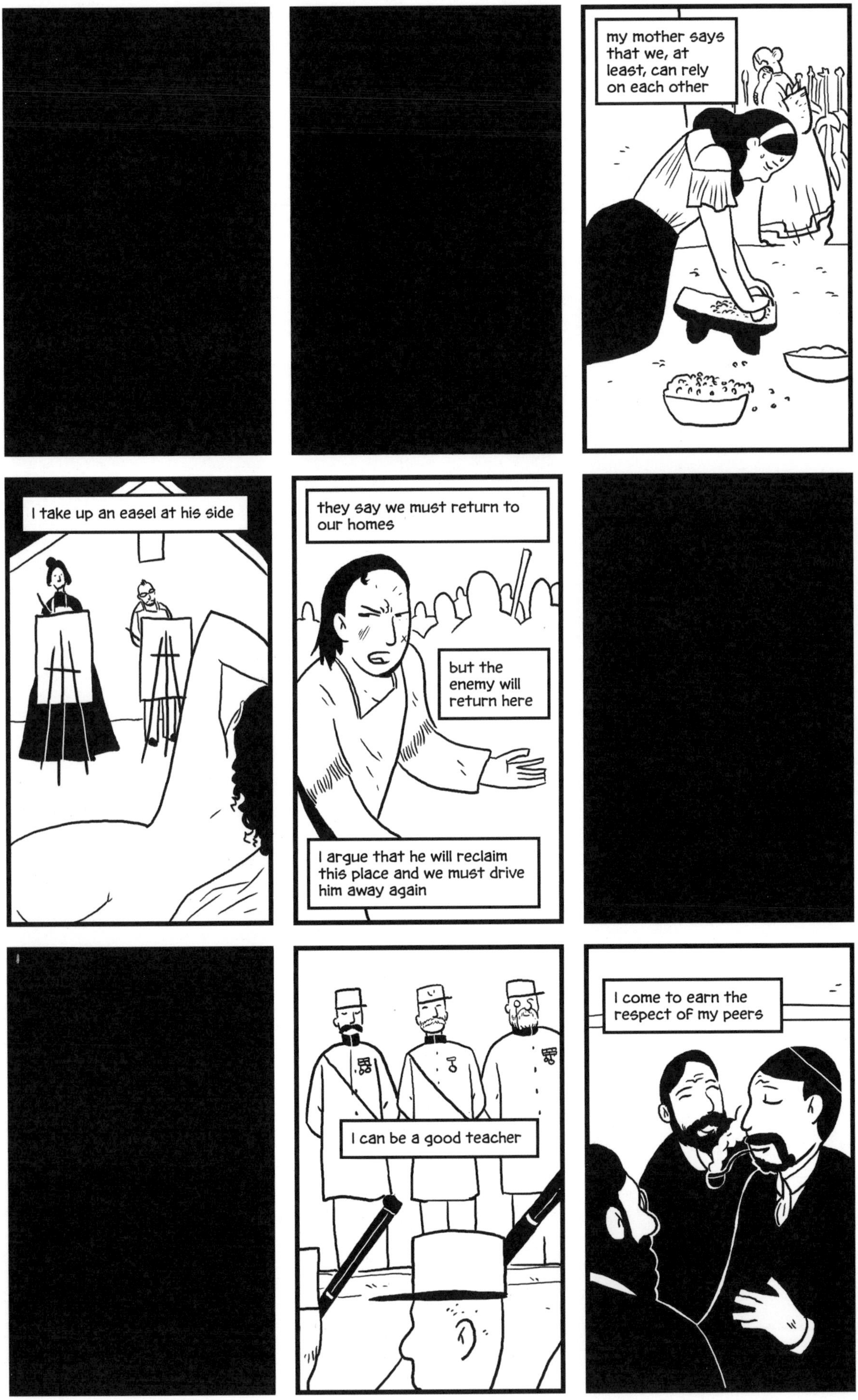
my mother says that we, at least, can rely on each other
I take up an easel at his side
they say we must return to our homes
but the enemy will return here
I argue that he will reclaim this place and we must drive him away again
I can be a good teacher
I come to earn the respect of my peers

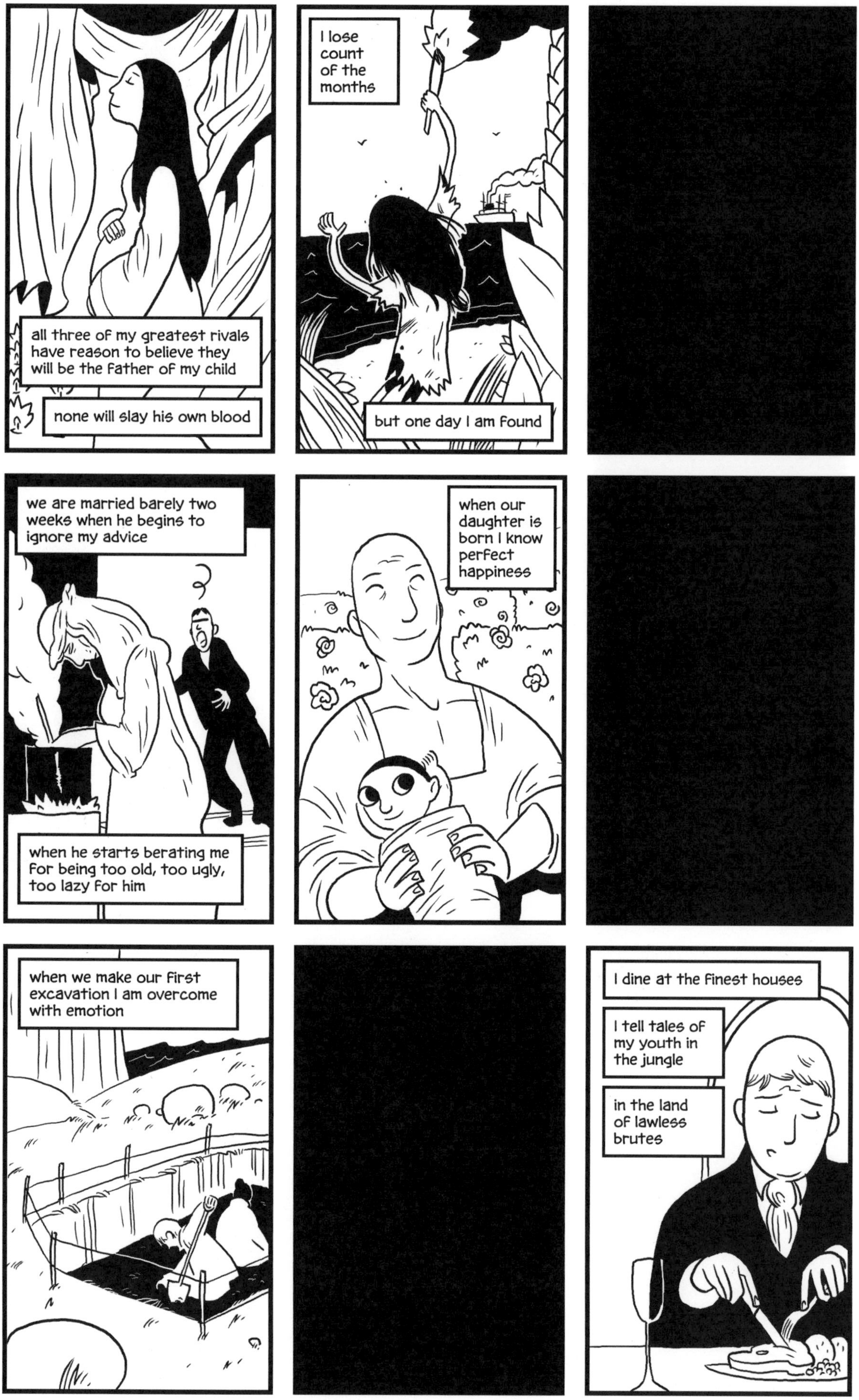
all three of my greatest rivals have reason to believe they will be the father of my child
none will slay his own blood
I lose count of the months
but one day I am found
we are married barely two weeks when he begins to ignore my advice
when he starts berating me for being too old, too ugly, too lazy for him
when our daughter is born I know perfect happiness
when we make our first excavation I am overcome with emotion
I dine at the finest houses
I tell tales of my youth in the jungle
in the land of lawless brutes

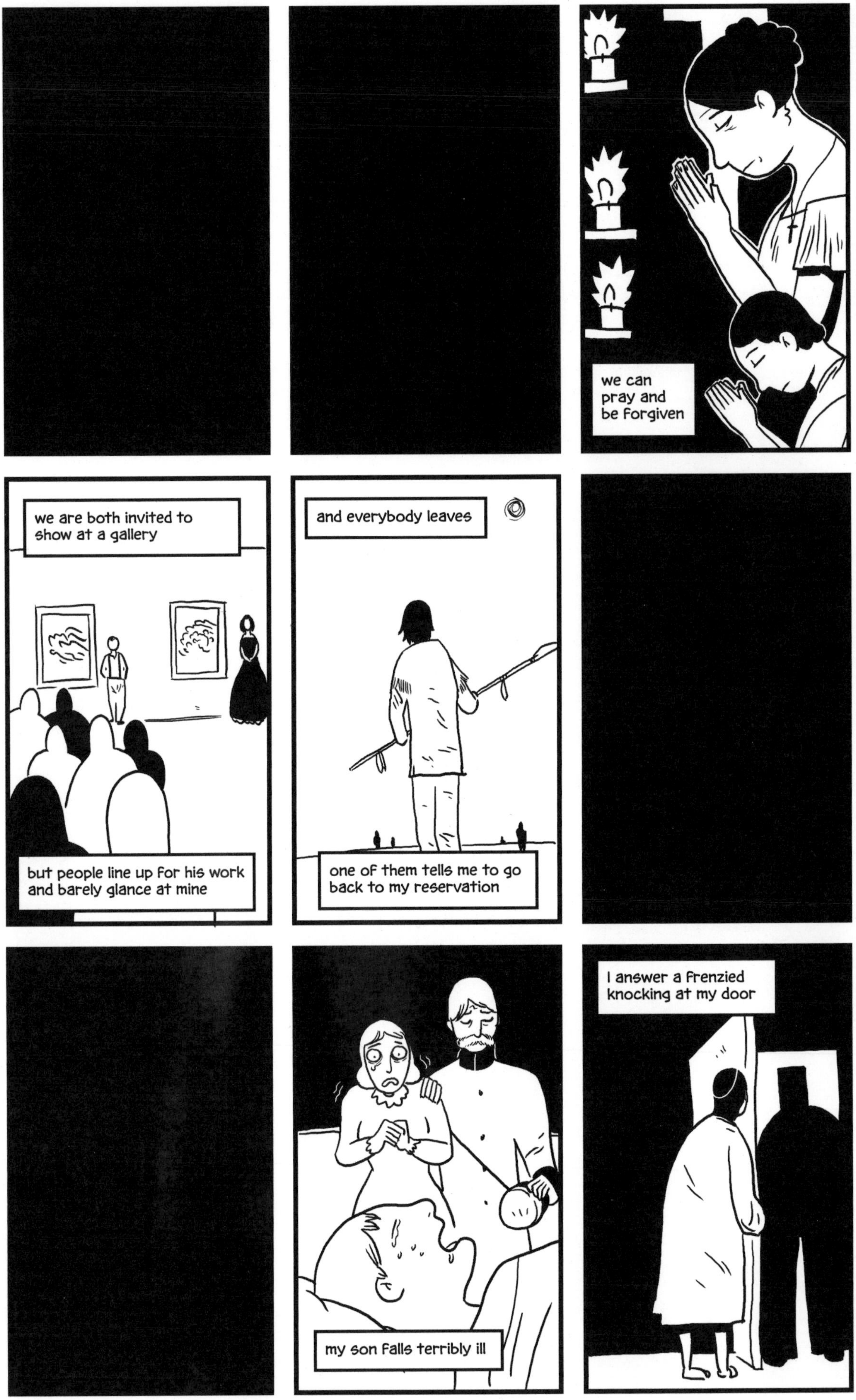
we can pray and be forgiven
we are both invited to show at a gallery
but people line up for his work and barely glance at mine
and everybody leaves
one of them tells me to go back to my reservation
my son falls terribly ill
I answer a frenzied knocking at my door

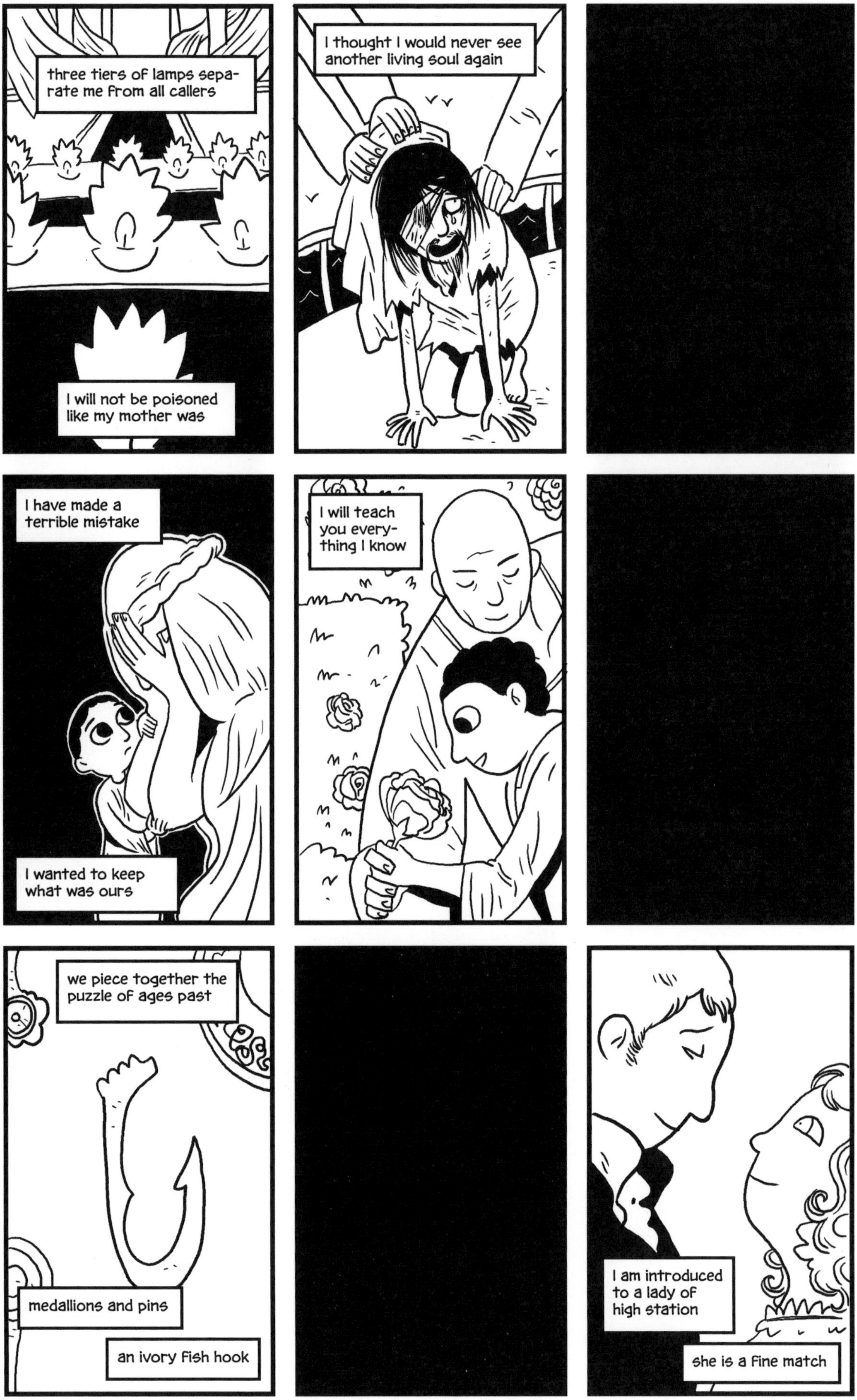
three tiers of lamps separate me from all callers
I will not be poisoned like my mother was
I thought I would never see another living soul again
I have made a terrible mistake
I wanted to keep what was ours
I will teach you everything I know
we piece together the puzzle of ages past
medallions and pins
an ivory fish hook
I am introduced to a lady of high station
she is a fine match

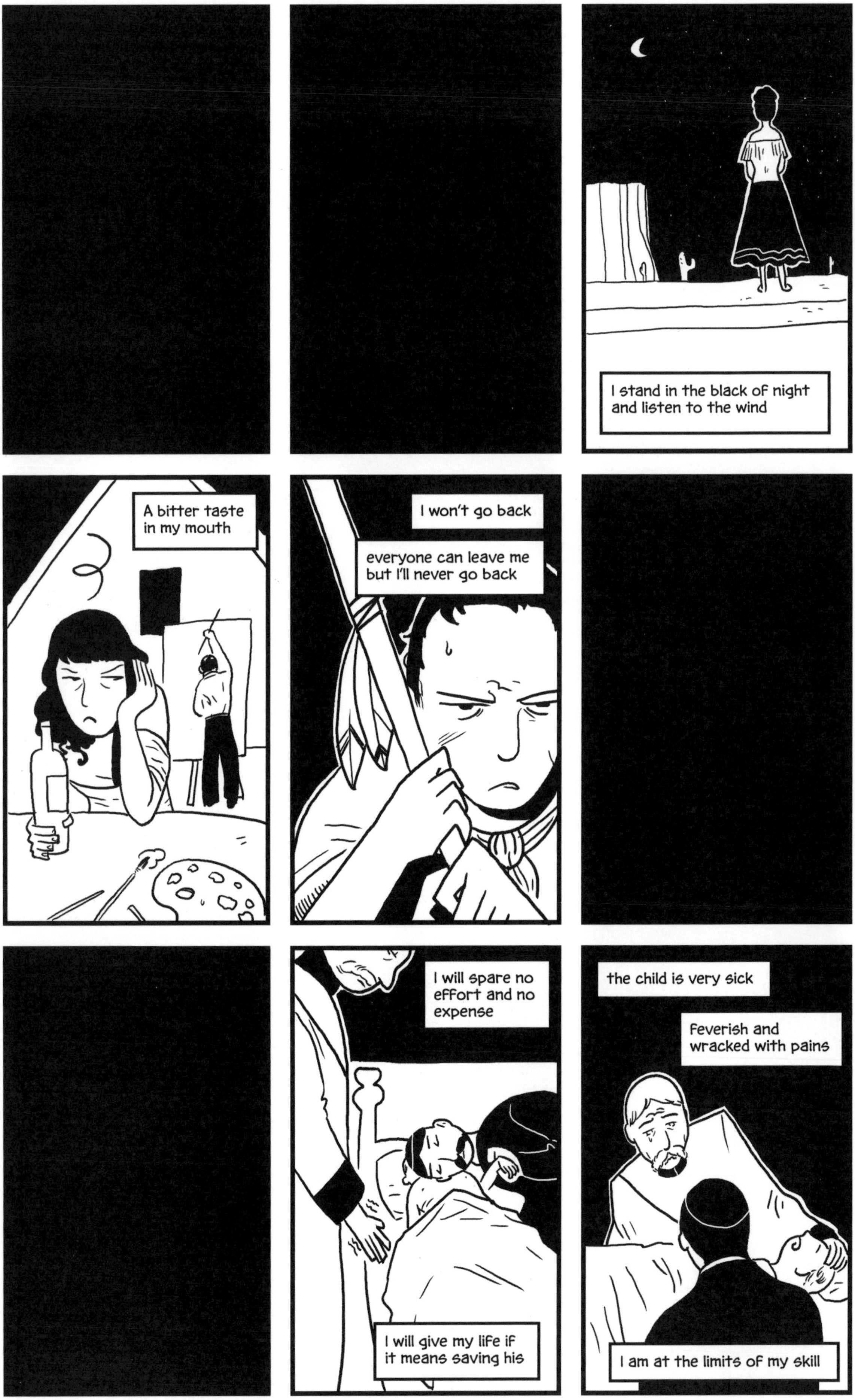
I stand in the black of night
and listen to the wind
A bitter taste
in my mouth
I won't go back
everyone can leave me
but I'll never go back
I will spare no
effort and no
expense
I will give my life if
it means saving his
the child is very sick
Feverish and
wracked with pains
I am at the limits of my skill

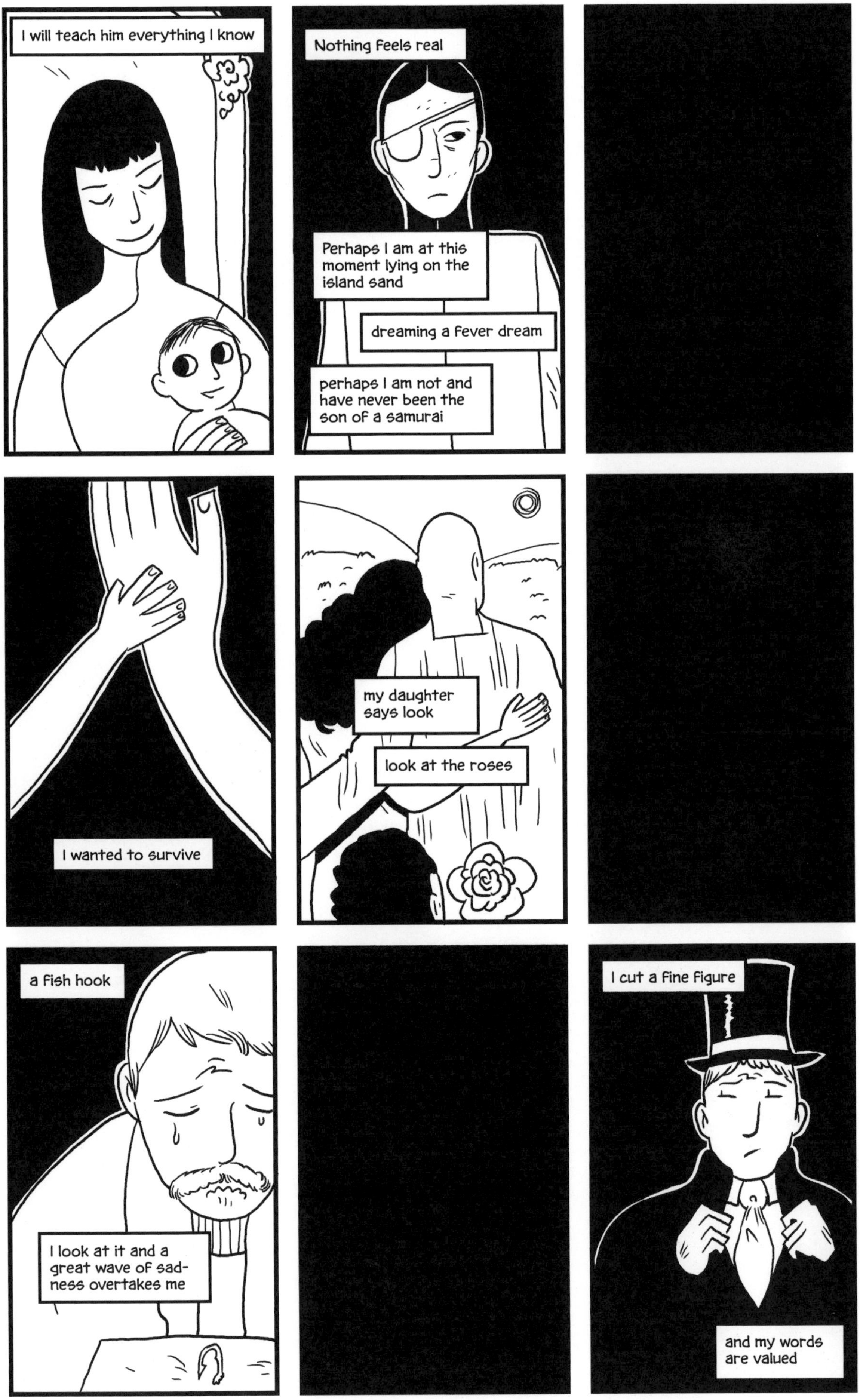
I will teach him everything I know
Nothing feels real
Perhaps I am at this moment lying on the island sand
dreaming a fever dream
perhaps I am not and have never been the son of a samurai
I wanted to survive
my daughter says look
look at the roses
a fish hook
I look at it and a great wave of sadness overtakes me
I cut a fine figure
and my words are valued

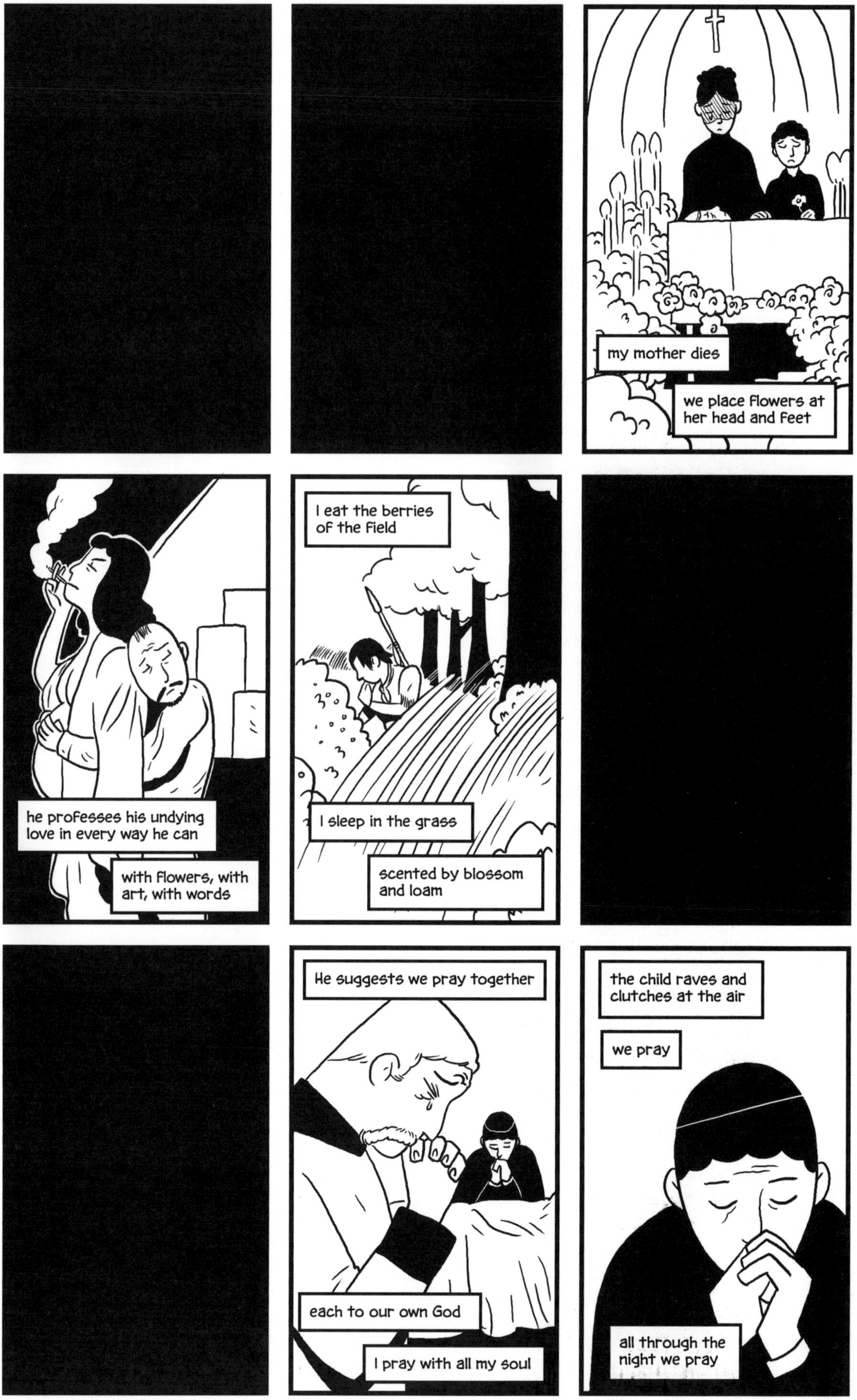
my mother dies
we place flowers at her head and feet
he professes his undying love in every way he can
with flowers, with art, with words
I eat the berries of the field
I sleep in the grass
scented by blossom and loam
He suggests we pray together
each to our own God
I pray with all my soul
the child raves and clutches at the air
we pray
all through the night we pray

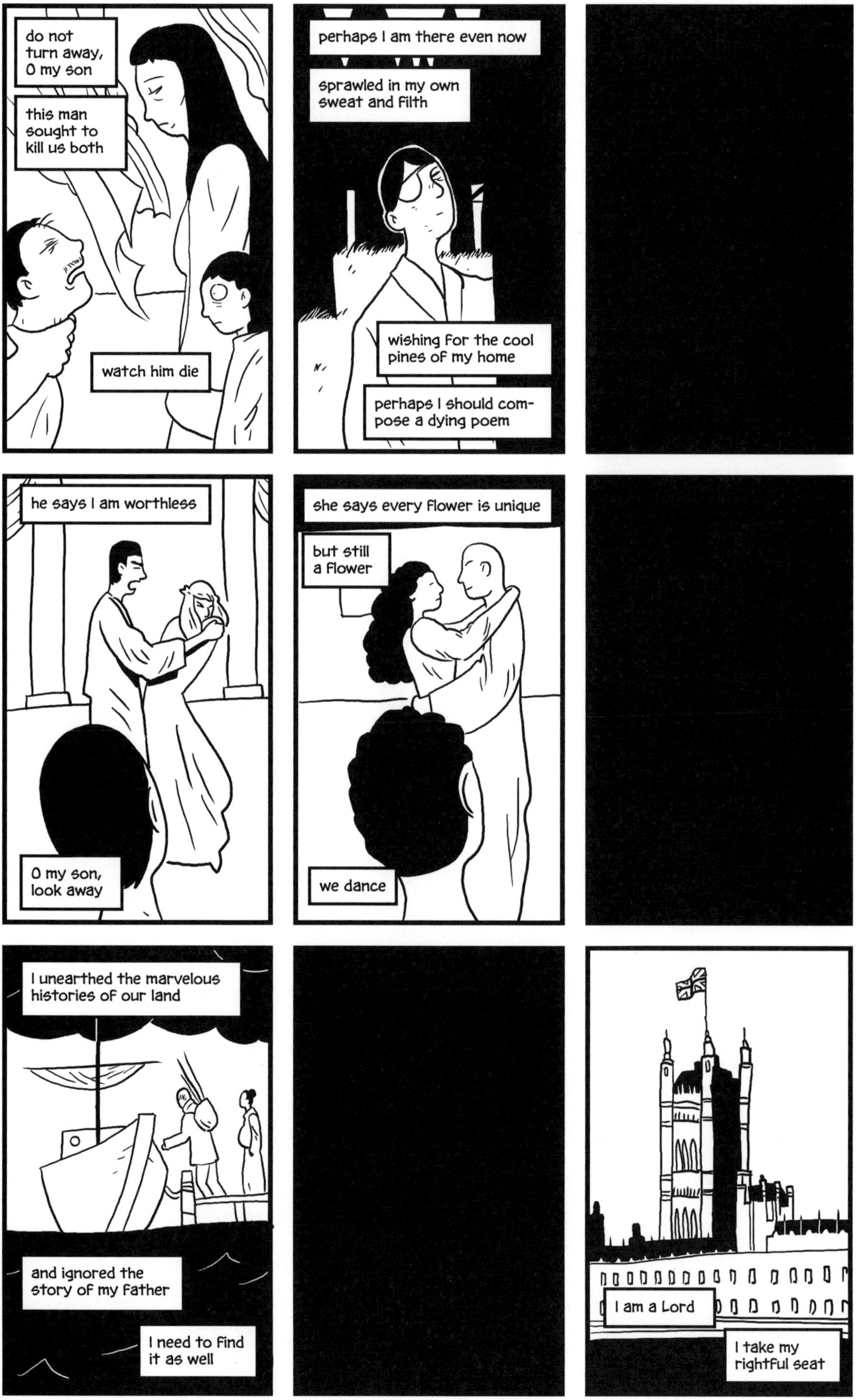
do not turn away, O my son
this man sought to kill us both
watch him die
perhaps I am there even now
sprawled in my own sweat and filth
wishing for the cool pines of my home
perhaps I should compose a dying poem
he says I am worthless
O my son, look away
she says every flower is unique
but still a flower
we dance
I unearthed the marvelous histories of our land
and ignored the story of my father
I need to find it as well
I am a Lord
I take my rightful seat

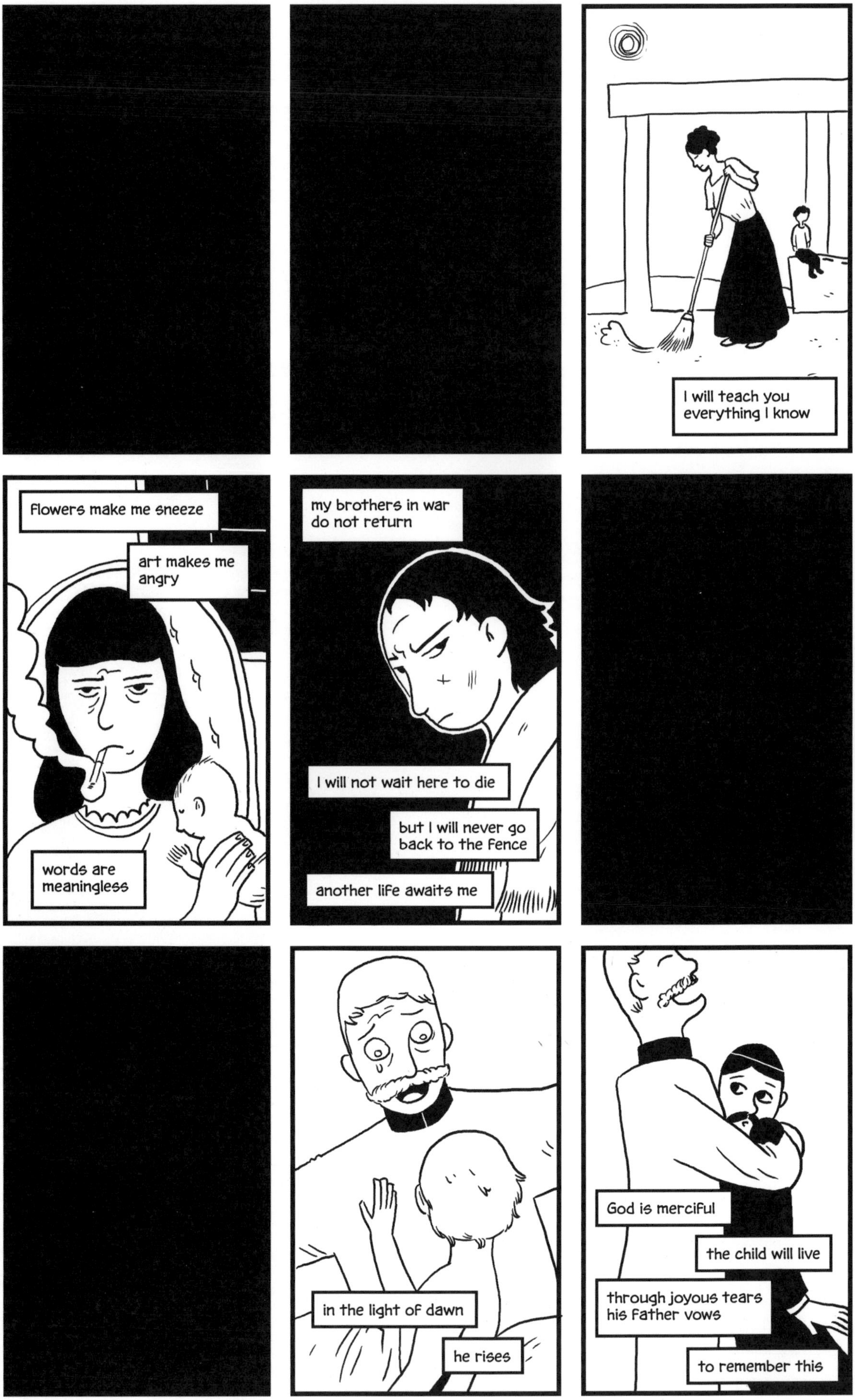
I will teach you everything I know
Flowers make me sneeze
art makes me angry
words are meaningless
my brothers in war do not return
I will not wait here to die
but I will never go back to the fence
another life awaits me
in the light of dawn
he rises
God is merciful
the child will live
through joyous tears his father vows
to remember this

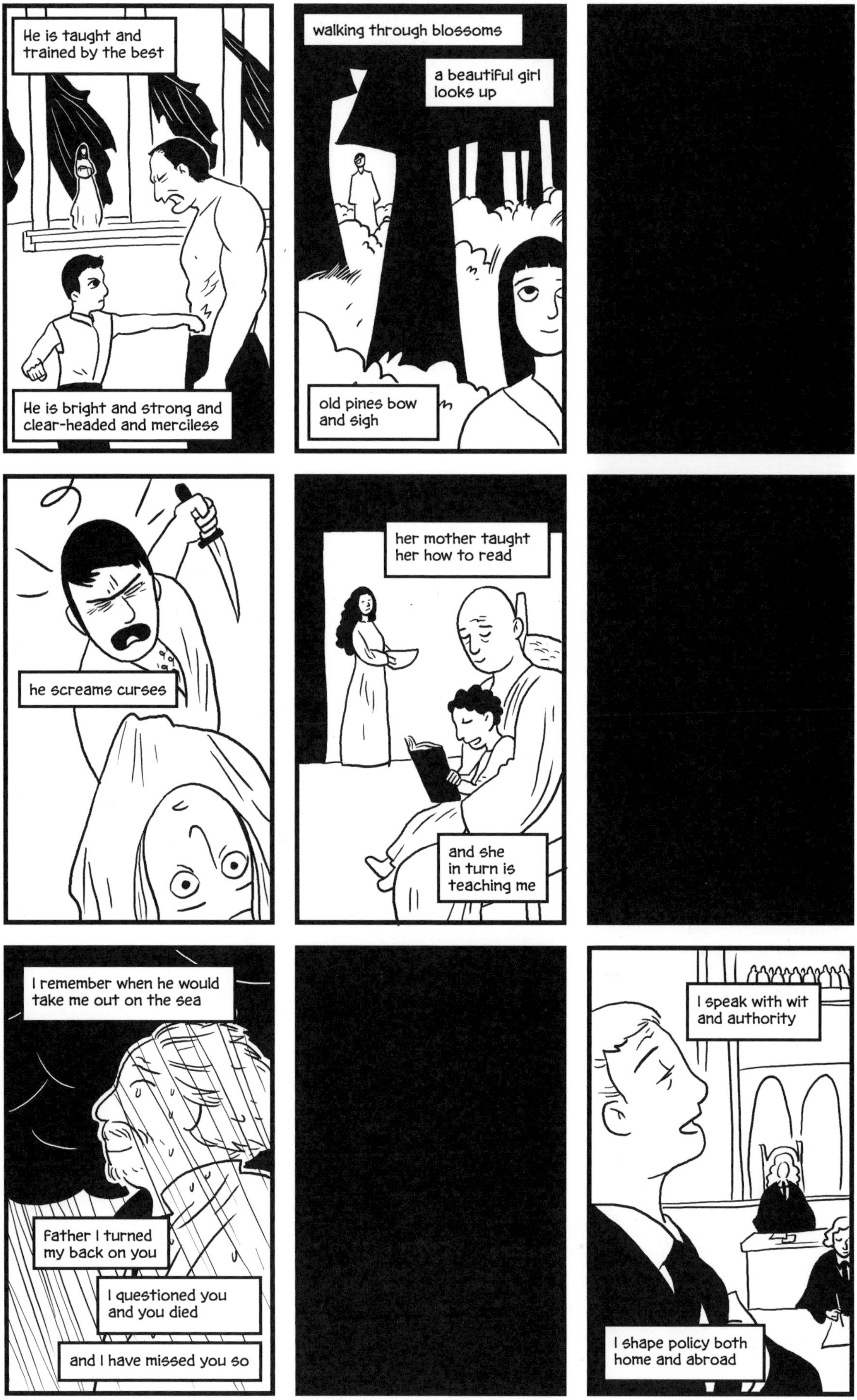
He is taught and trained by the best
He is bright and strong and clear-headed and merciless
walking through blossoms
a beautiful girl looks up
old pines bow and sigh
he screams curses
her mother taught her how to read
and she in turn is teaching me
I remember when he would take me out on the sea
Father I turned my back on you
I questioned you and you died
and I have missed you so
I speak with wit and authority
I shape policy both home and abroad

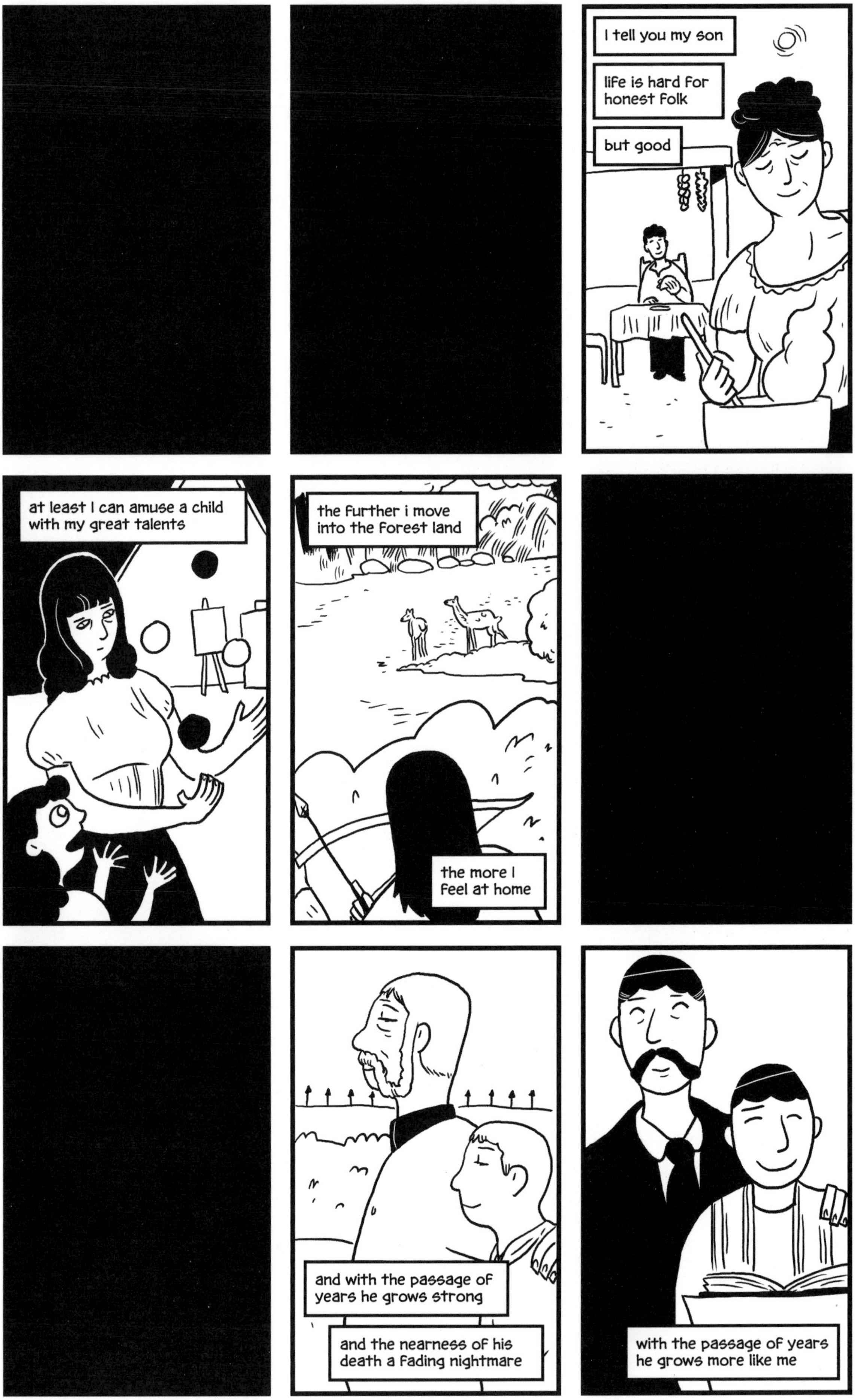
I tell you my son
life is hard for honest folk
but good
at least I can amuse a child with my great talents
the further i move into the forest land
the more I feel at home
and with the passage of years he grows strong
and the nearness of his death a fading nightmare
with the passage of years he grows more like me

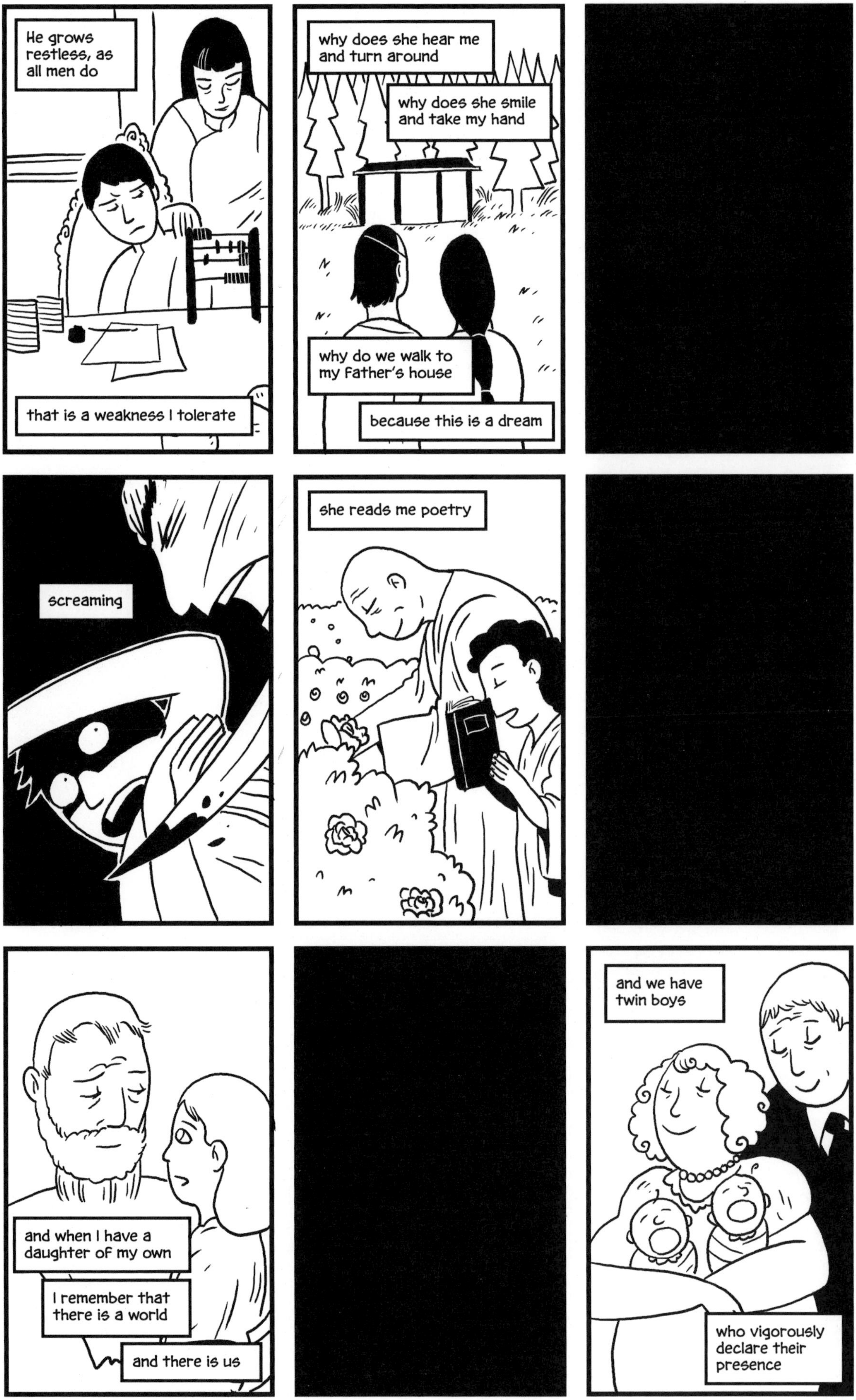
He grows restless, as all men do
that is a weakness I tolerate
why does she hear me and turn around
why does she smile and take my hand
why do we walk to my father's house
because this is a dream
screaming
she reads me poetry
and when I have a daughter of my own
I remember that there is a world
and there is us
and we have twin boys
who vigorously declare their presence

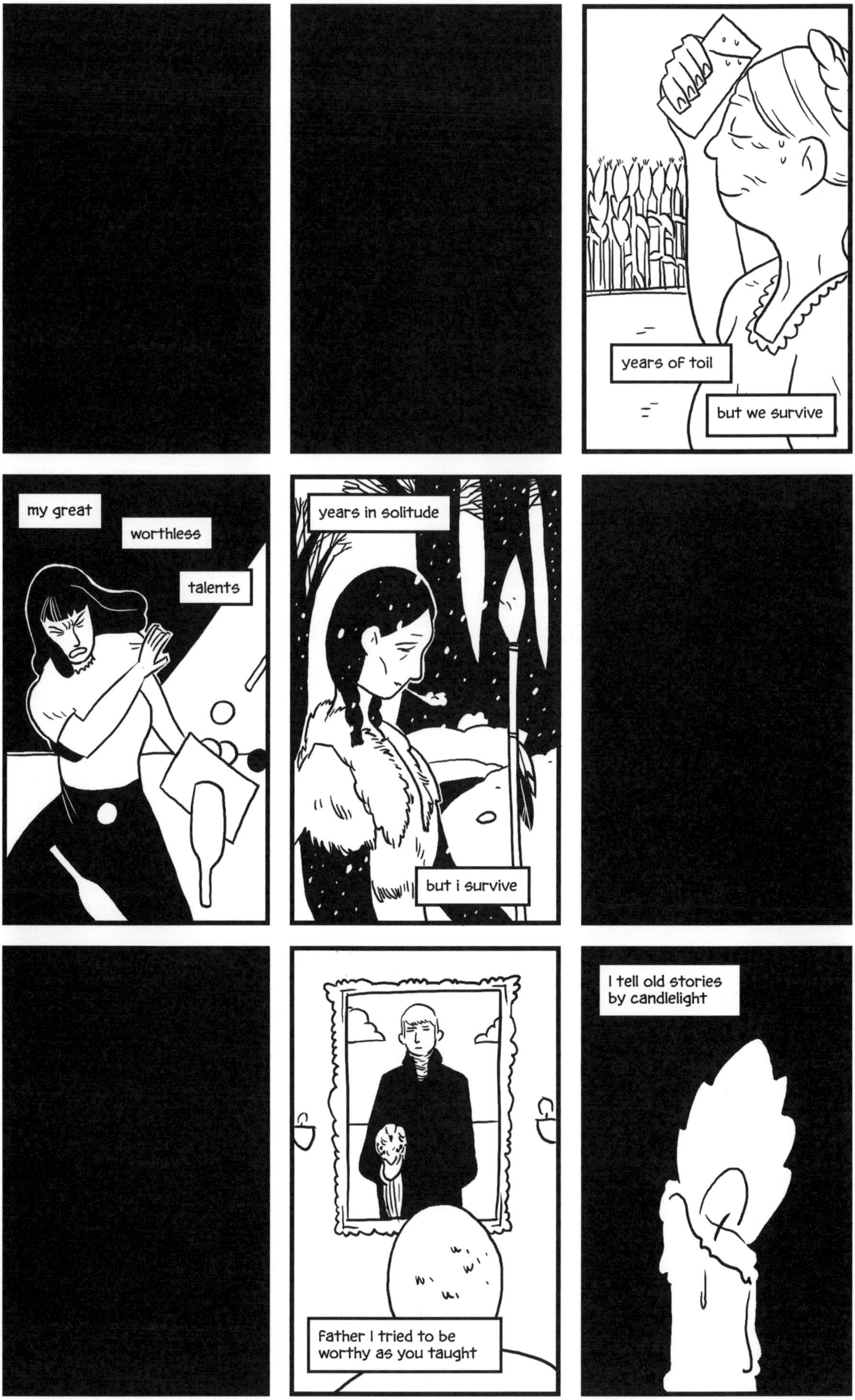
years of toil
but we survive
my great
worthless
talents
years in solitude
but i survive
father I tried to be worthy as you taught
I tell old stories by candlelight

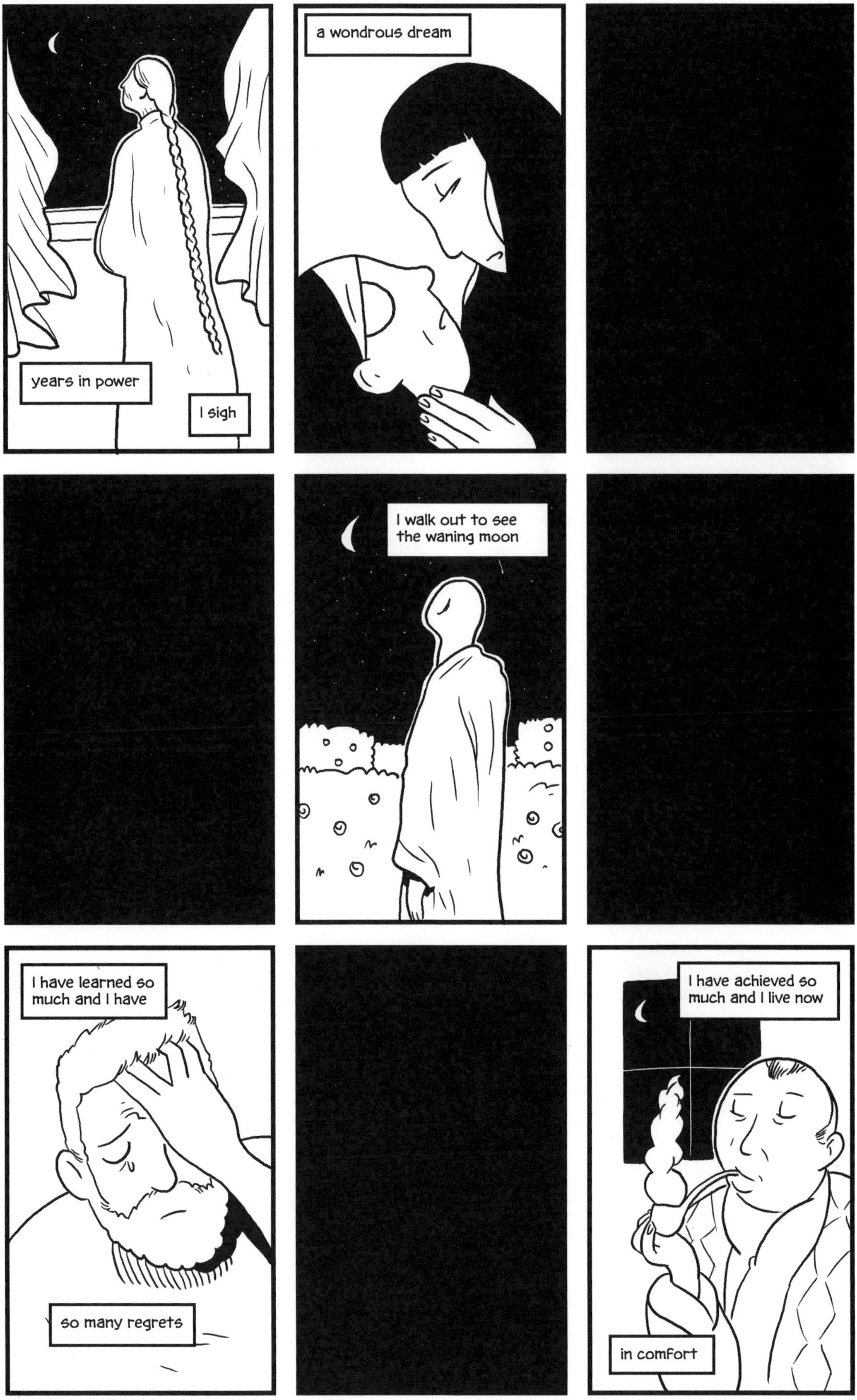
years in power
I sigh
a wondrous dream
I walk out to see the waning moon
I have learned so much and I have
so many regrets
I have achieved so much and I live now
in comfort

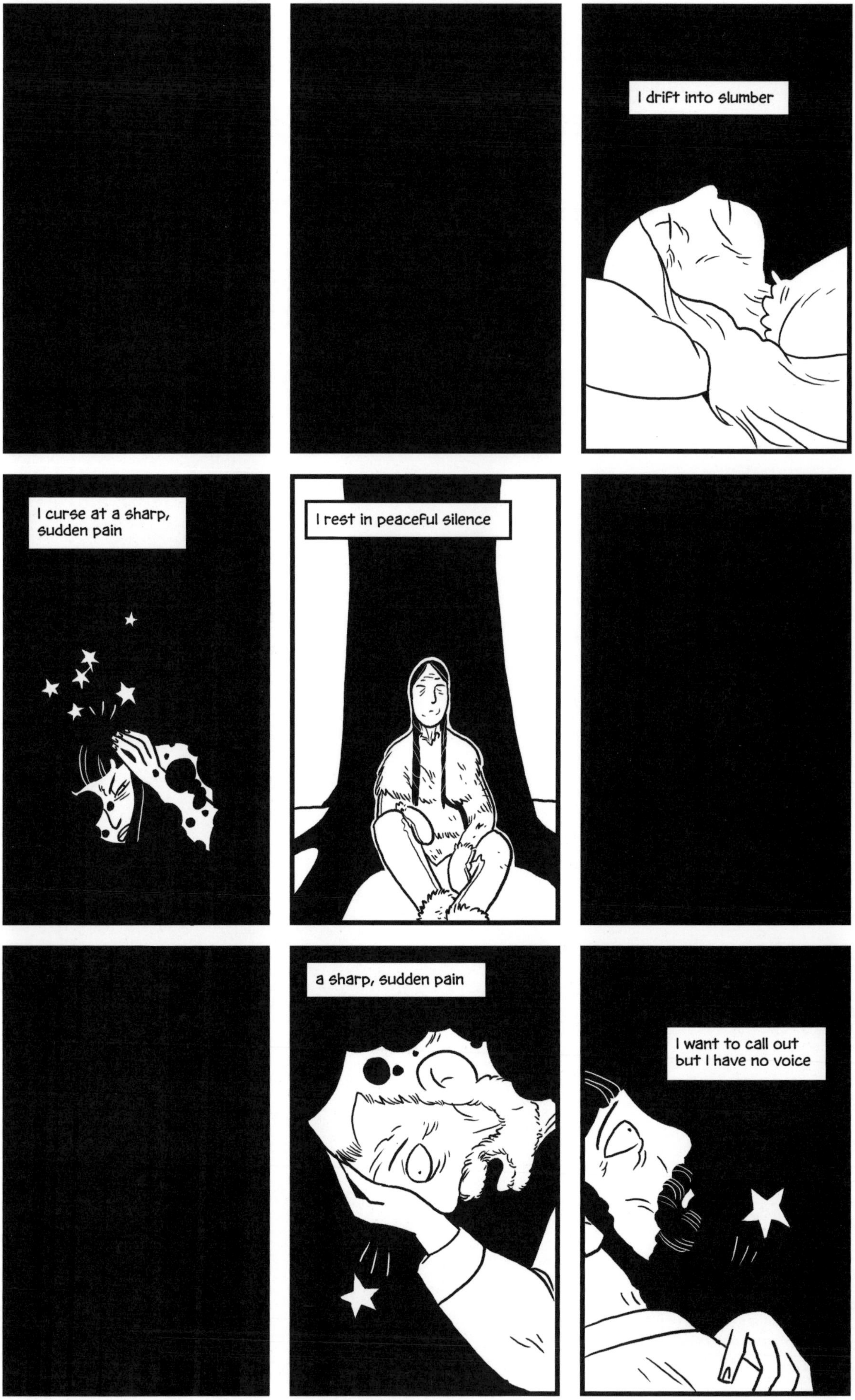
I drift into slumber
I curse at a sharp, sudden pain
I rest in peaceful silence
a sharp, sudden pain
I want to call out but I have no voice

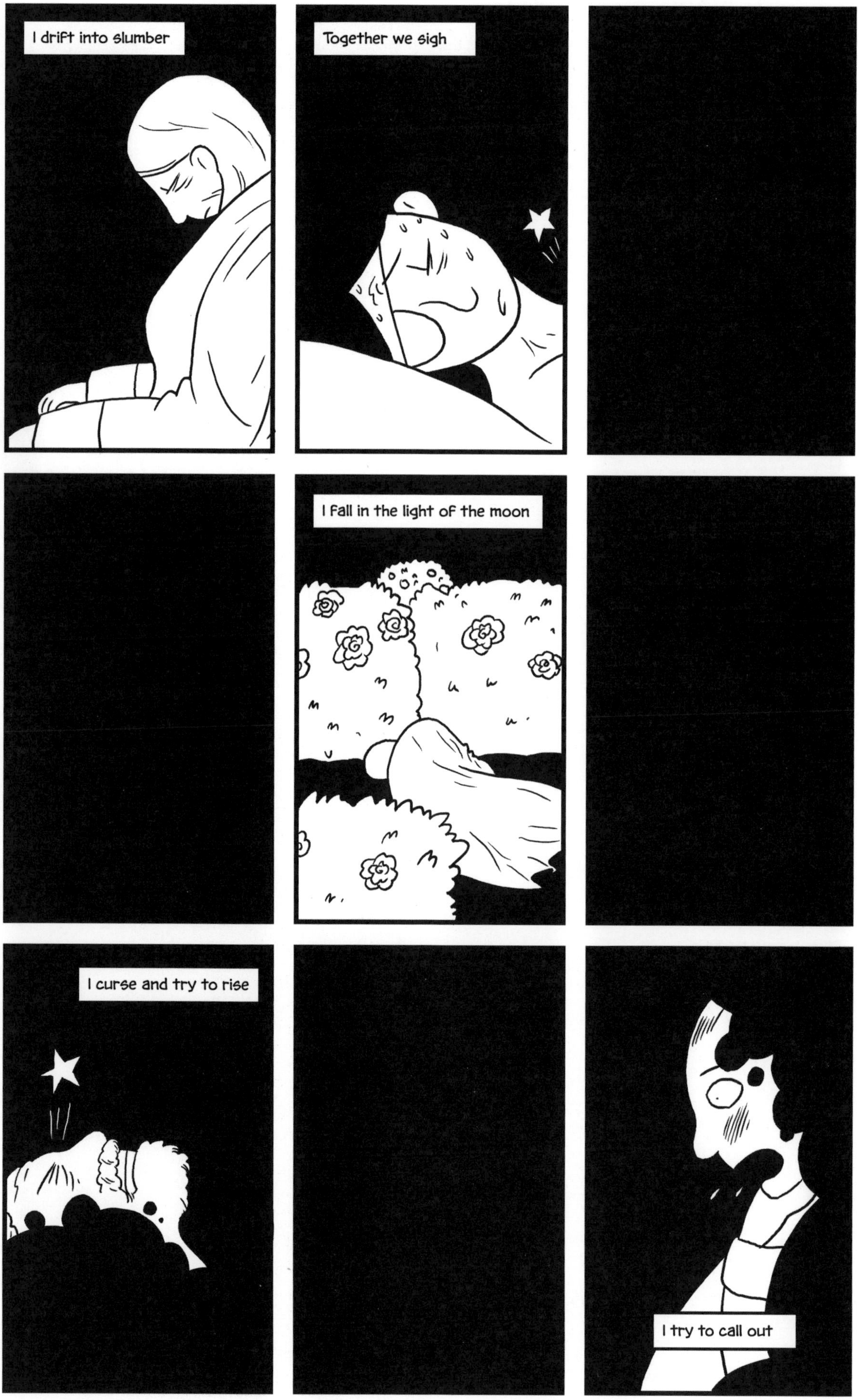
I drift into slumber
Together we sigh
I fall in the light of the moon
I curse and try to rise
I try to call out

PART FOUR

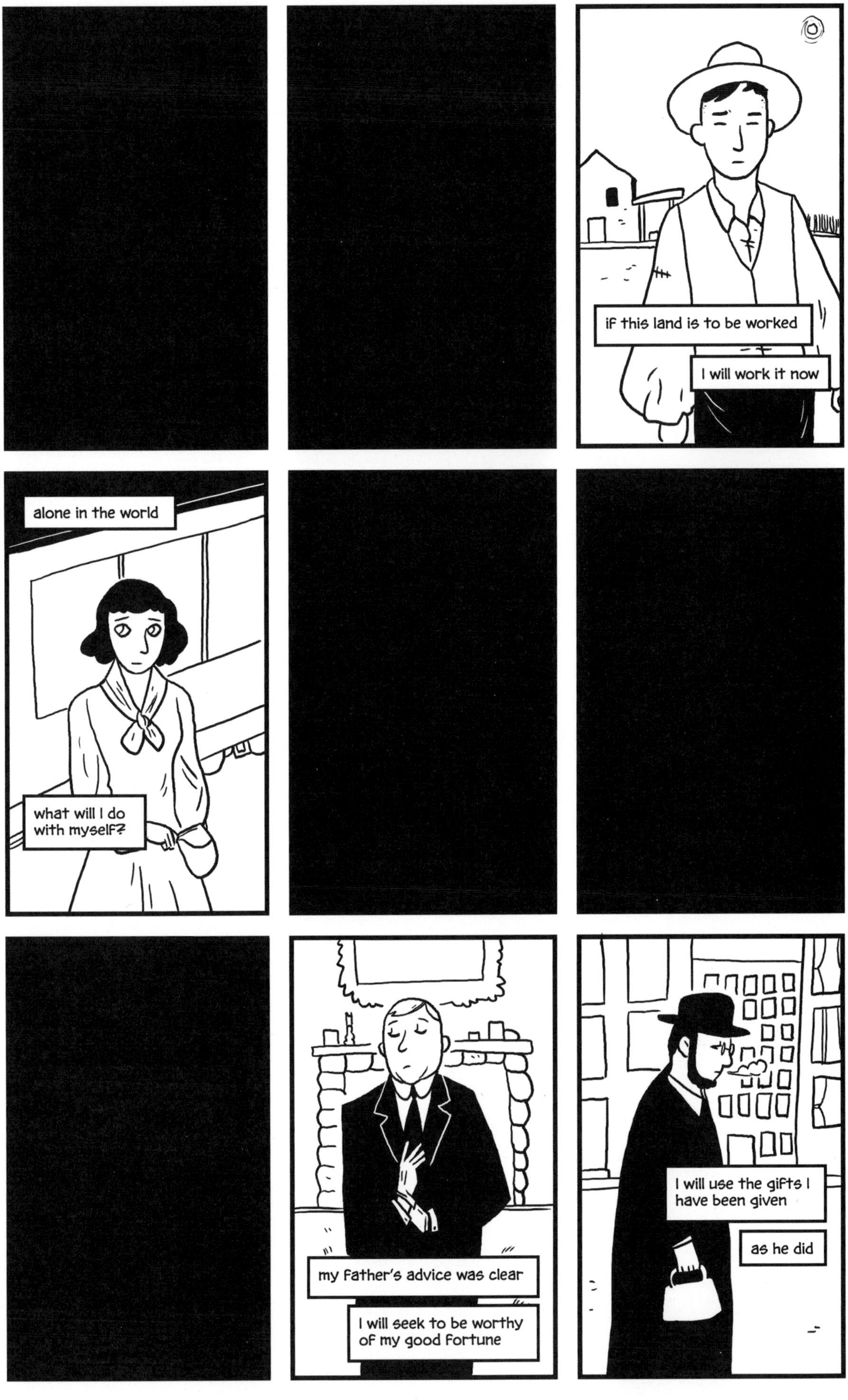
if this land is to be worked
I will work it now
alone in the world
what will I do
with myself?
my father's advice was clear
I will seek to be worthy
of my good fortune
I will use the gifts I
have been given
as he did

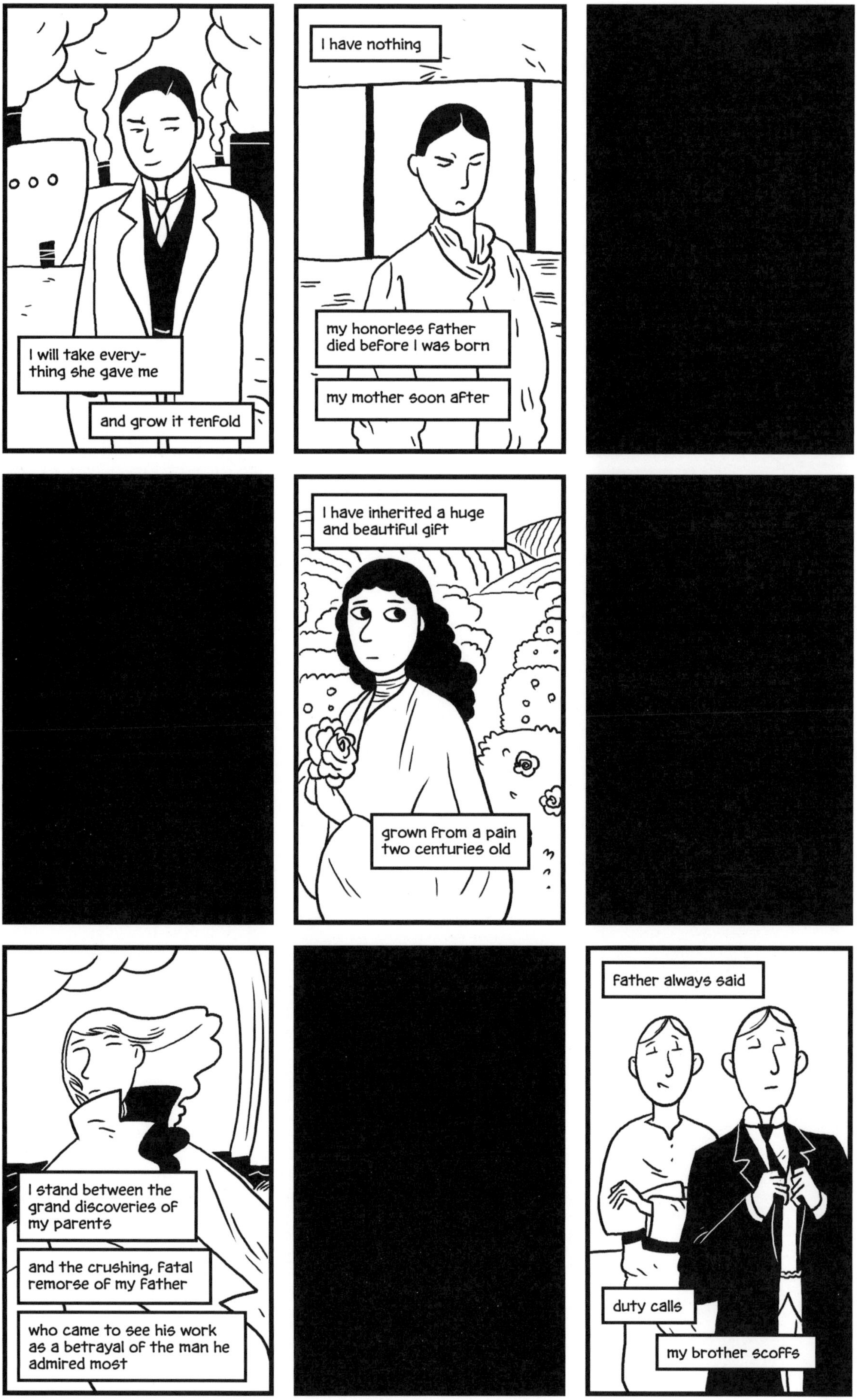
I will take every-thing she gave me
and grow it tenfold
I have nothing
my honorless father died before I was born
my mother soon after
I have inherited a huge and beautiful gift
grown from a pain two centuries old
I stand between the grand discoveries of my parents
and the crushing, fatal remorse of my father
who came to see his work as a betrayal of the man he admired most
father always said
duty calls
my brother scoffs

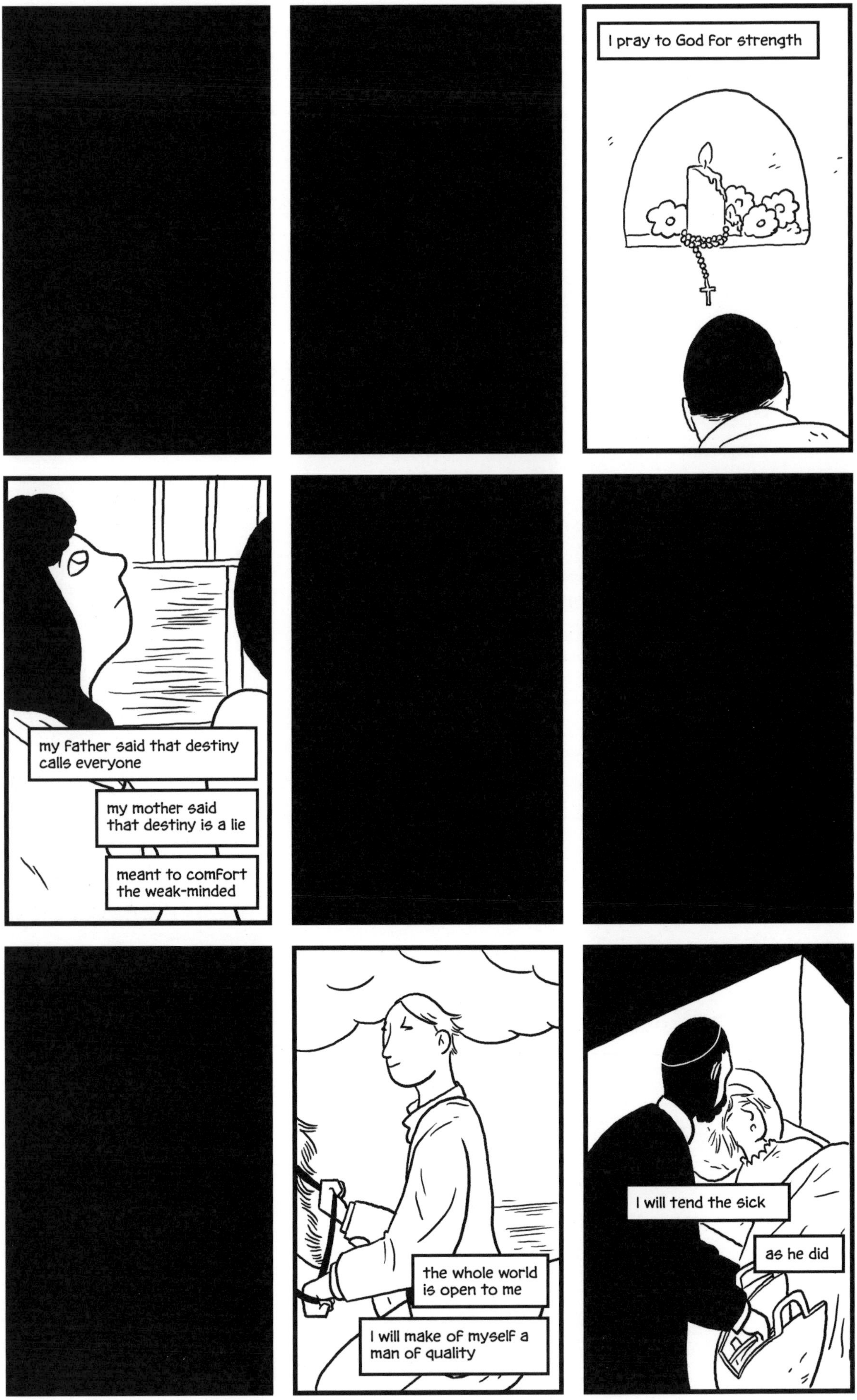
I pray to God for strength
my father said that destiny calls everyone
my mother said that destiny is a lie
meant to comfort the weak-minded
the whole world is open to me
I will make of myself a man of quality
I will tend the sick
as he did

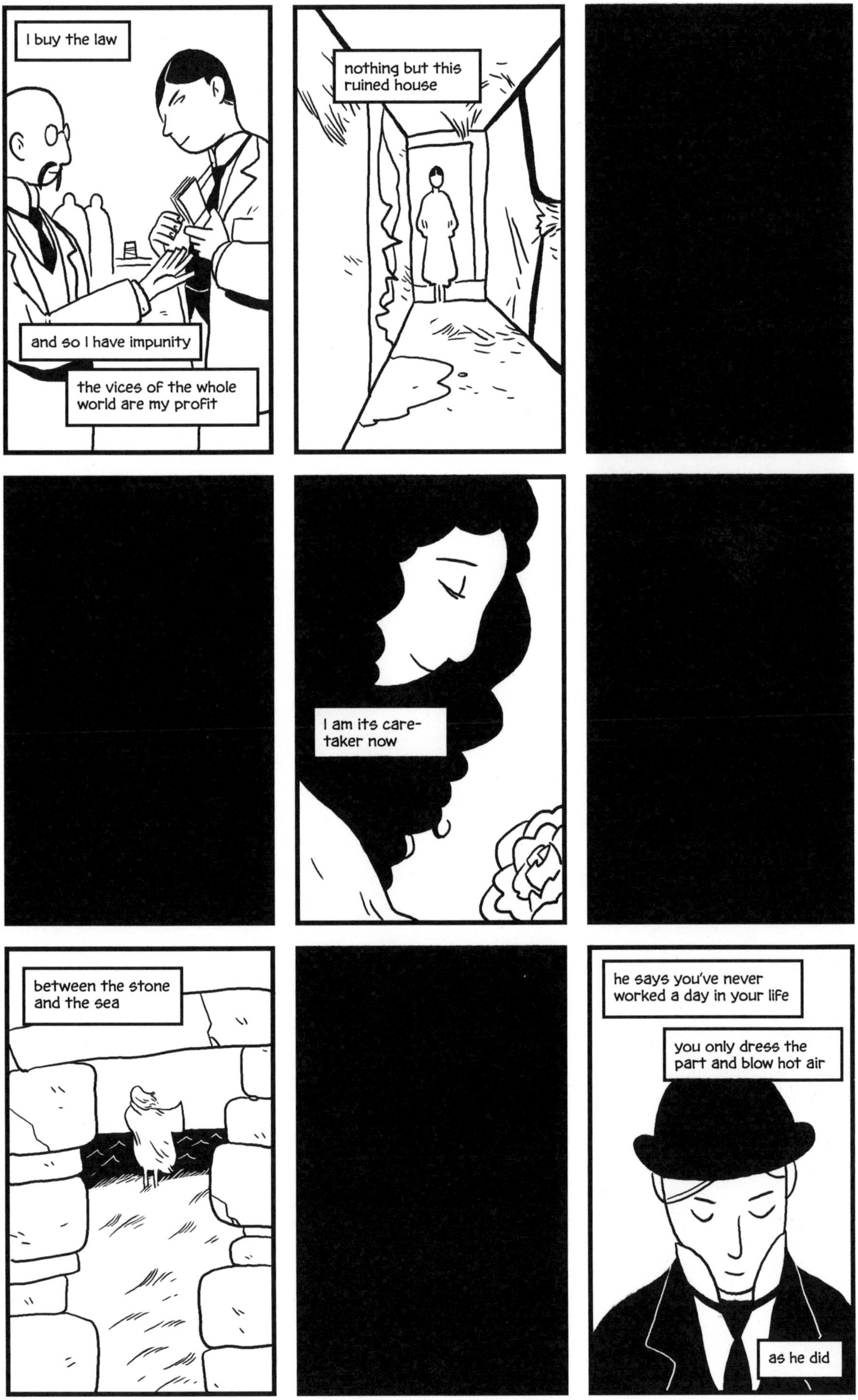
I buy the law
and so I have impunity
the vices of the whole world are my profit
nothing but this ruined house
I am its care-taker now
between the stone and the sea
he says you've never worked a day in your life
you only dress the part and blow hot air
as he did

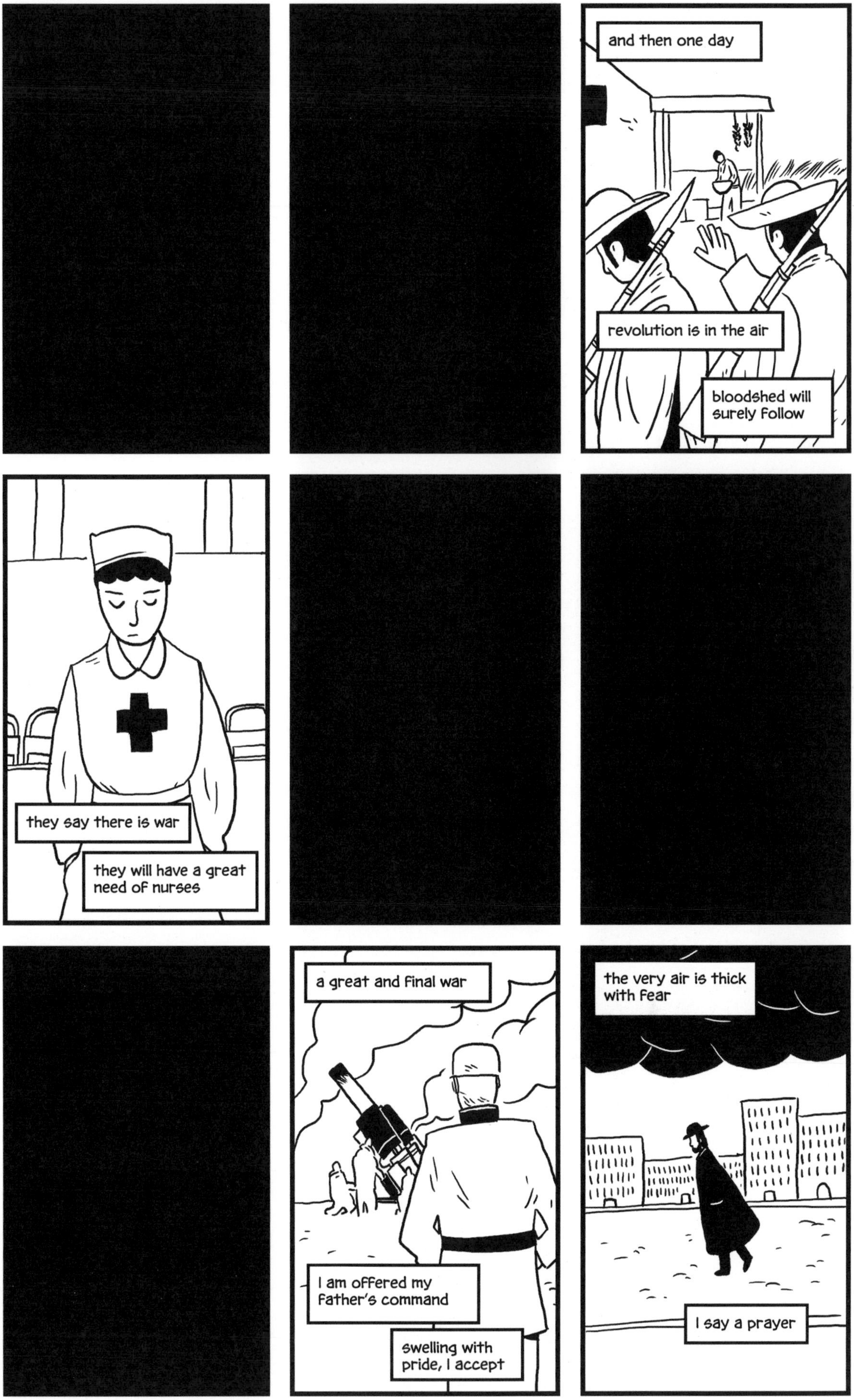
and then one day
revolution is in the air
bloodshed will surely follow
they say there is war
they will have a great need of nurses
a great and final war
I am offered my father's command
swelling with pride, I accept
the very air is thick with fear
I say a prayer

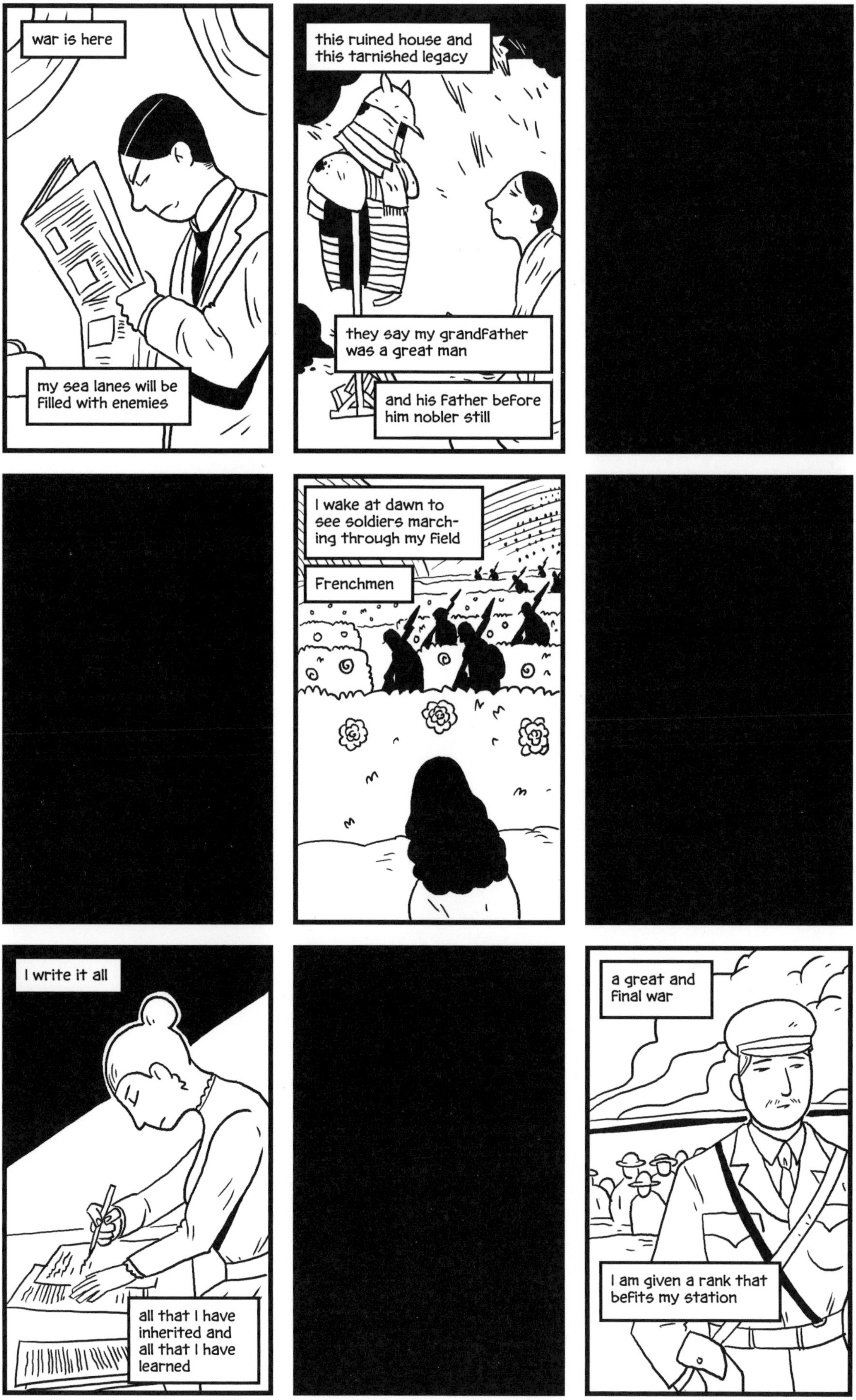
war is here
my sea lanes will be filled with enemies
this ruined house and this tarnished legacy
they say my grandfather was a great man
and his father before him nobler still
I wake at dawn to see soldiers march-ing through my field
Frenchmen
I write it all
all that I have inherited and all that I have learned
a great and final war
I am given a rank that befits my station

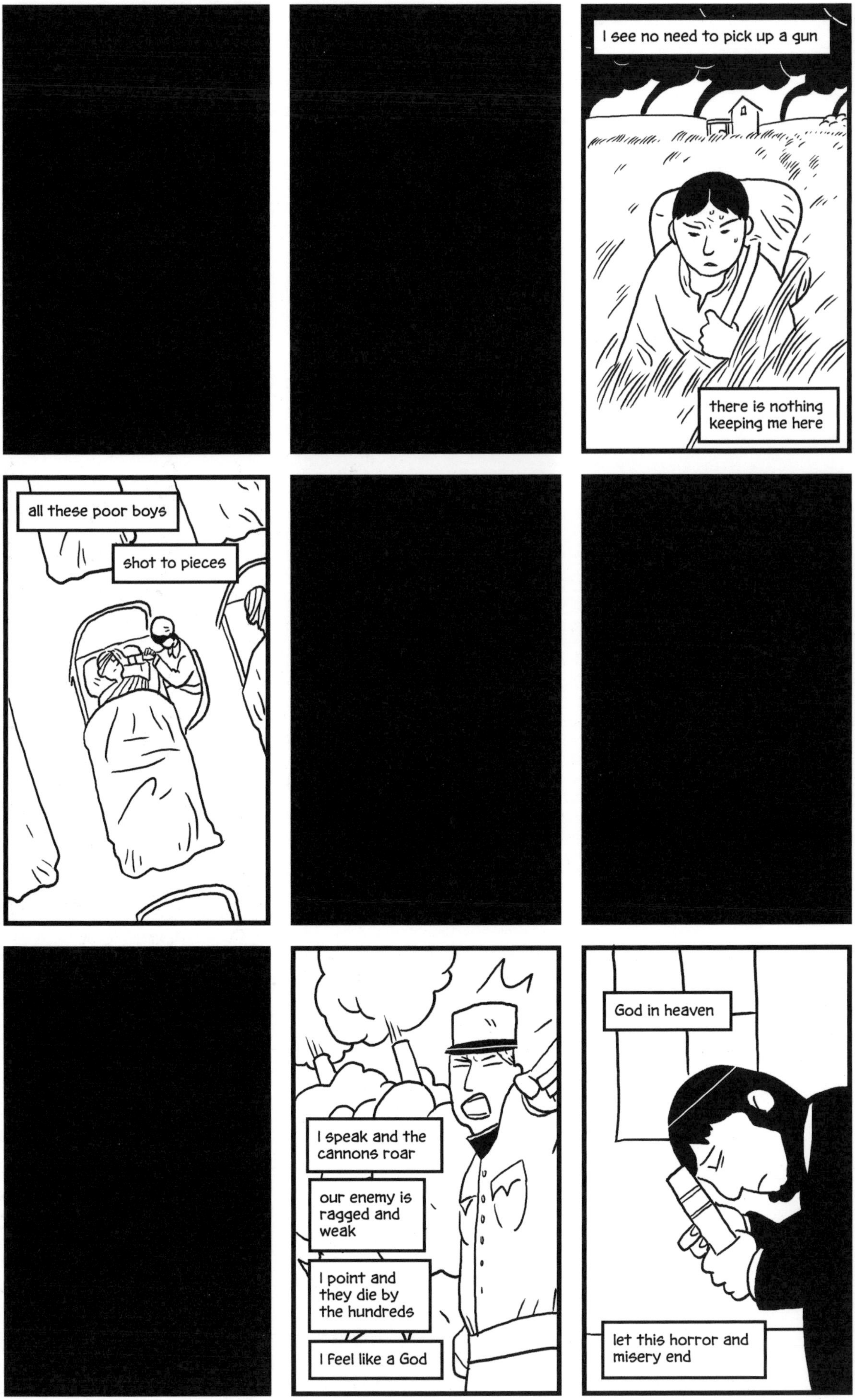
I see no need to pick up a gun
there is nothing keeping me here
all these poor boys
shot to pieces
I speak and the cannons roar
our enemy is ragged and weak
I point and they die by the hundreds
I feel like a God
God in heaven
let this horror and misery end

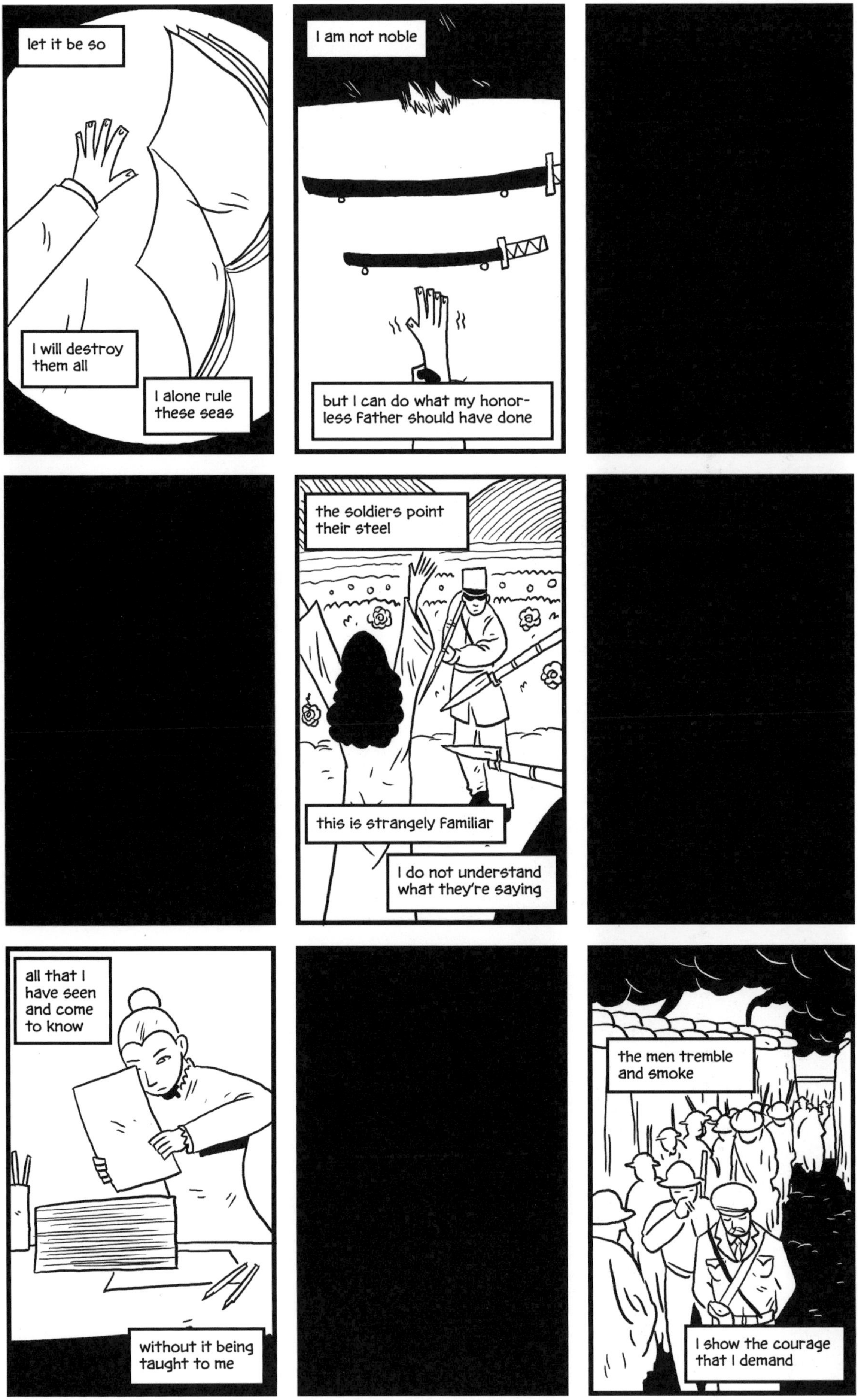
let it be so
I will destroy them all
I alone rule these seas
I am not noble
but I can do what my honor-less father should have done
the soldiers point their steel
this is strangely familiar
I do not understand what they're saying
all that I have seen and come to know
without it being taught to me
the men tremble and smoke
I show the courage that I demand

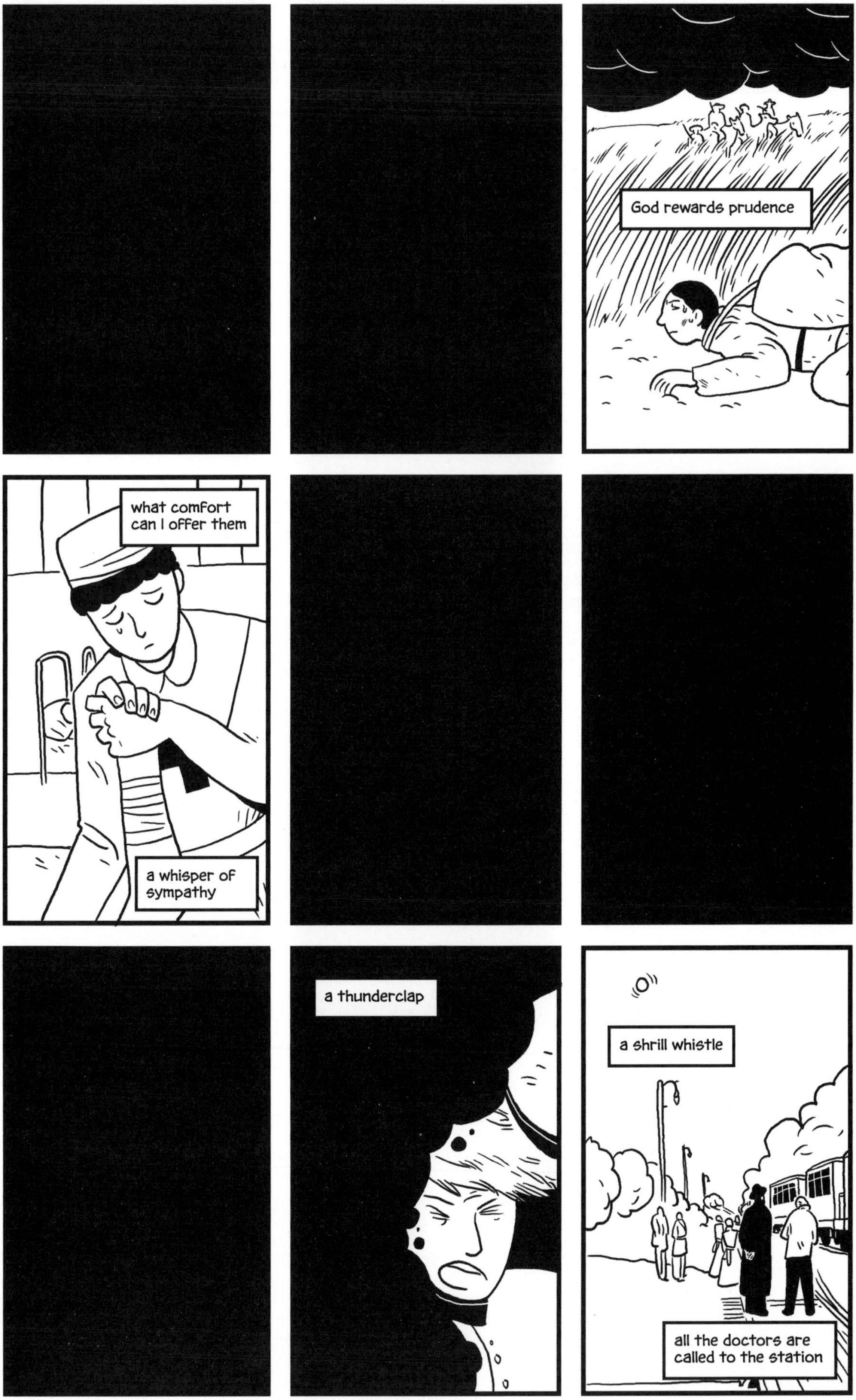
God rewards prudence
what comfort can I offer them
a whisper of sympathy
a thunderclap
a shrill whistle
all the doctors are called to the station

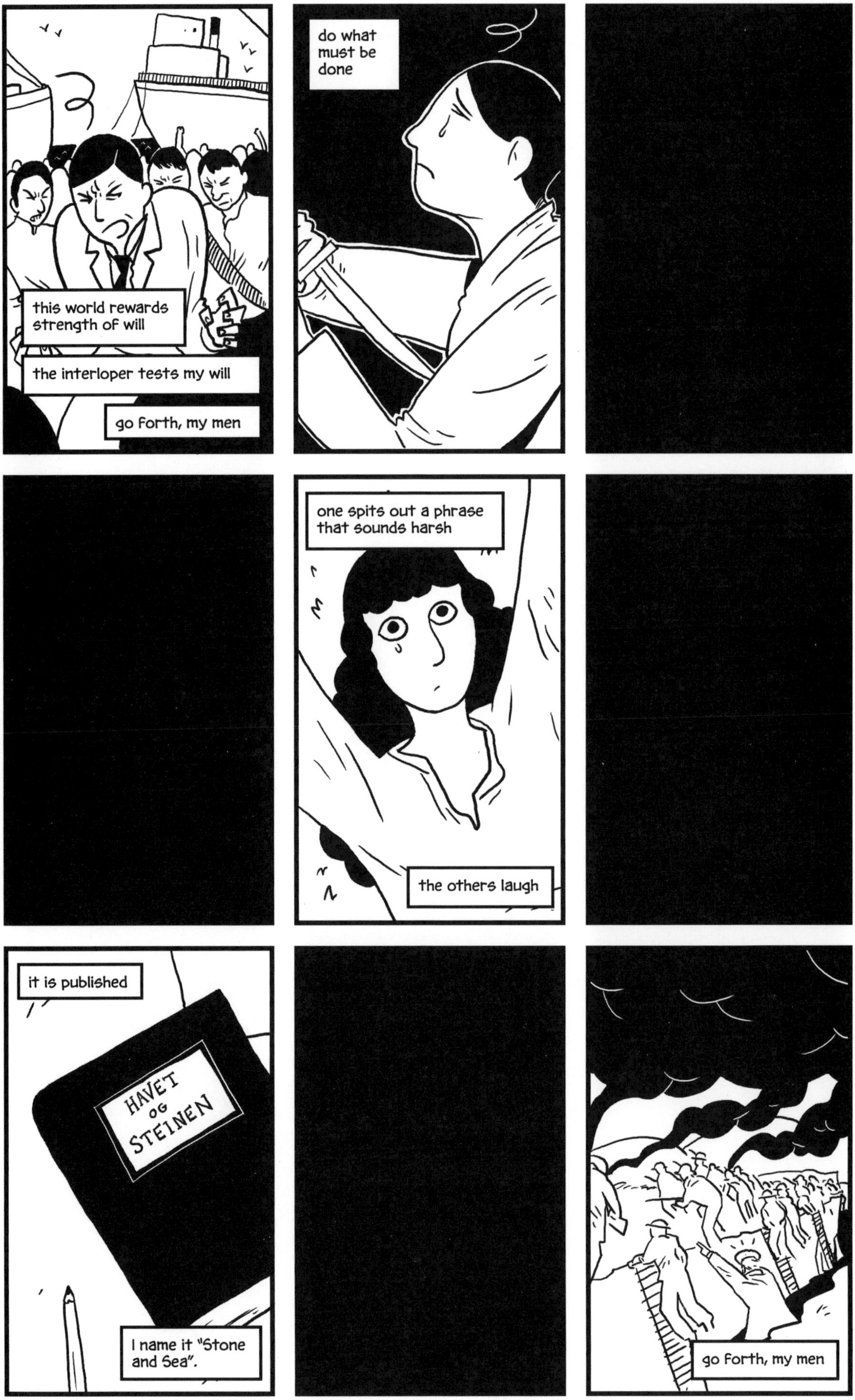
this world rewards strength of will
the interloper tests my will
go forth, my men
do what must be done
one spits out a phrase that sounds harsh
the others laugh
it is published
HAVET OG STEINEN
I name it "Stone and Sea".
go forth, my men

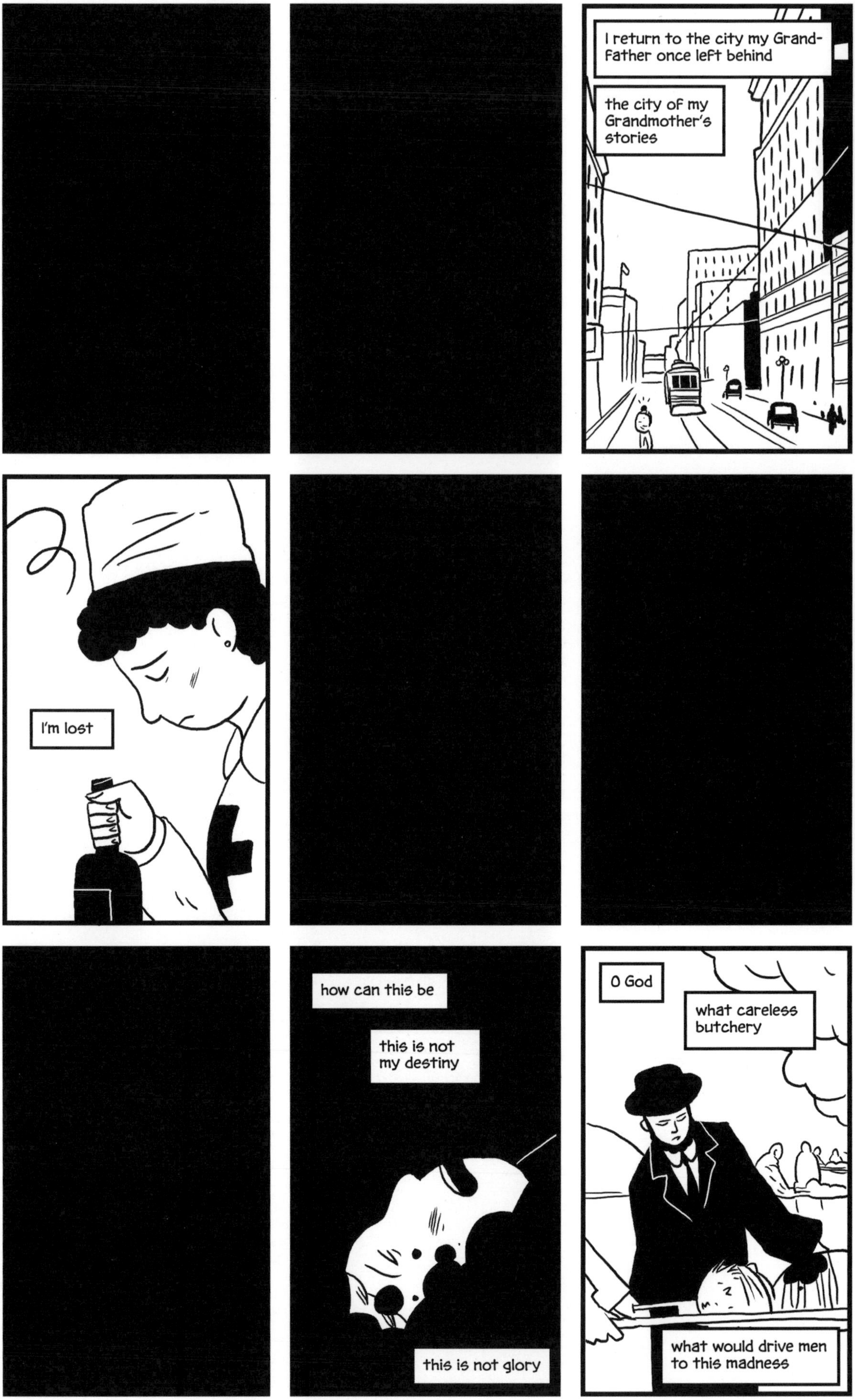
I return to the city my Grand-
Father once left behind
the city of my
Grandmother's
stories
I'm lost
how can this be
this is not
my destiny
this is not glory
O God
what careless
butchery
what would drive men
to this madness

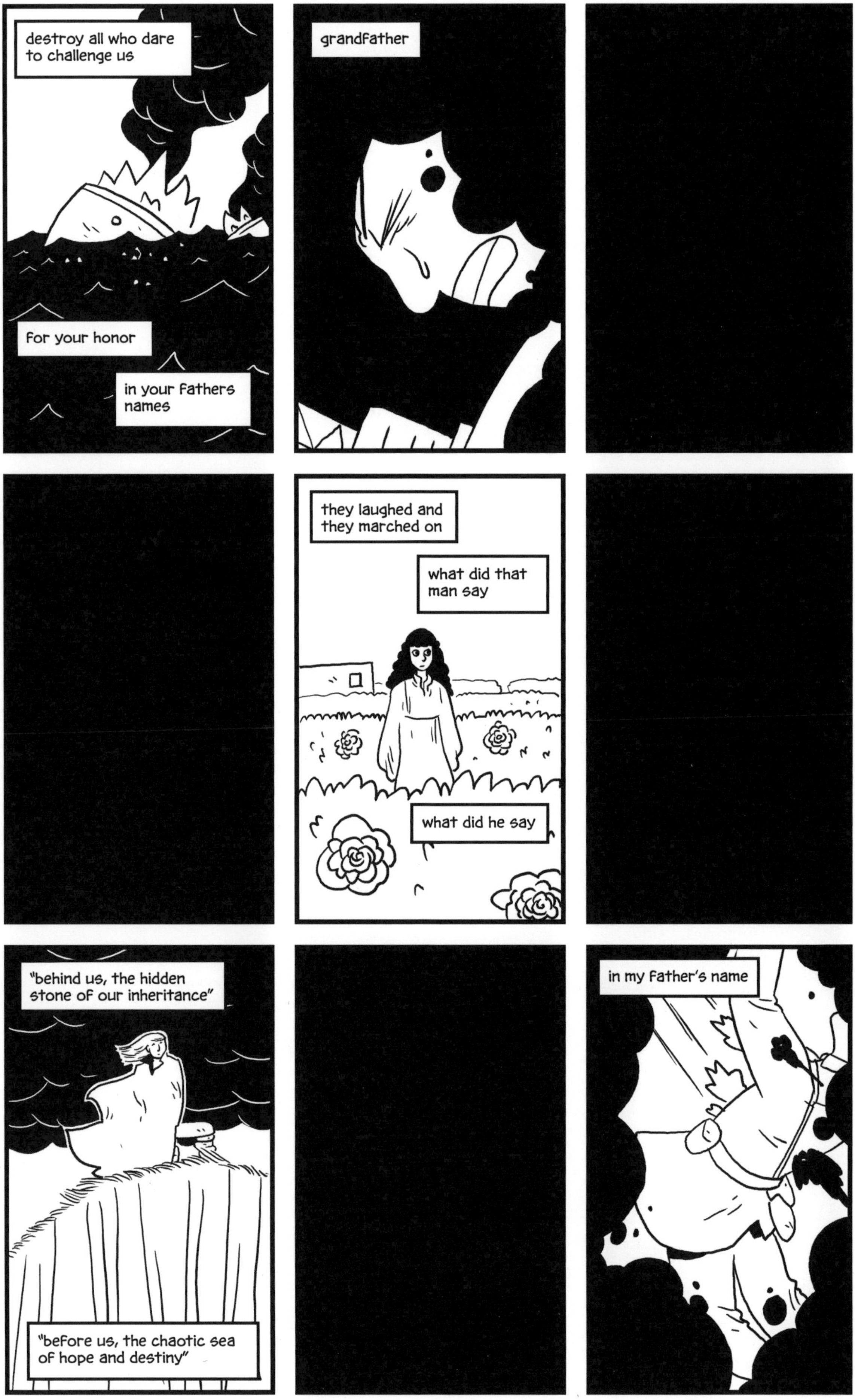
destroy all who dare to challenge us
for your honor
in your fathers names
grandfather
they laughed and they marched on
what did that man say
what did he say
"behind us, the hidden stone of our inheritance"
"before us, the chaotic sea of hope and destiny"
in my father's name

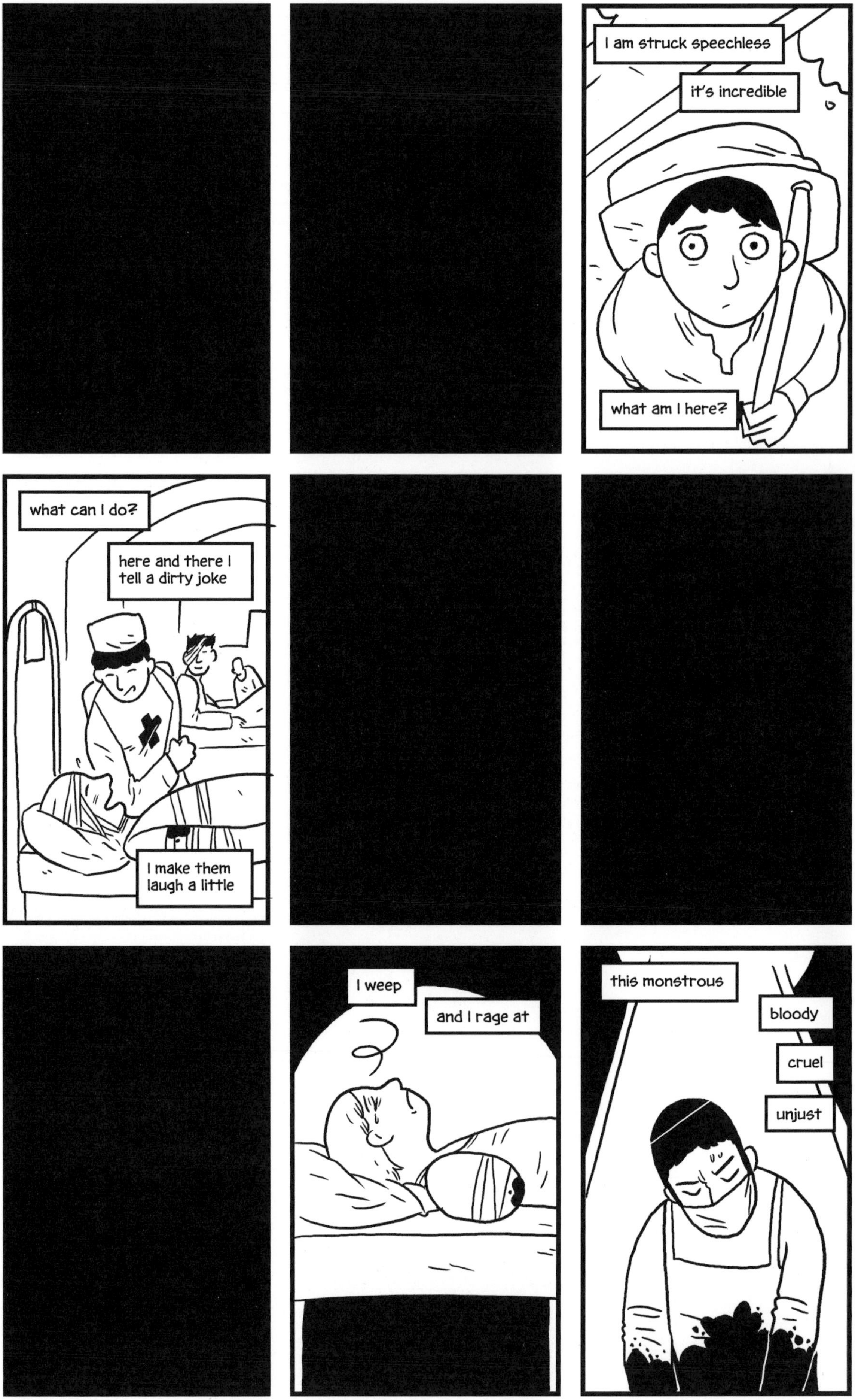
I am struck speechless
it's incredible
what am I here?
what can I do?
here and there I tell a dirty joke
I make them laugh a little
I weep
and I rage at
this monstrous
bloody
cruel
unjust

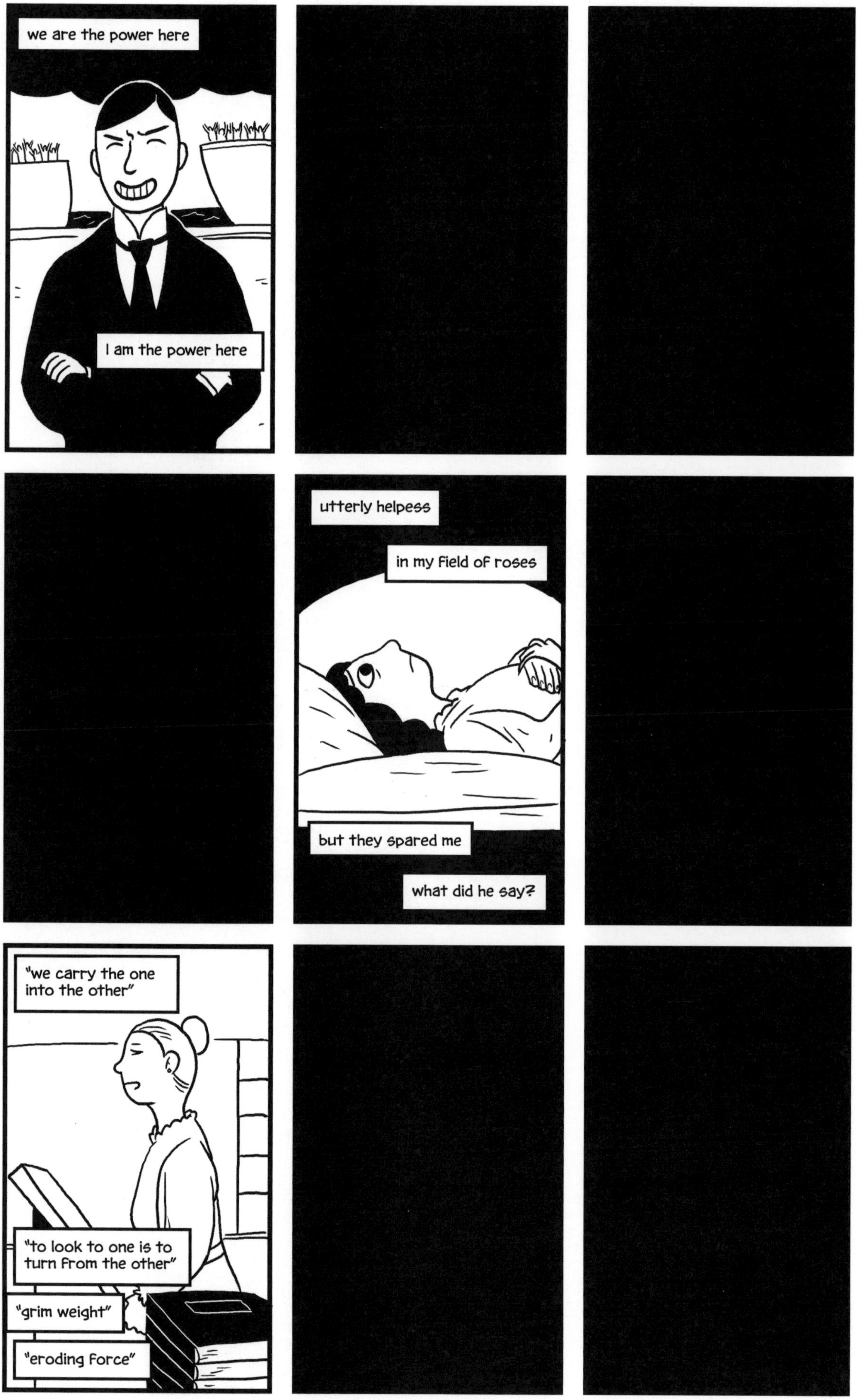
we are the power here
I am the power here
utterly helpess
in my field of roses
but they spared me
what did he say?
"we carry the one into the other"
"to look to one is to turn from the other"
"grim weight"
"eroding force"

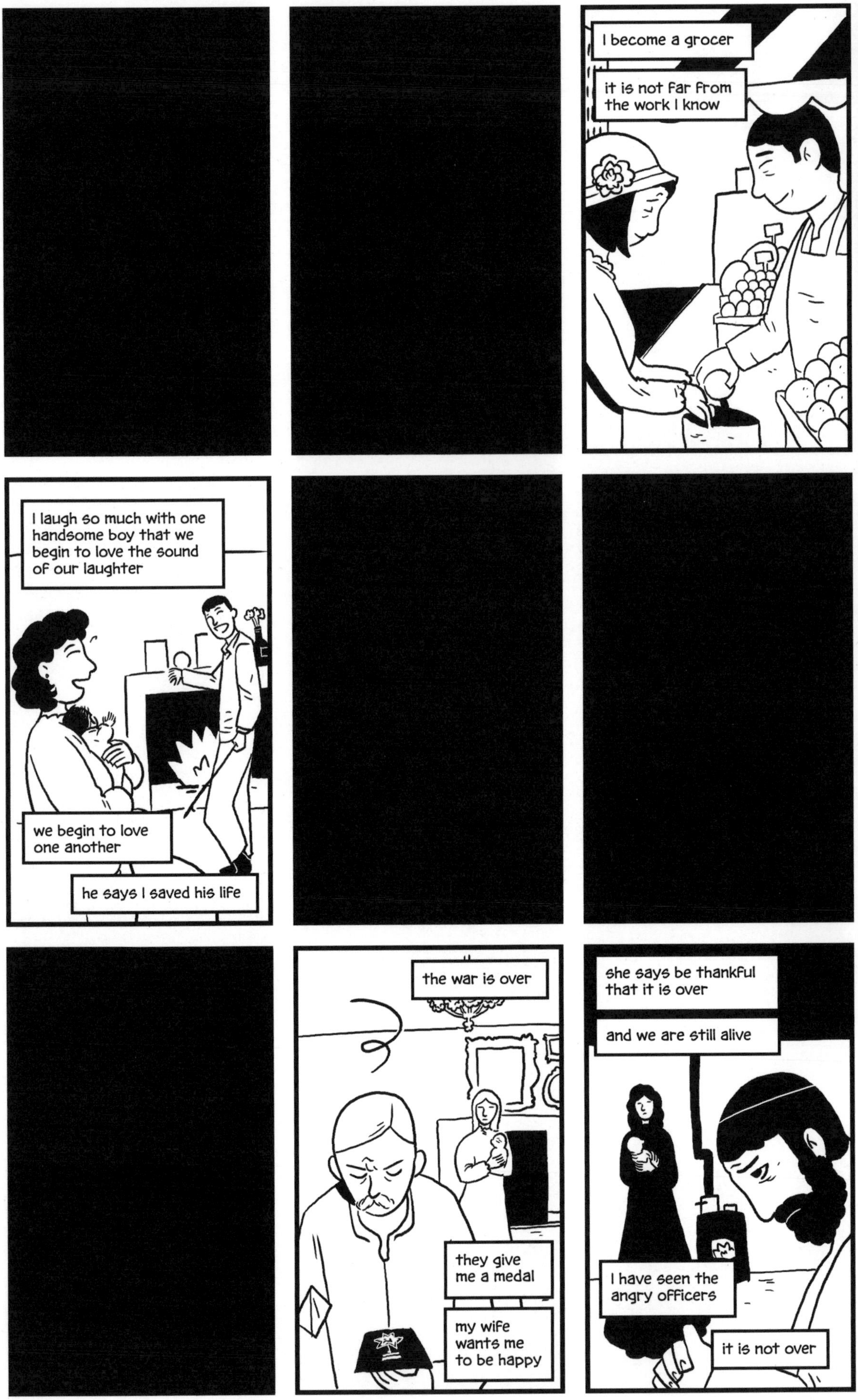
[redacted]
I become a grocer
it is not far from the work I know
I laugh so much with one handsome boy that we begin to love the sound of our laughter
we begin to love one another
he says I saved his life
[redacted]
the war is over
they give me a medal
my wife wants me to be happy
she says be thankful that it is over
and we are still alive
I have seen the angry officers
it is not over

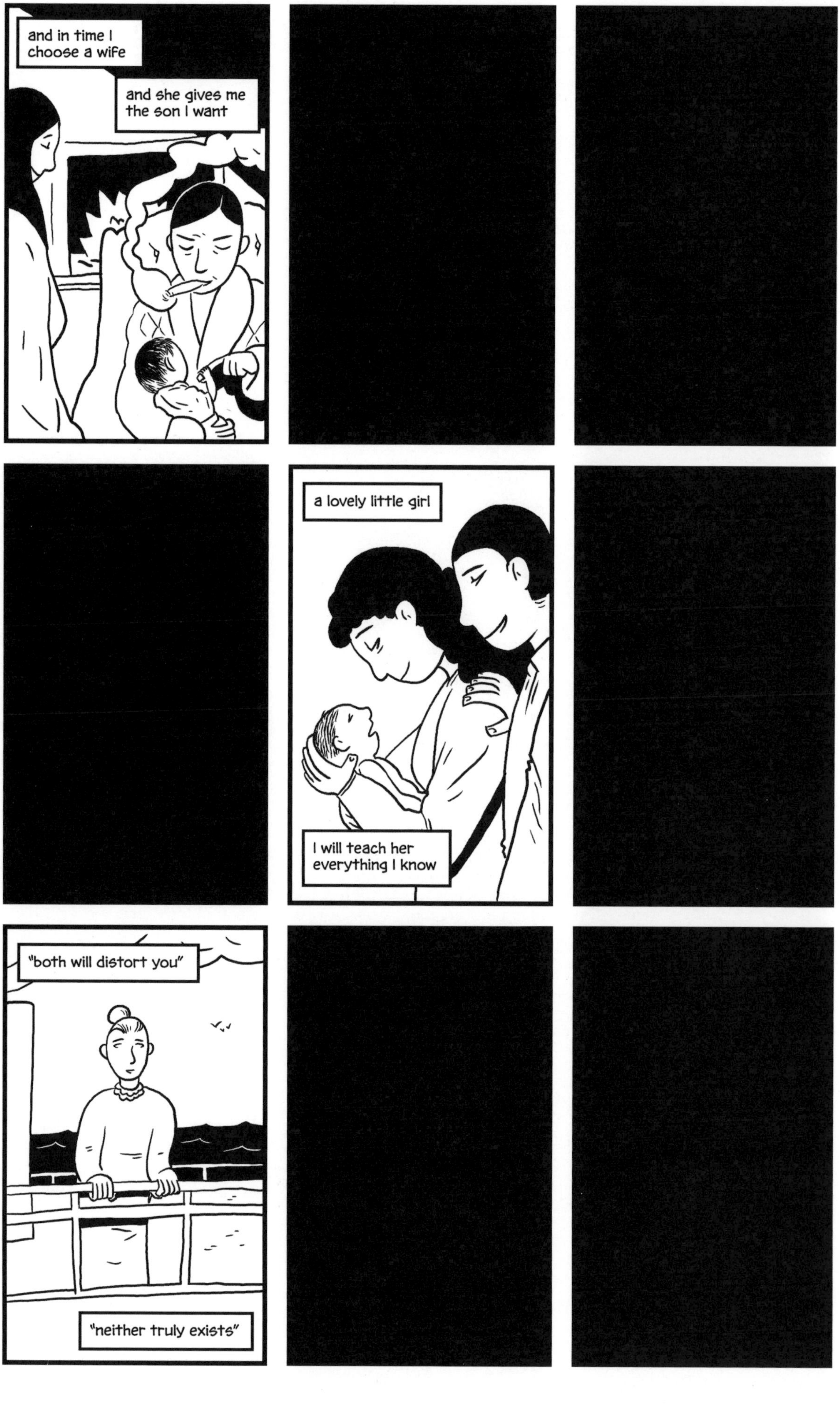
and in time I choose a wife
and she gives me the son I want
a lovely little girl
I will teach her everything I know
"both will distort you"
"neither truly exists"

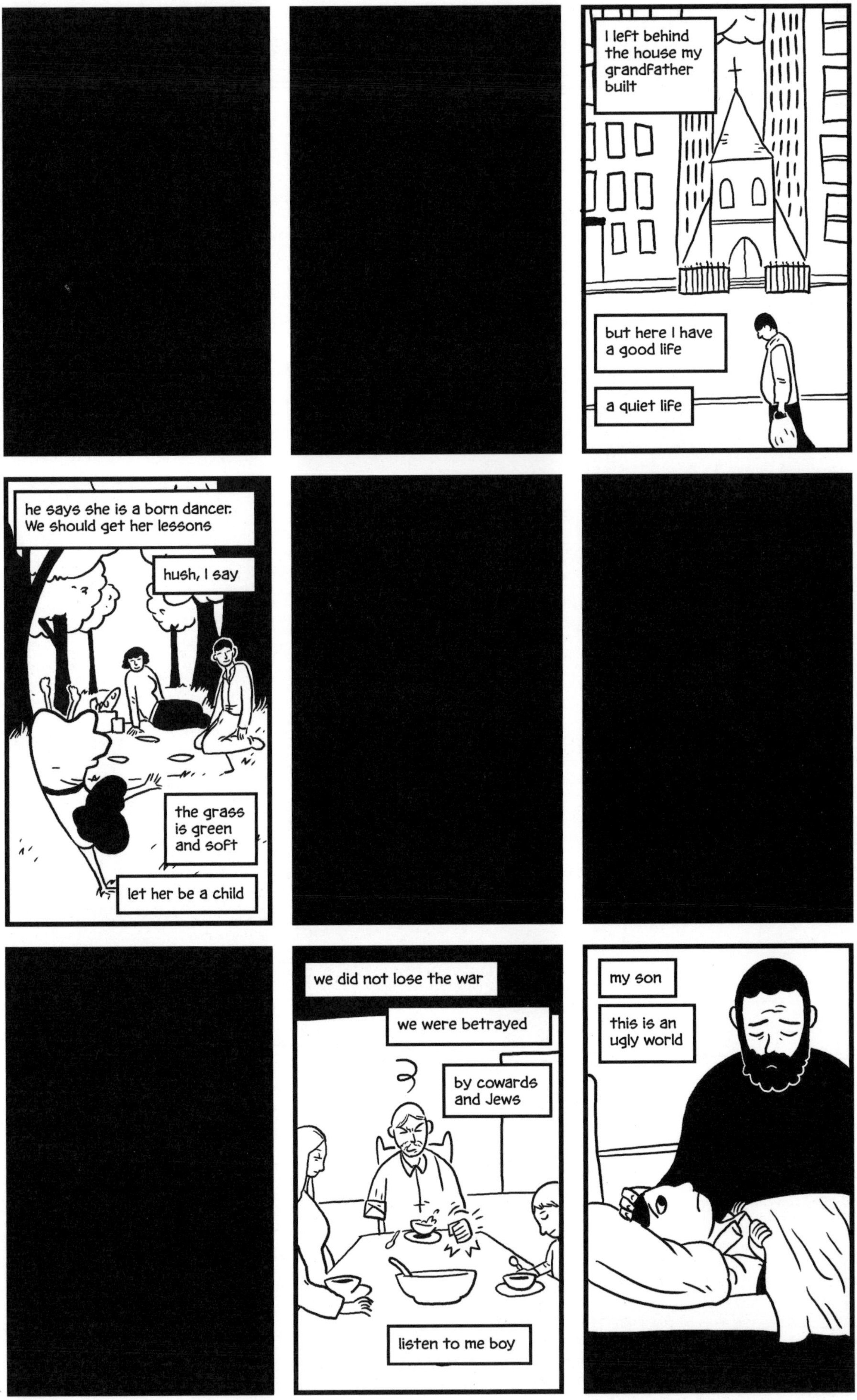
I left behind the house my grandfather built
but here I have a good life
a quiet life
he says she is a born dancer. We should get her lessons
hush, I say
the grass is green and soft
let her be a child
we did not lose the war
we were betrayed
by cowards and Jews
listen to me boy
my son
this is an ugly world

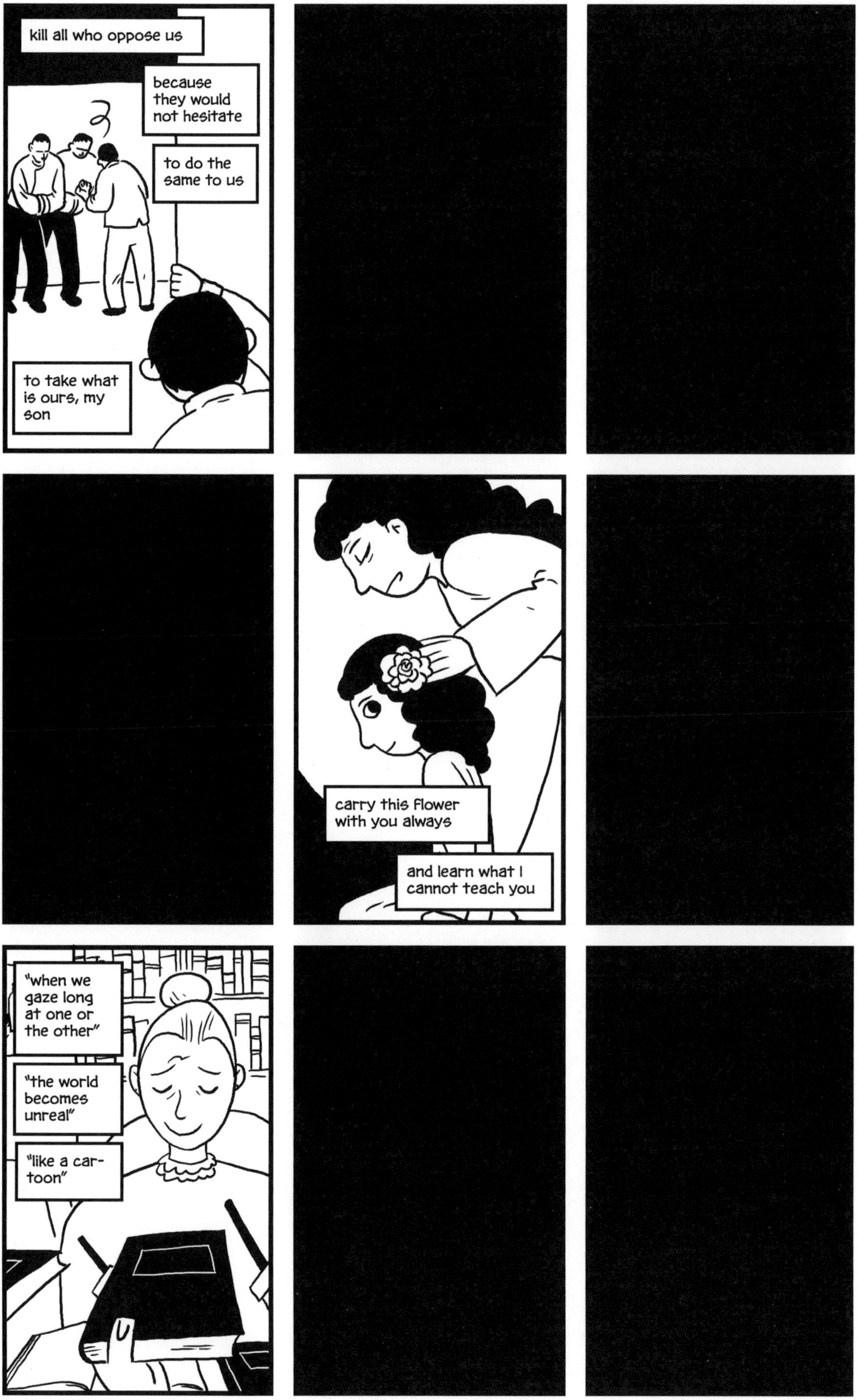
kill all who oppose us
because they would not hesitate
to do the same to us
to take what is ours, my son
carry this flower with you always
and learn what I cannot teach you
"when we gaze long at one or the other"
"the world becomes unreal"
"like a car-toon"

PART FIVE

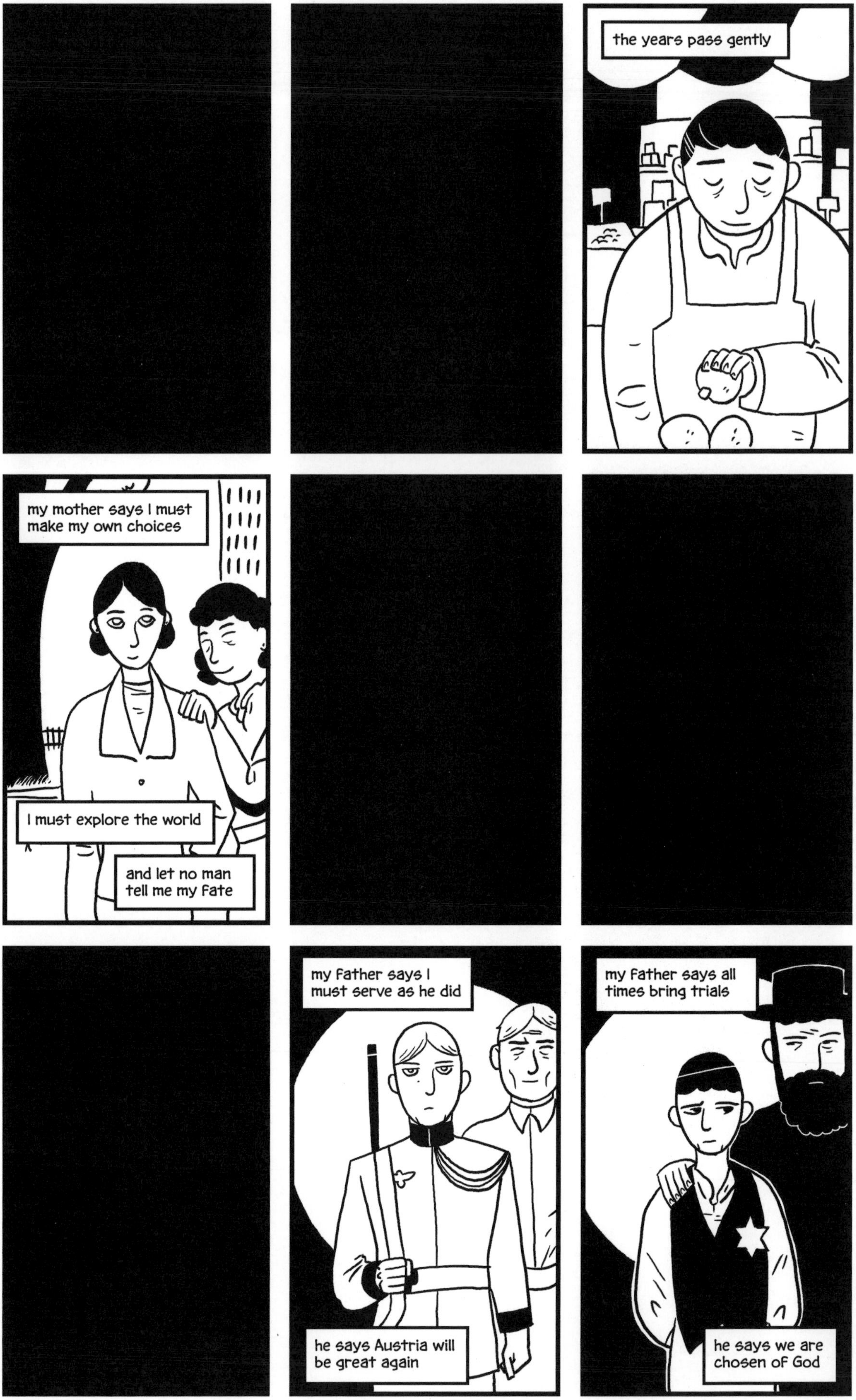
the years pass gently
my mother says I must make my own choices
I must explore the world
and let no man tell me my fate
my father says I must serve as he did
he says Austria will be great again
my father says all times bring trials
he says we are chosen of God

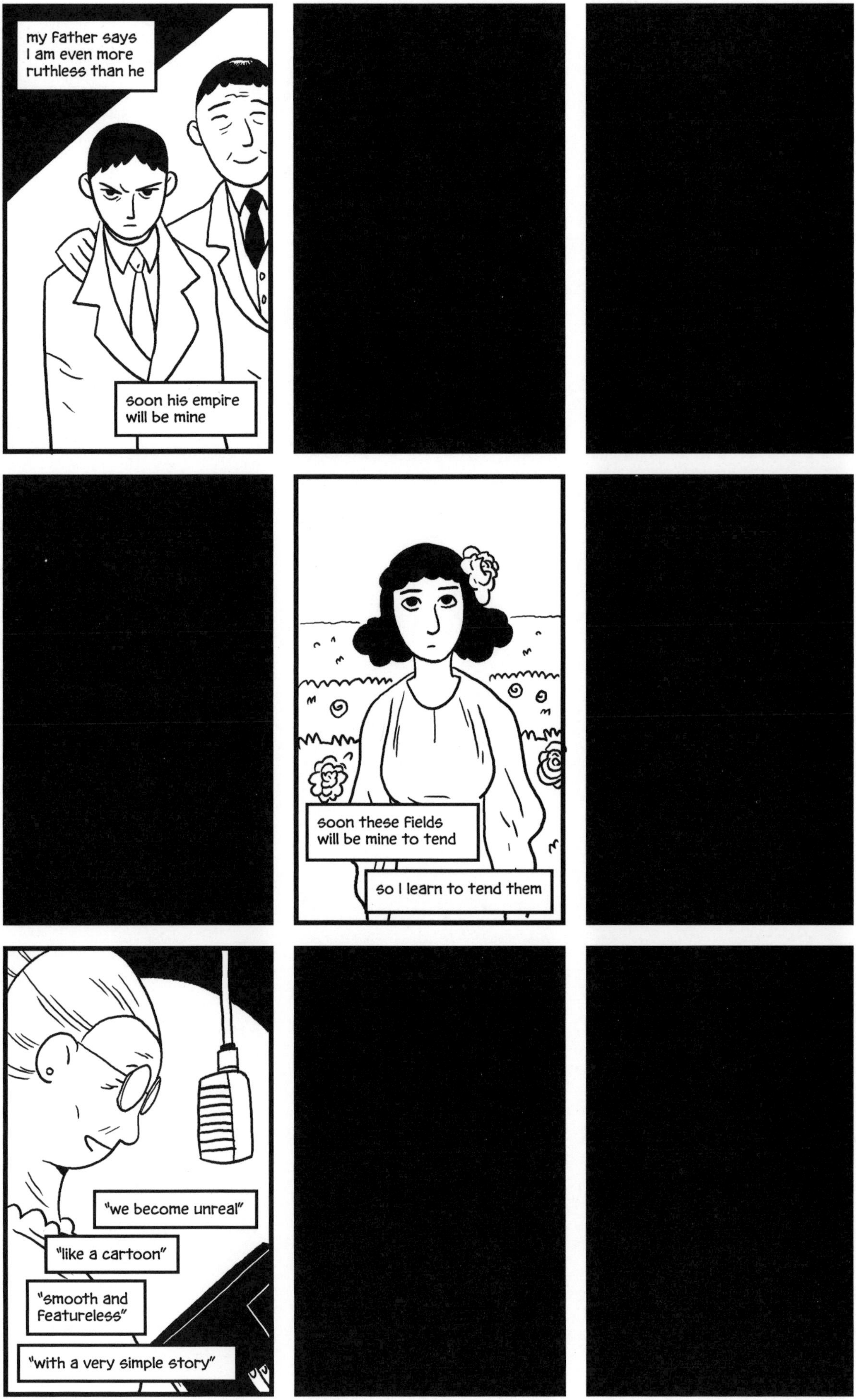
my father says
I am even more
ruthless than he
soon his empire
will be mine
soon these fields
will be mine to tend
so I learn to tend them
"we become unreal"
"like a cartoon"
"smooth and
featureless"
"with a very simple story"

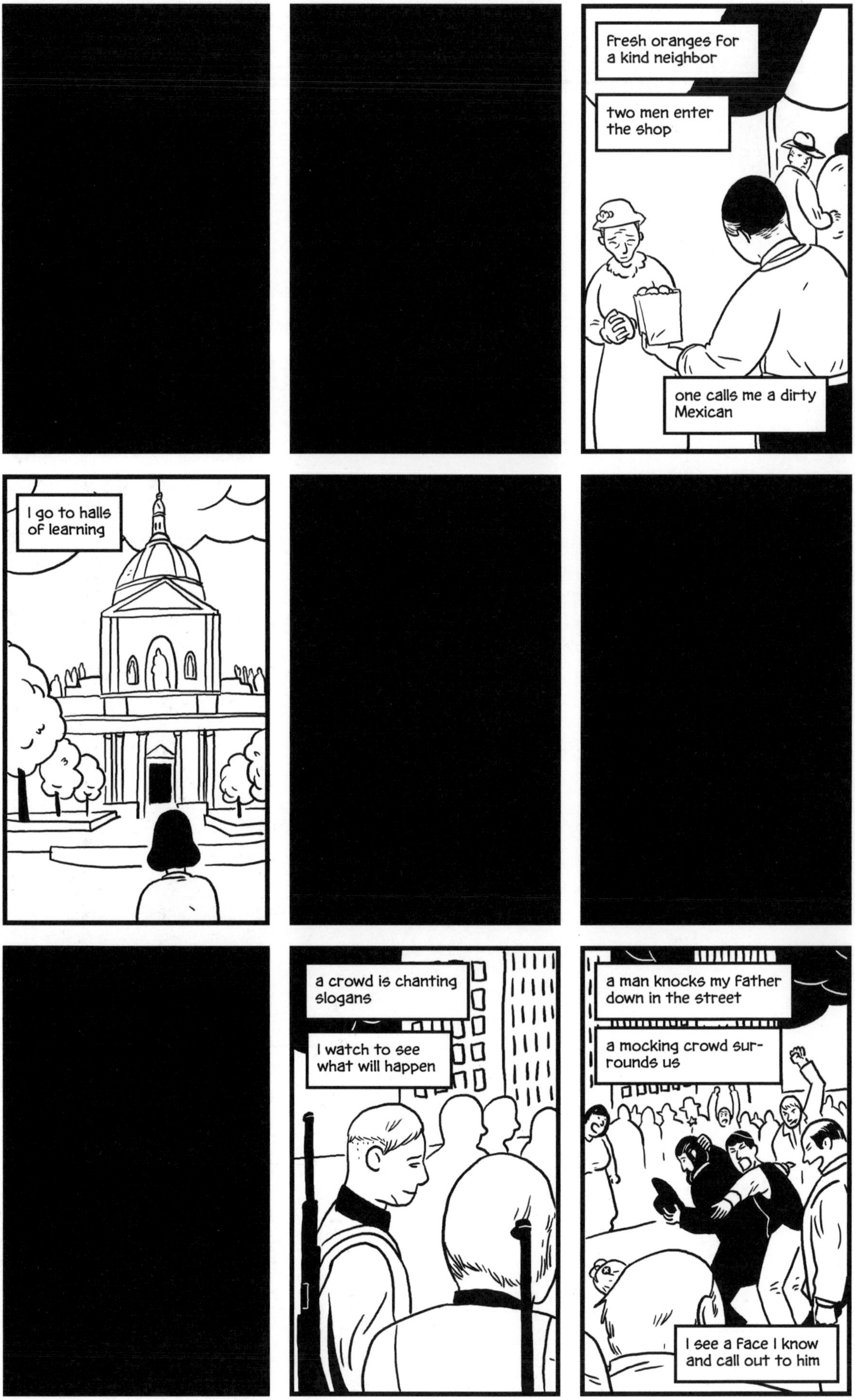
fresh oranges for a kind neighbor
two men enter the shop
one calls me a dirty Mexican
I go to halls of learning
a crowd is chanting slogans
I watch to see what will happen
a man knocks my father down in the street
a mocking crowd surrounds us
I see a face I know and call out to him

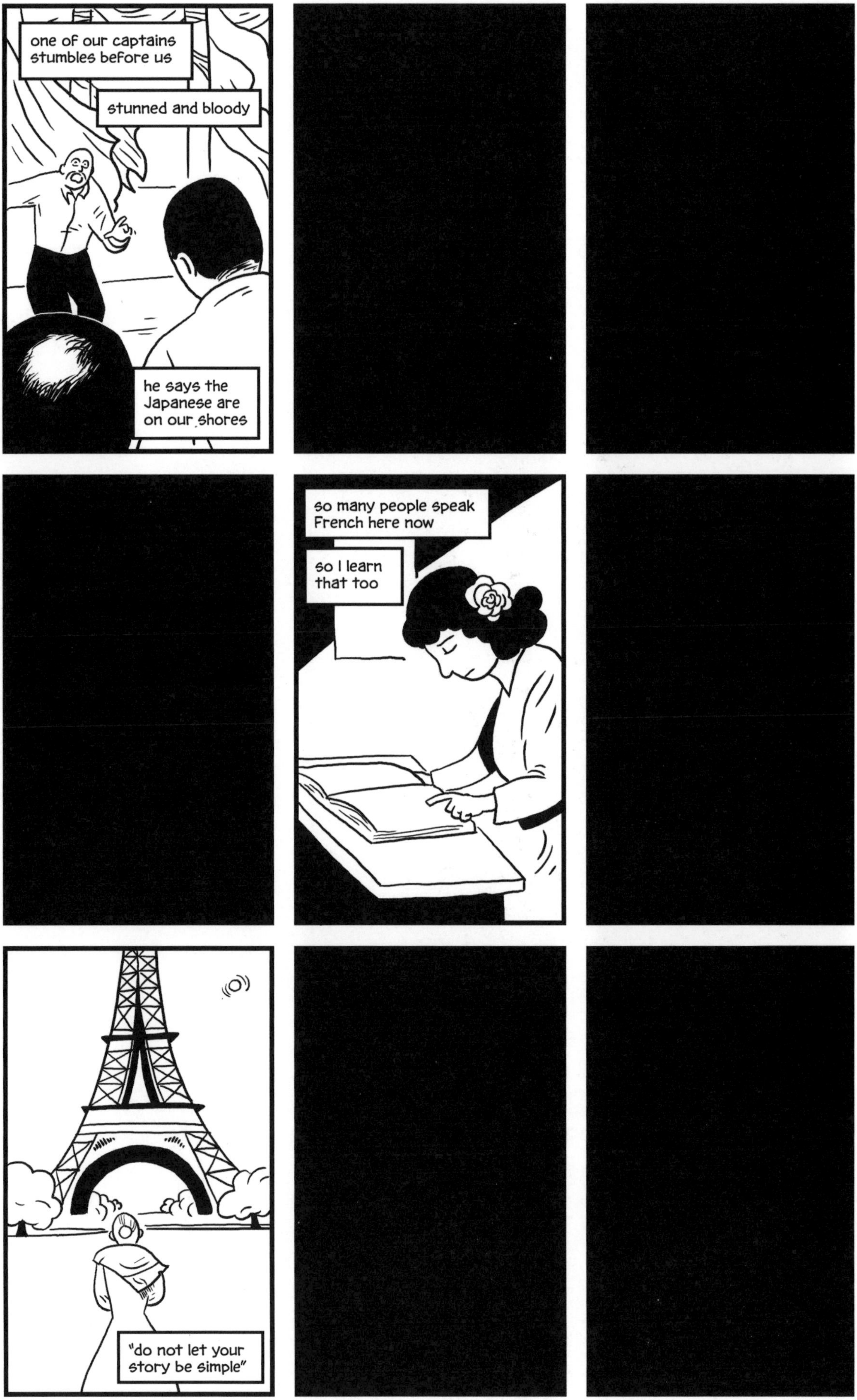
one of our captains stumbles before us
stunned and bloody
he says the Japanese are on our shores
so many people speak French here now
so I learn that too
"do not let your story be simple"

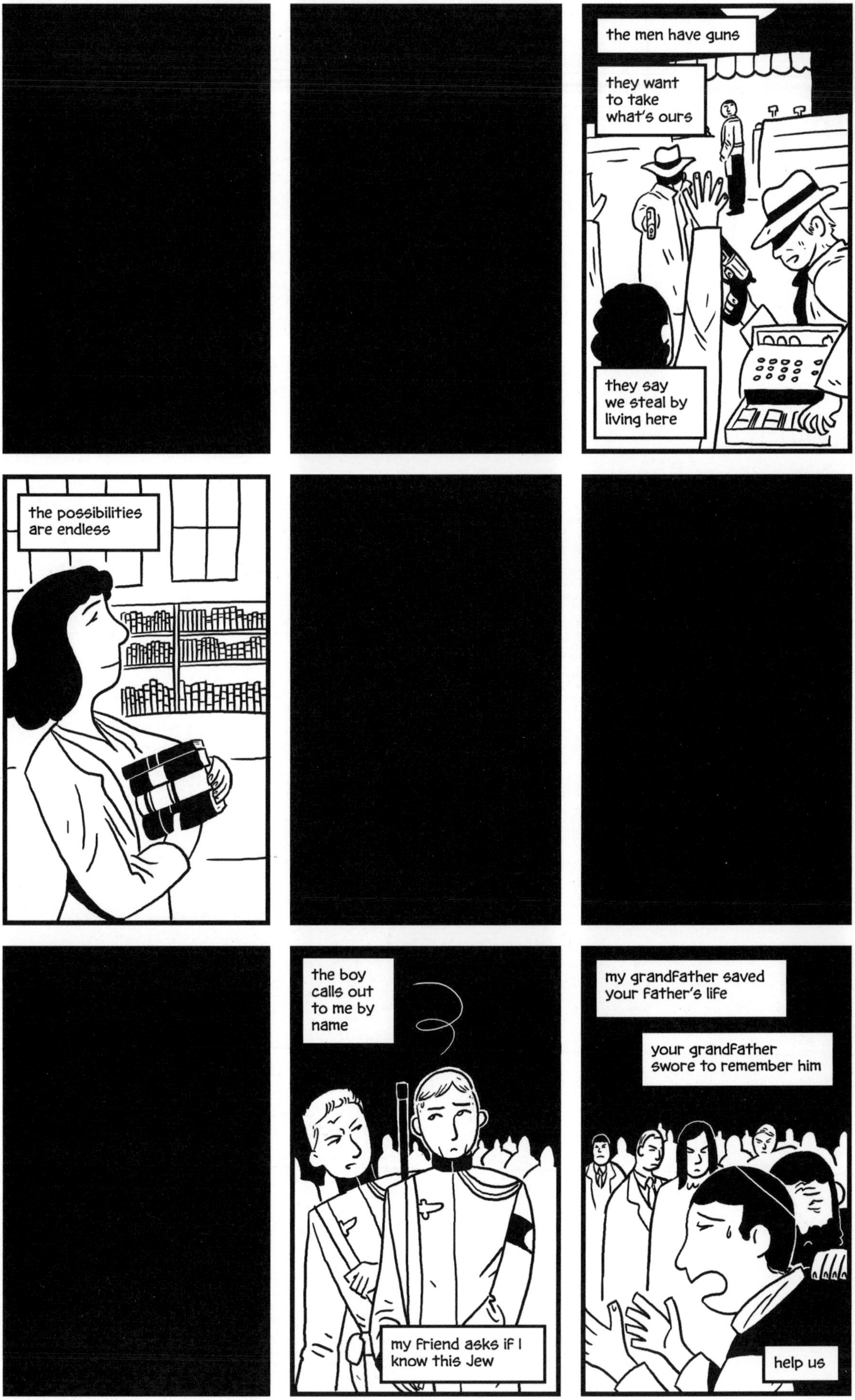
the men have guns
they want to take what's ours
they say we steal by living here
the possibilities are endless
the boy calls out to me by name
my friend asks if I know this Jew
my grandfather saved your father's life
your grandfather swore to remember him
help us

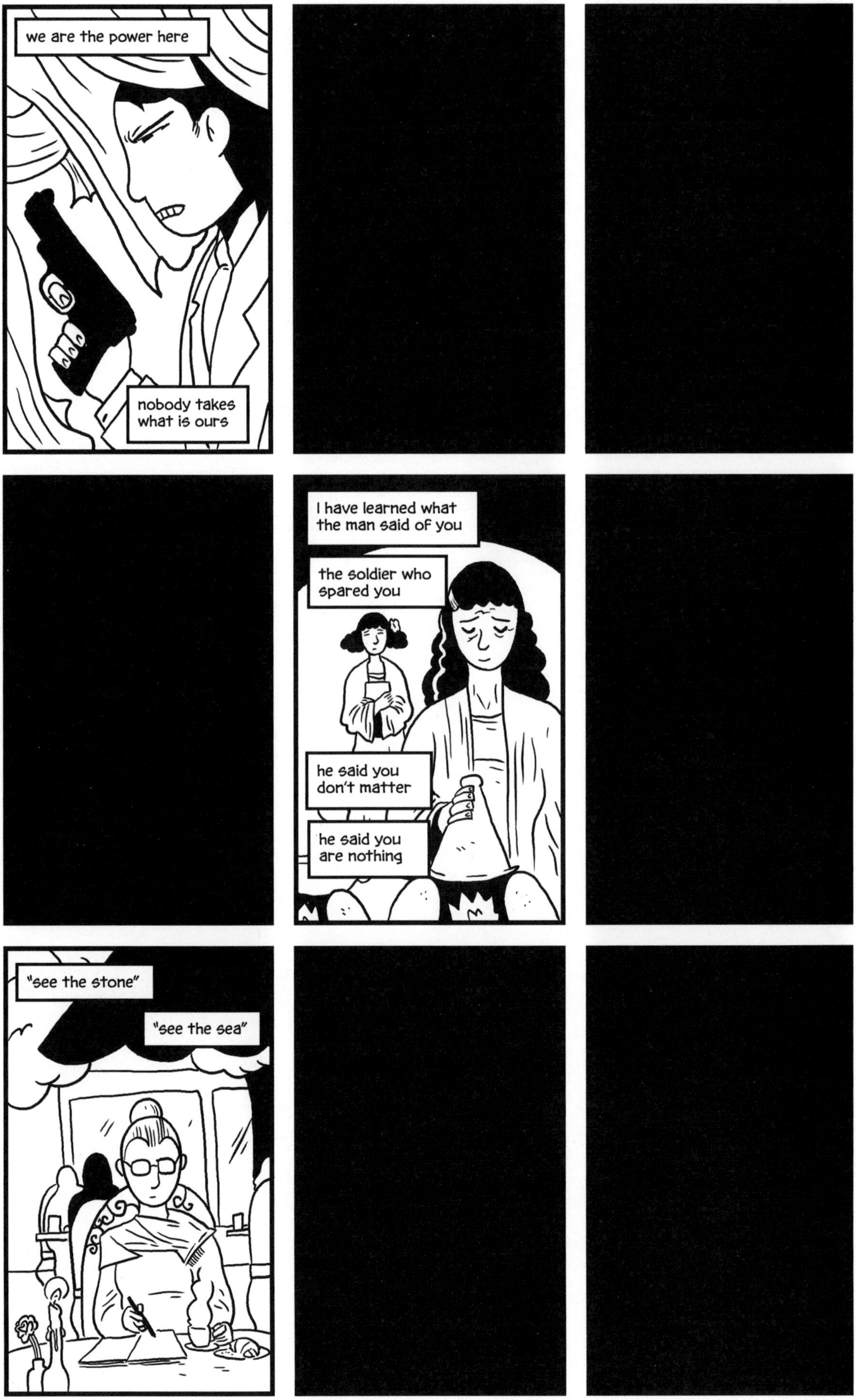

we are the power here
nobody takes what is ours
I have learned what the man said of you
the soldier who spared you
he said you don't matter
he said you are nothing
"see the stone"
"see the sea"

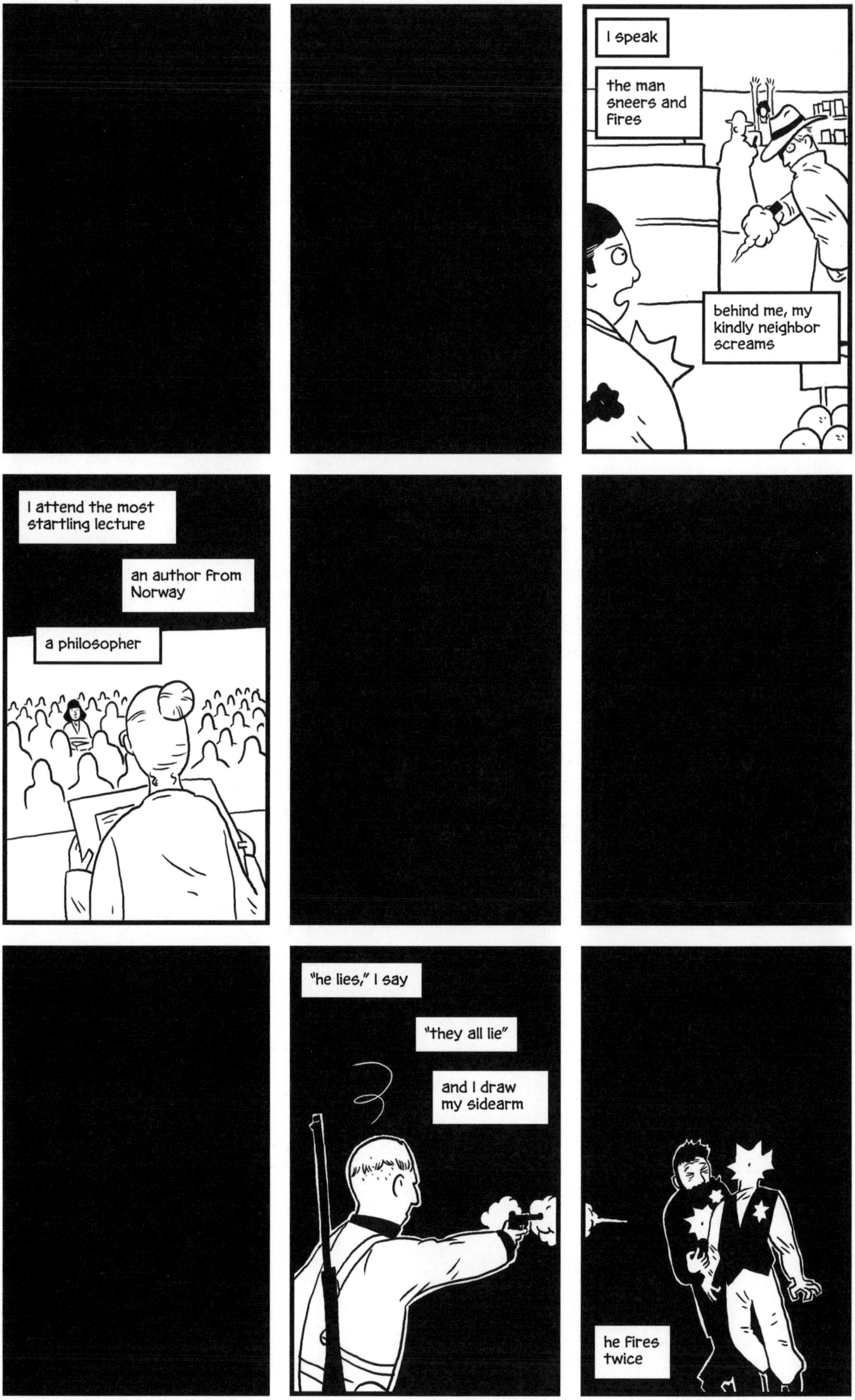
I speak
the man sneers and fires
behind me, my kindly neighbor screams
I attend the most startling lecture
an author from Norway
a philosopher
"he lies," I say
"they all lie"
and I draw my sidearm
he fires twice

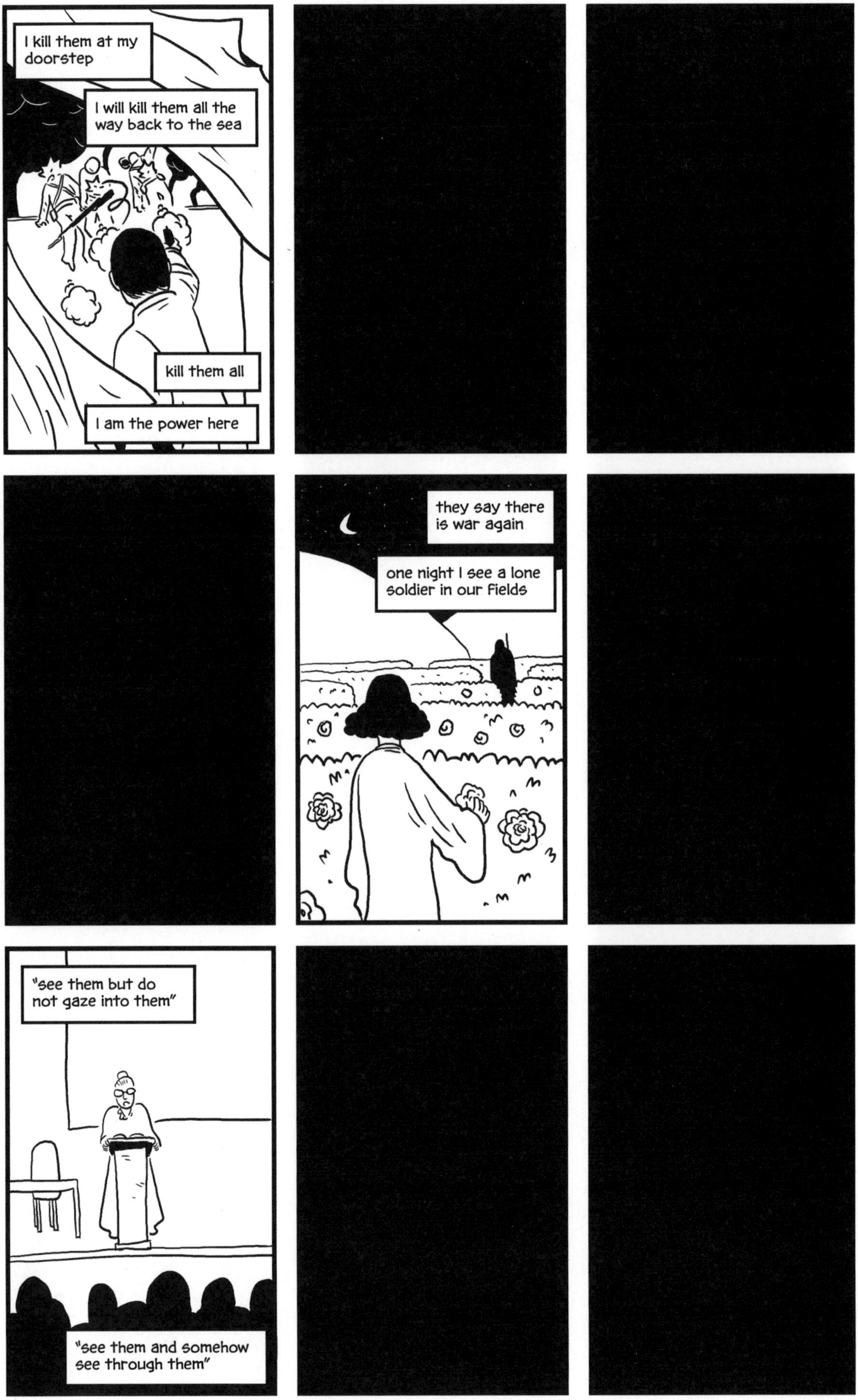
I kill them at my doorstep
I will kill them all the way back to the sea
kill them all
I am the power here
they say there is war again
one night I see a lone soldier in our fields
"see them but do not gaze into them"
"see them and somehow see through them"

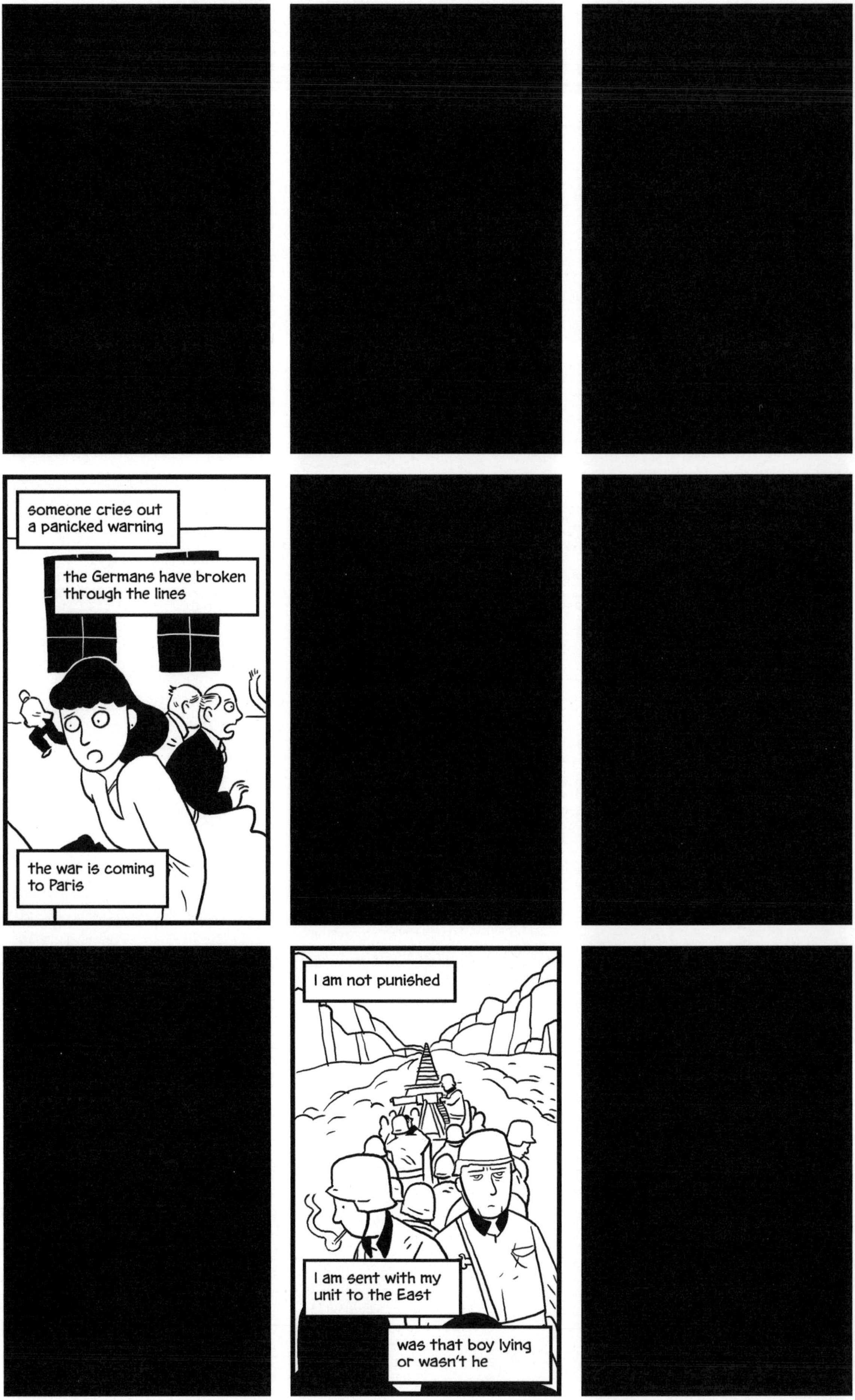
someone cries out
a panicked warning
the Germans have broken
through the lines
the war is coming
to Paris
I am not punished
I am sent with my
unit to the East
was that boy lying
or wasn't he

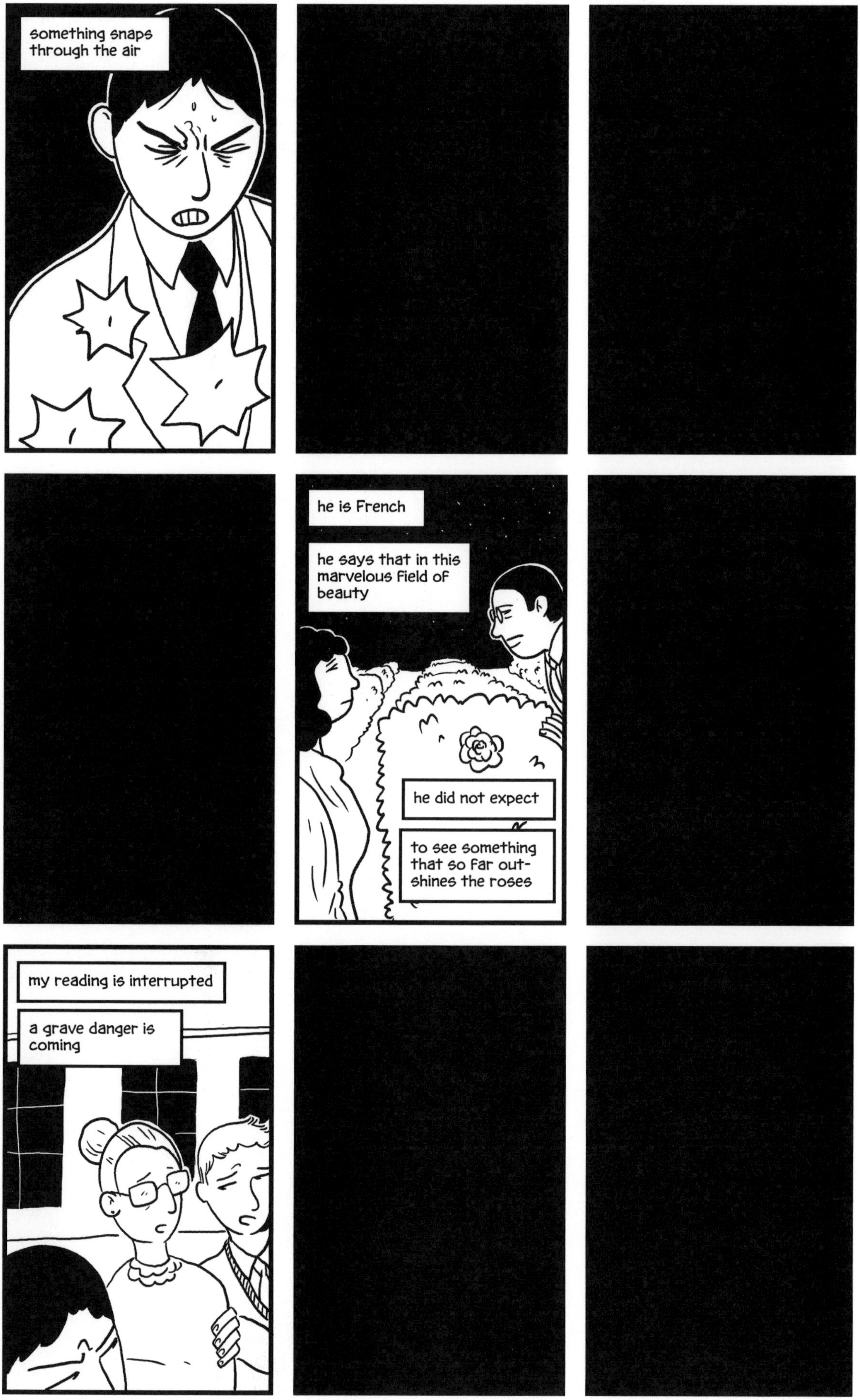
something snaps through the air
he is French
he says that in this marvelous field of beauty
he did not expect
to see something that so far outshines the roses
my reading is interrupted
a grave danger is coming

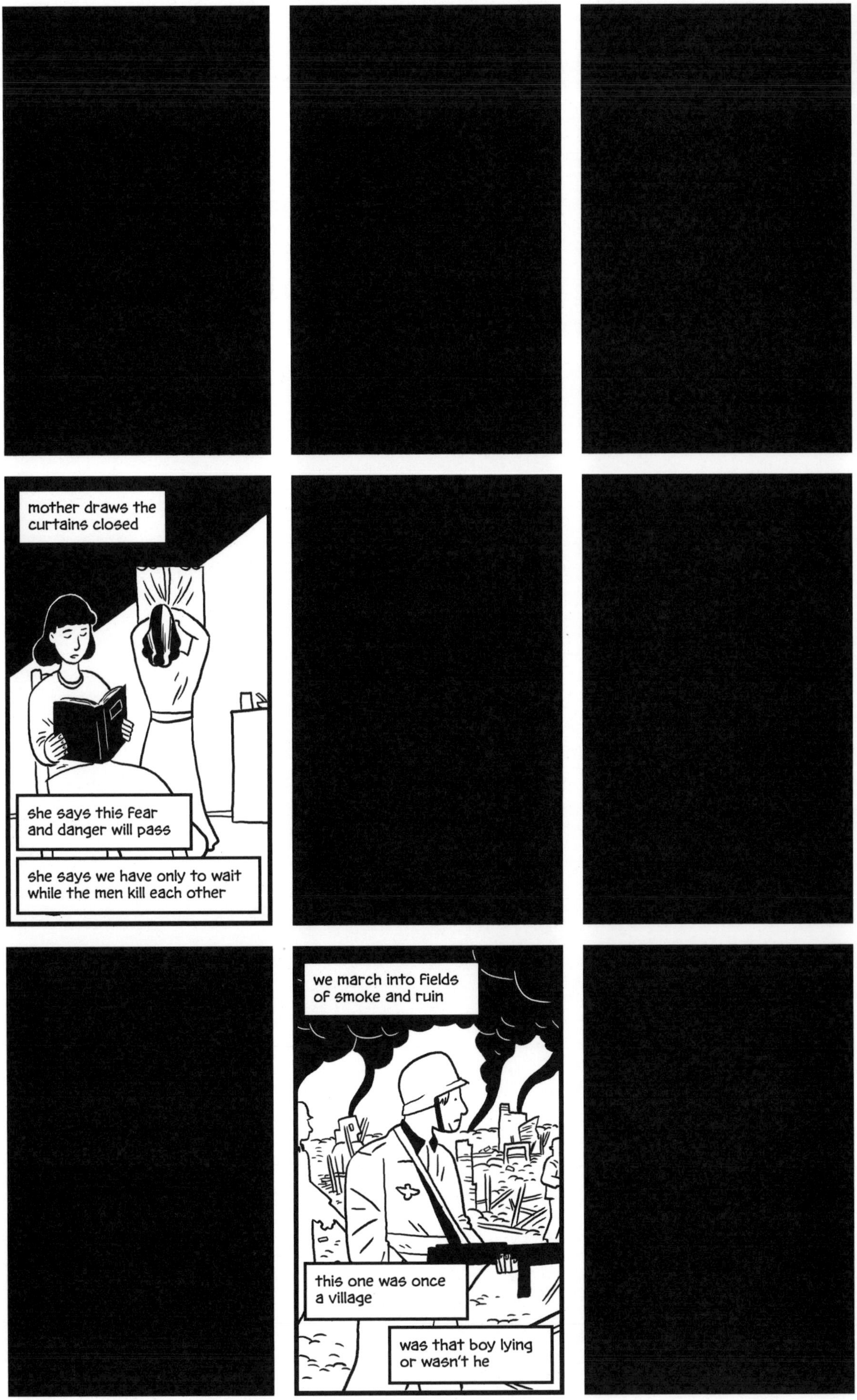
mother draws the curtains closed
she says this fear and danger will pass
she says we have only to wait while the men kill each other
we march into fields of smoke and ruin
this one was once a village
was that boy lying or wasn't he

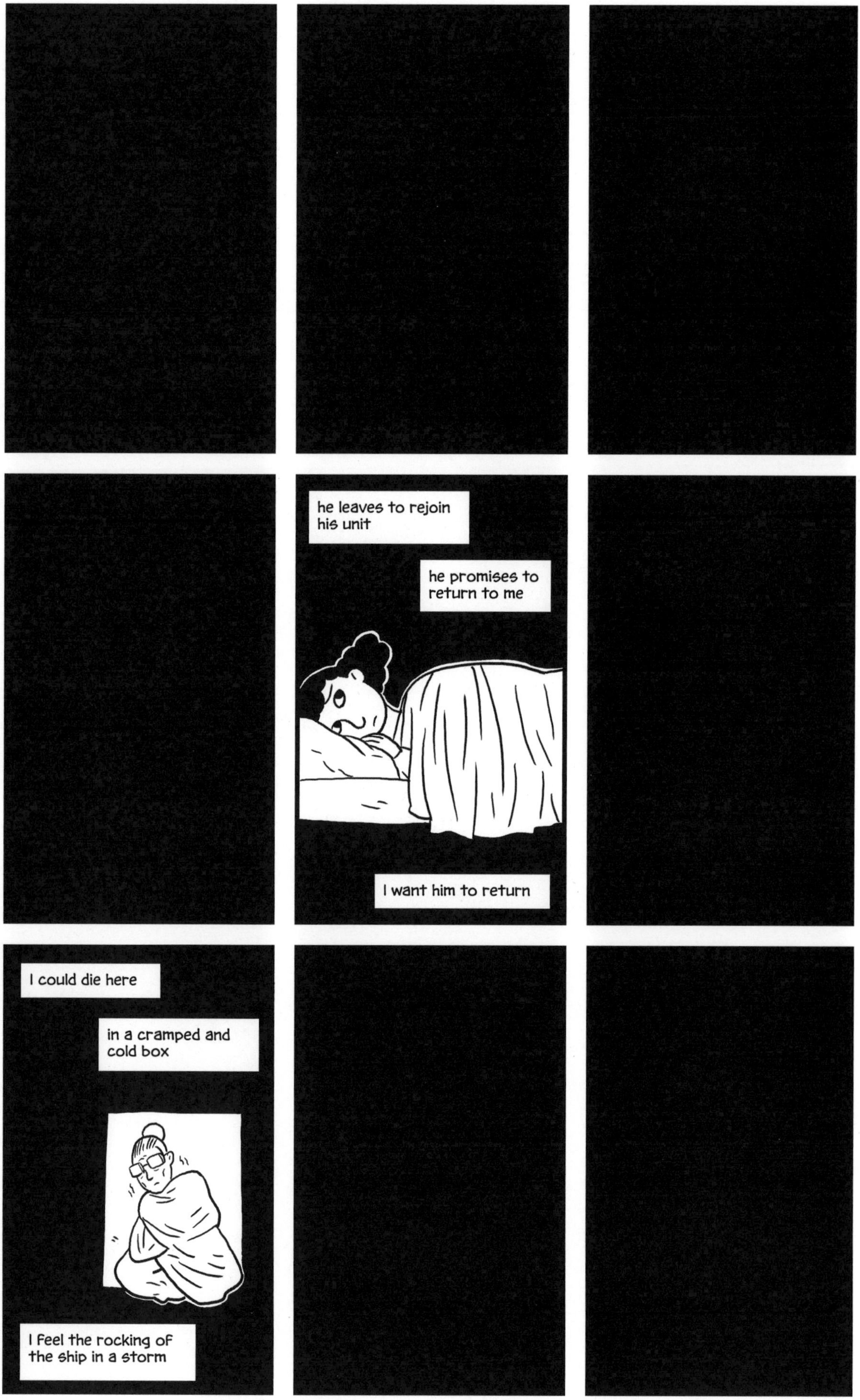
he leaves to rejoin his unit
he promises to return to me
I want him to return
I could die here
in a cramped and cold box
I feel the rocking of the ship in a storm

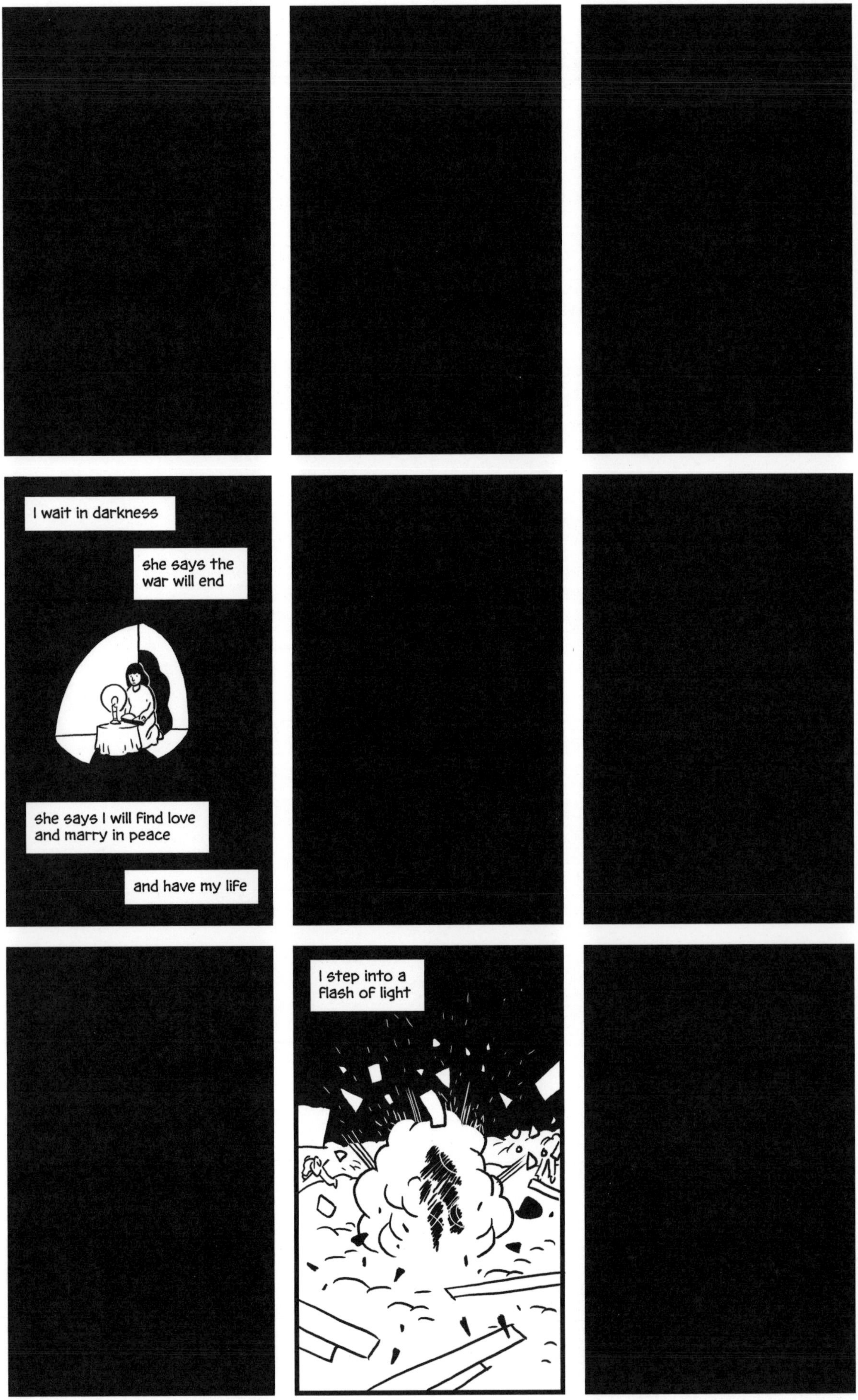
I wait in darkness
she says the war will end
she says I will find love and marry in peace
and have my life
I step into a flash of light

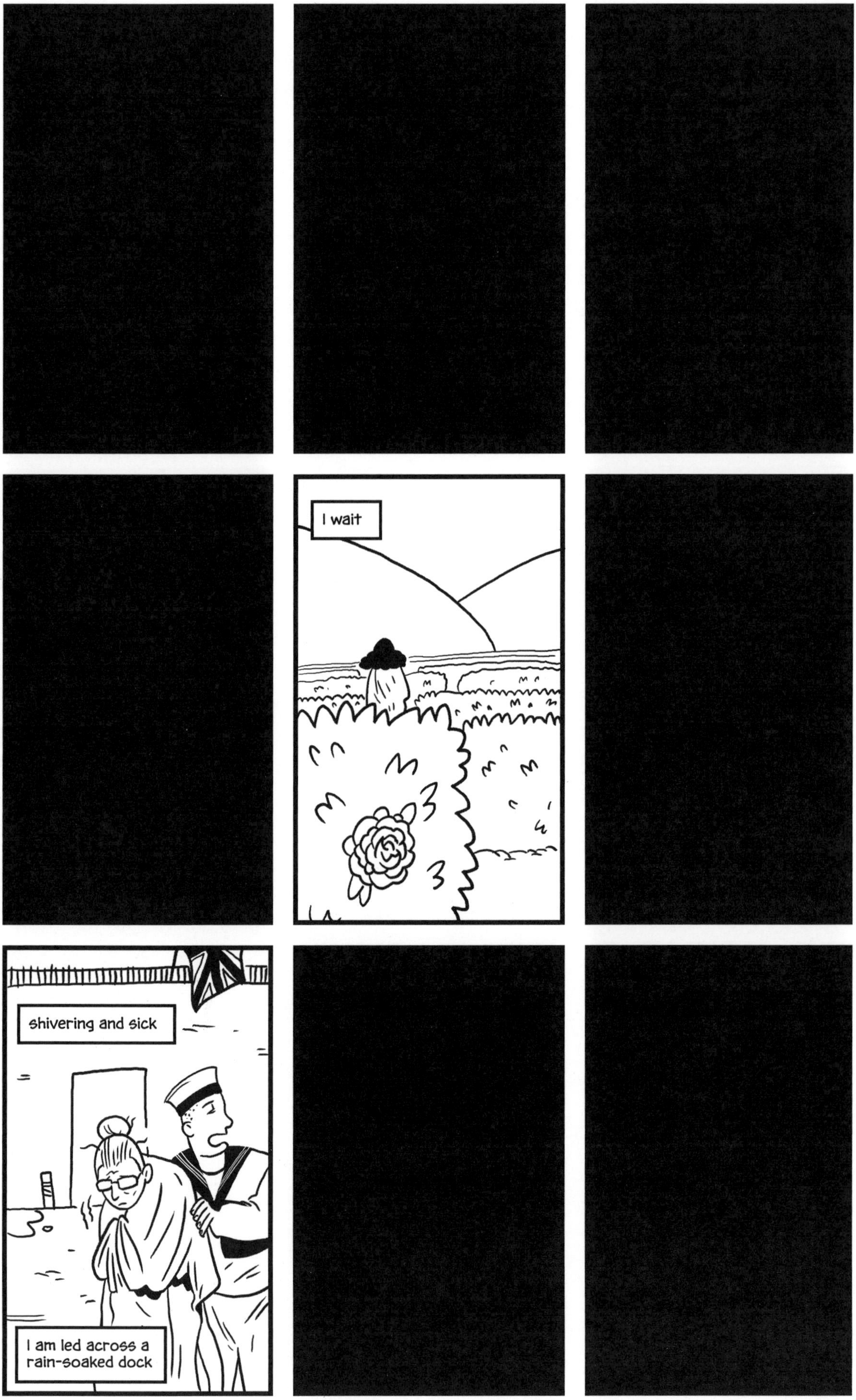
I wait
shivering and sick
I am led across a
rain-soaked dock

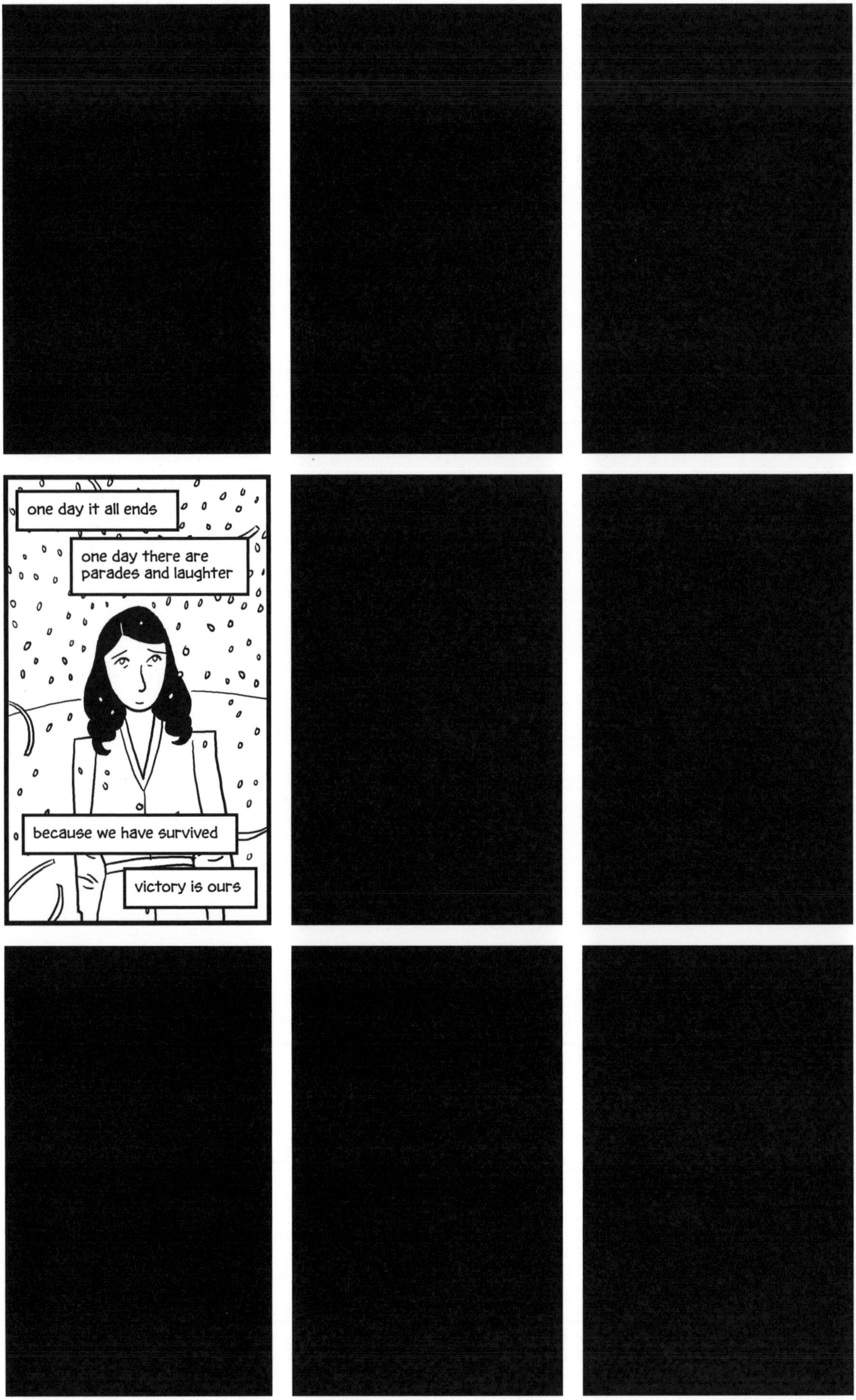
one day it all ends
one day there are parades and laughter
because we have survived
victory is ours

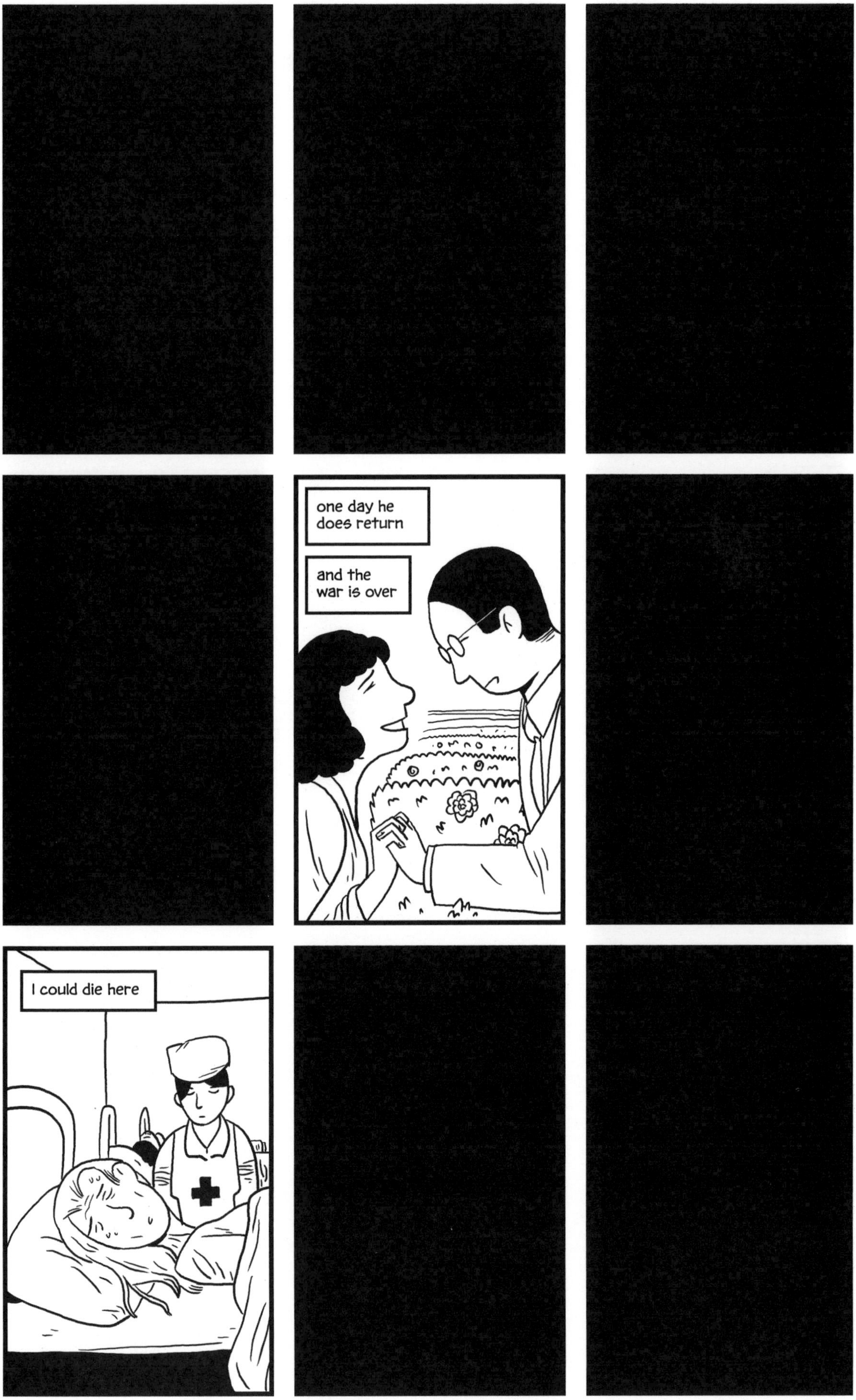
one day he does return
and the war is over
I could die here

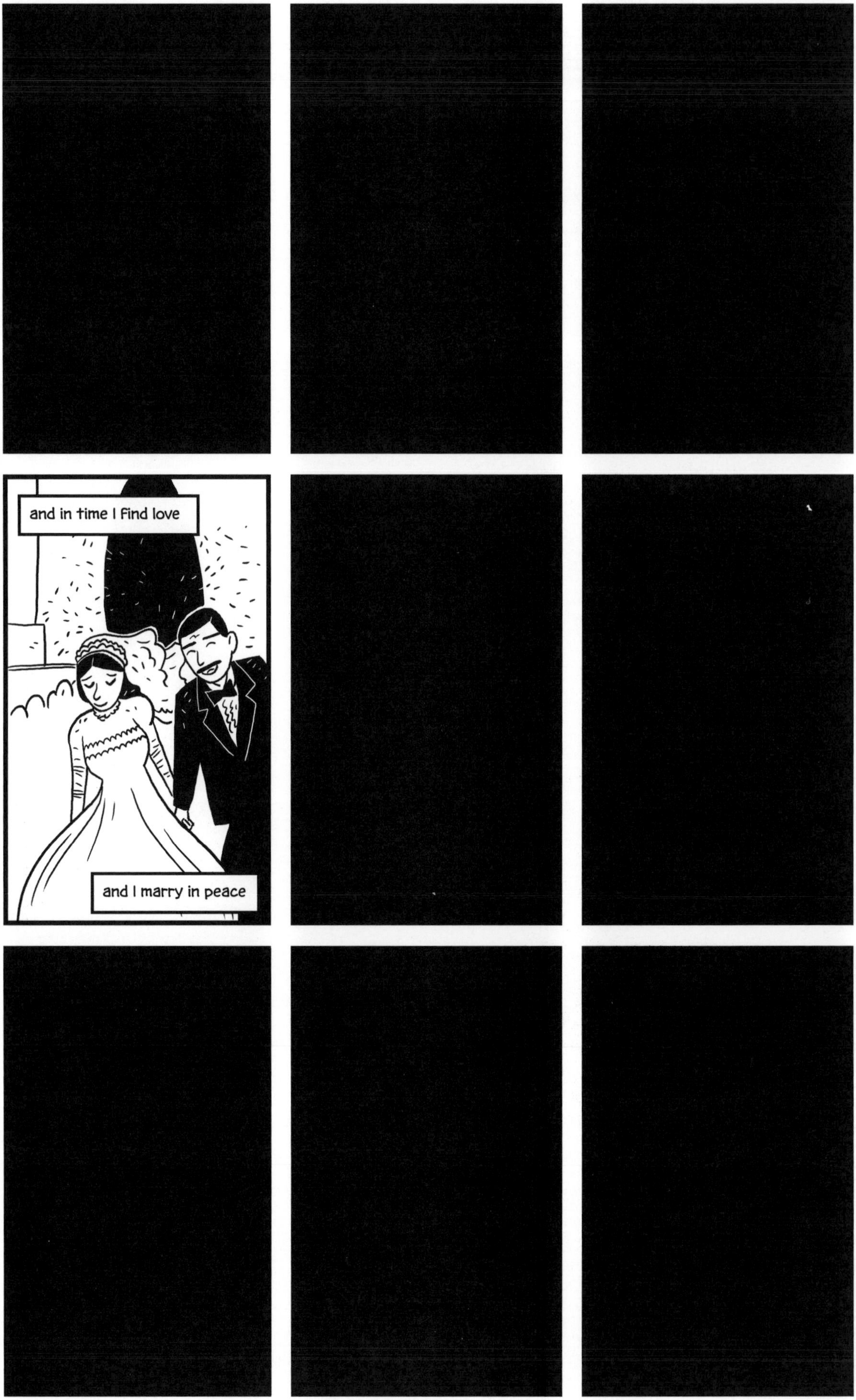
and in time I find love
and I marry in peace

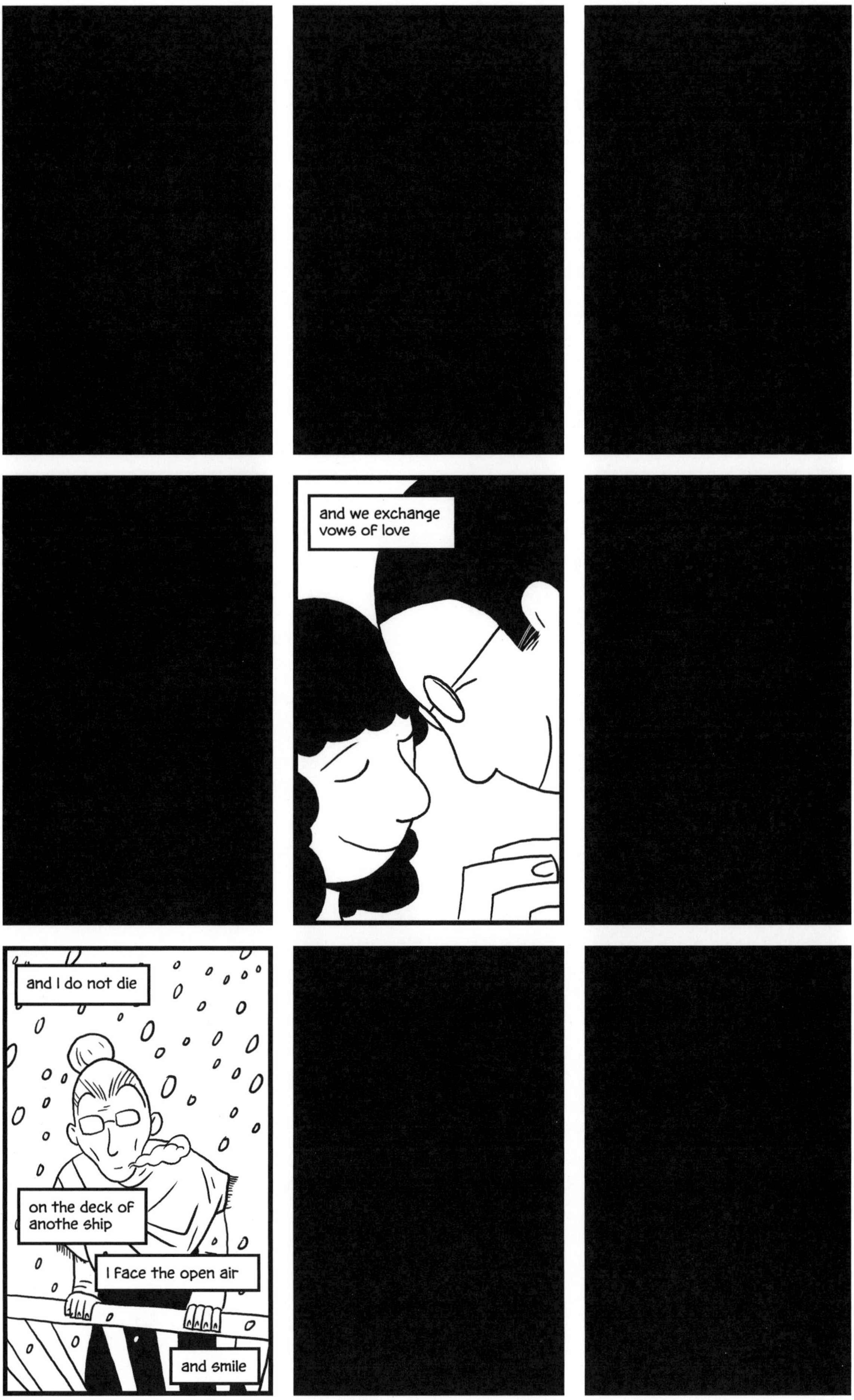
and we exchange vows of love
and I do not die
on the deck of anothe ship
I face the open air
and smile

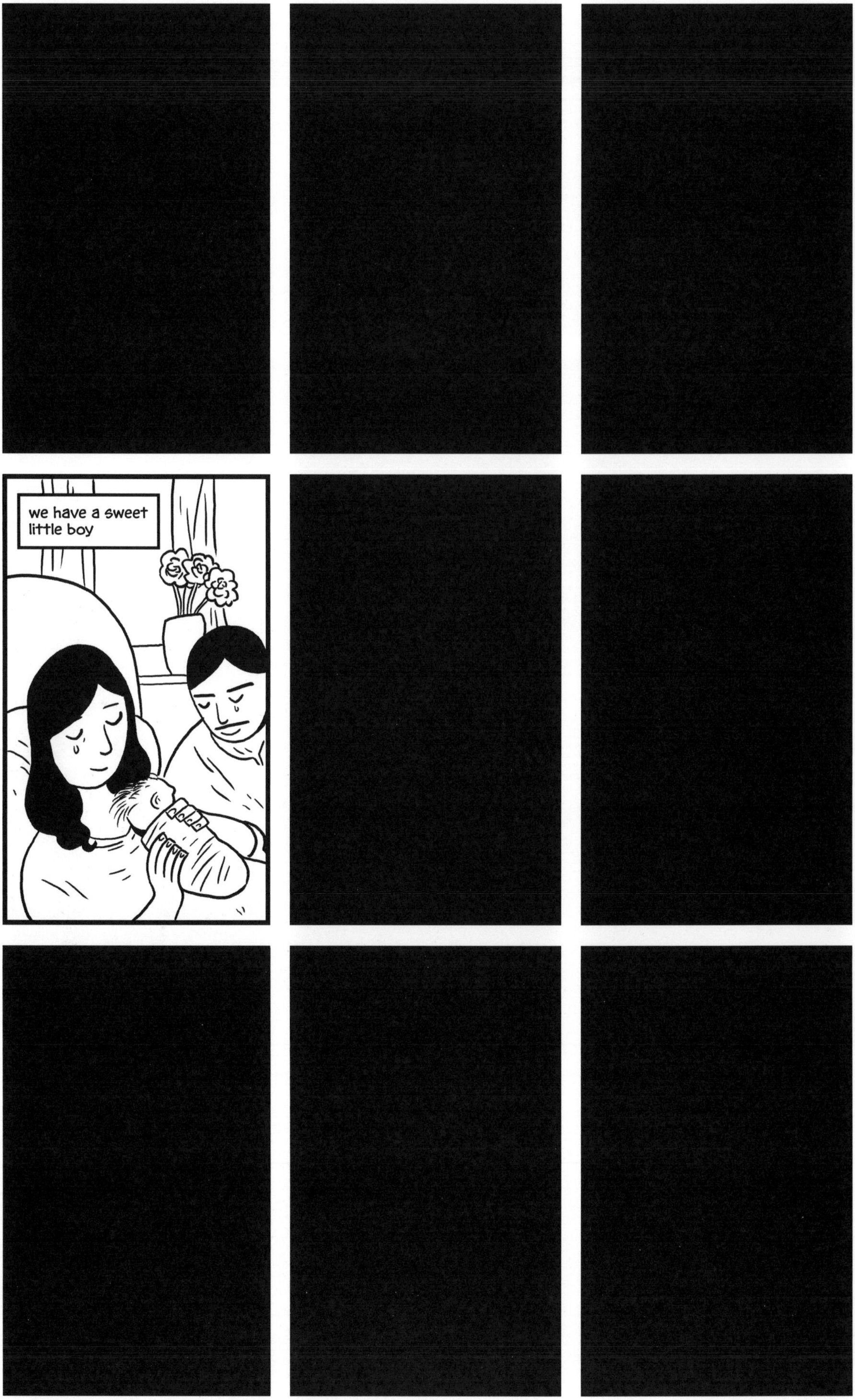
we have a sweet little boy

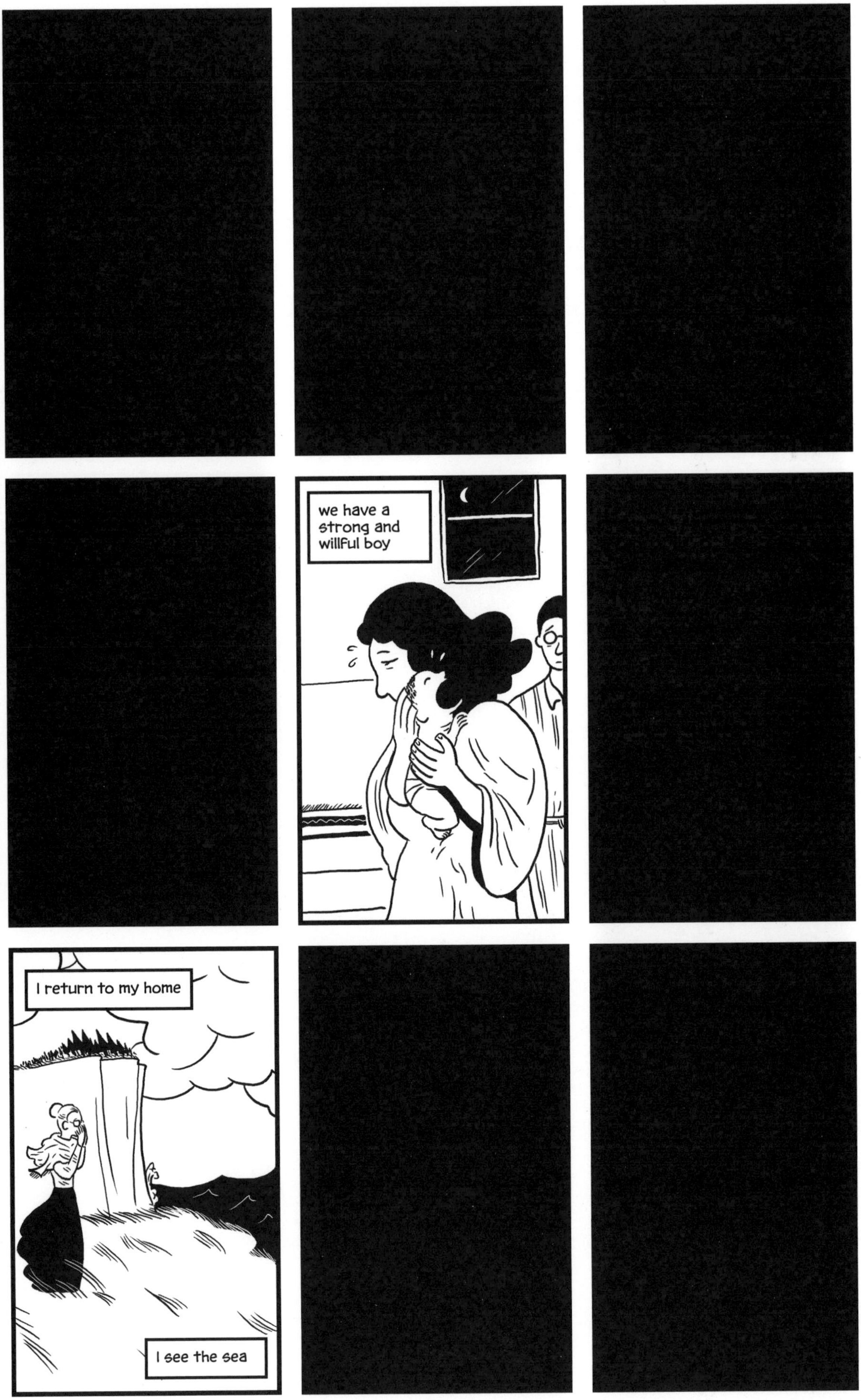
we have a strong and willful boy
I return to my home
I see the sea

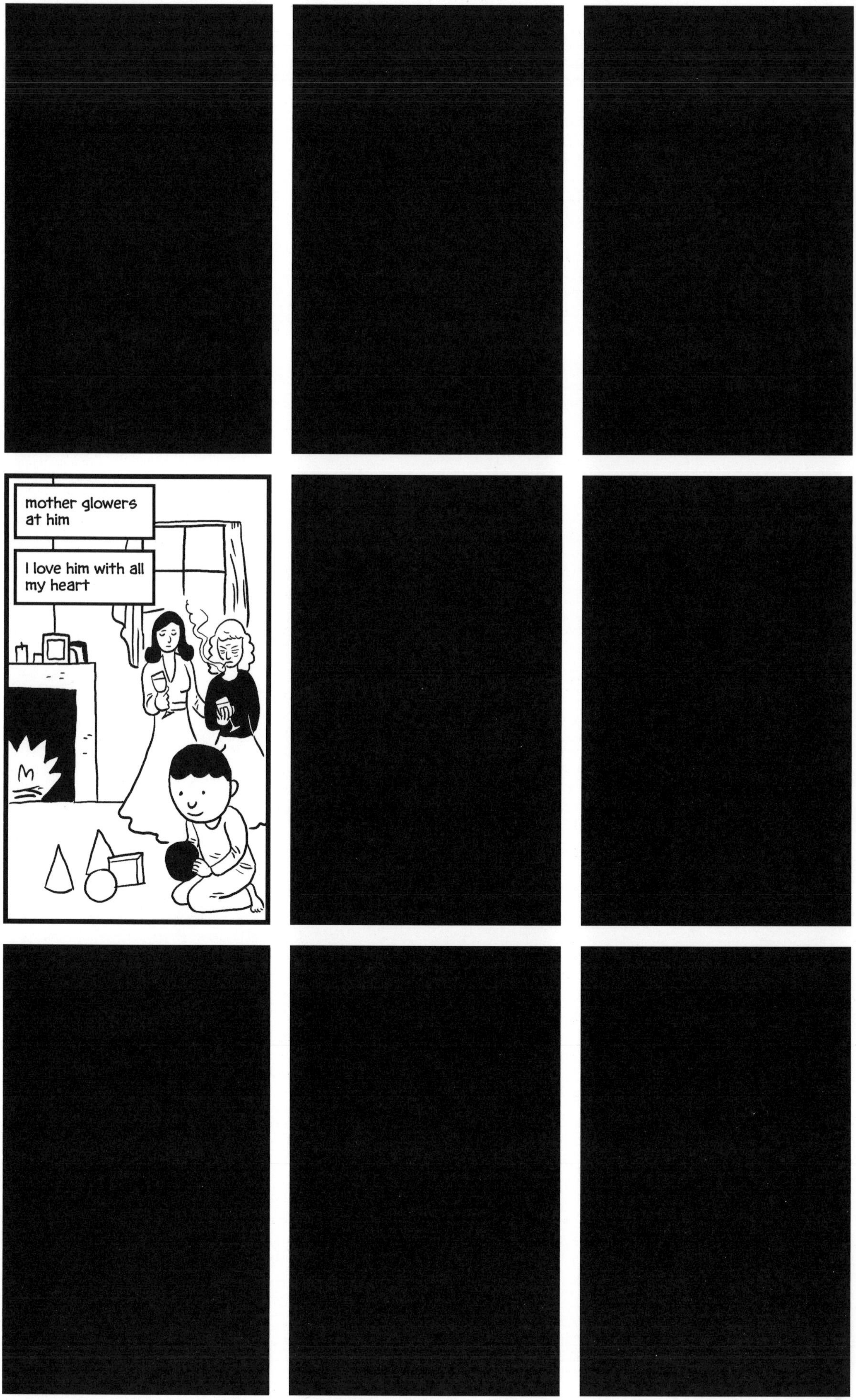
mother glowers at him
I love him with all my heart

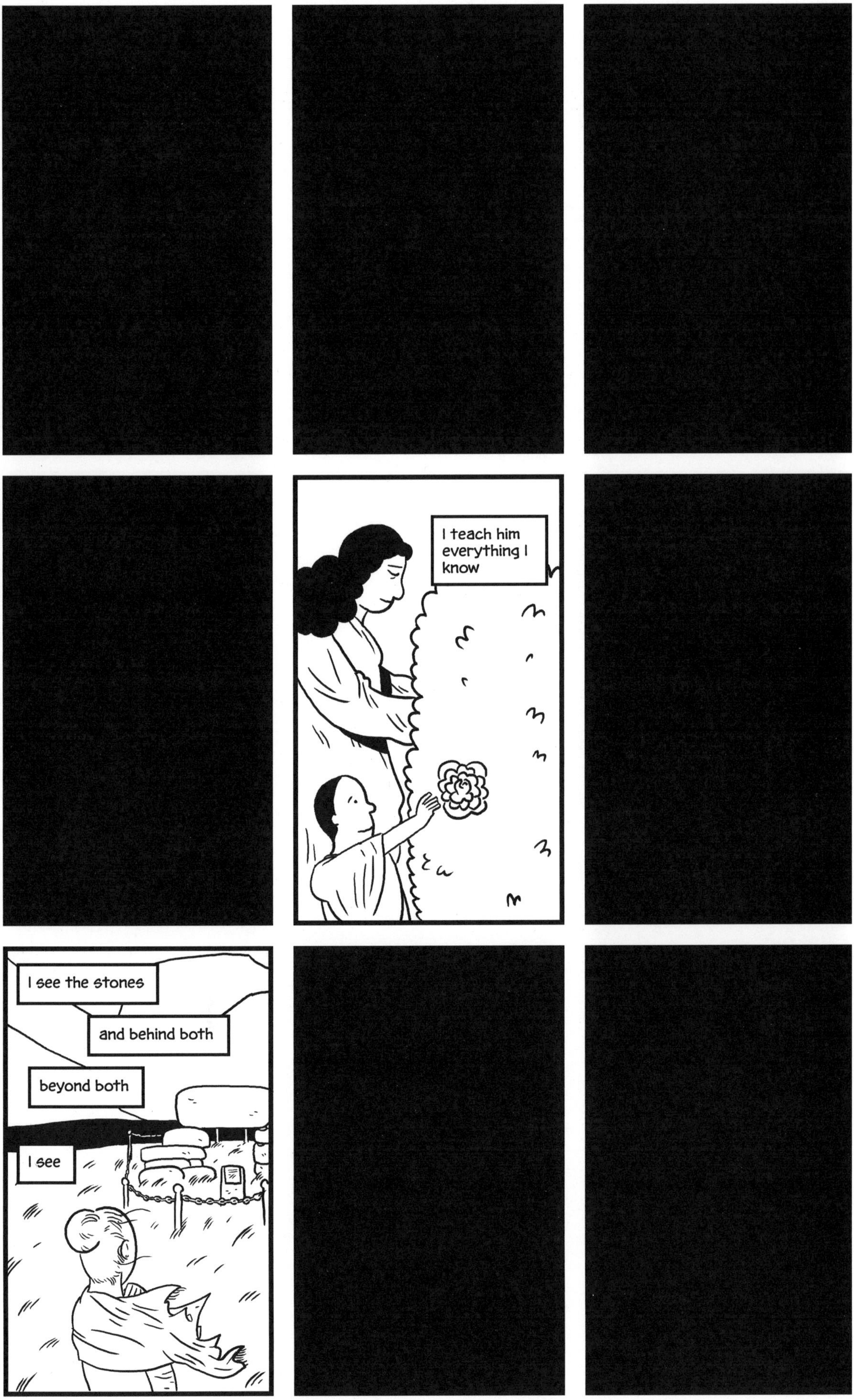
I teach him everything I know
I see the stones
and behind both
beyond both
I see

PART SIX

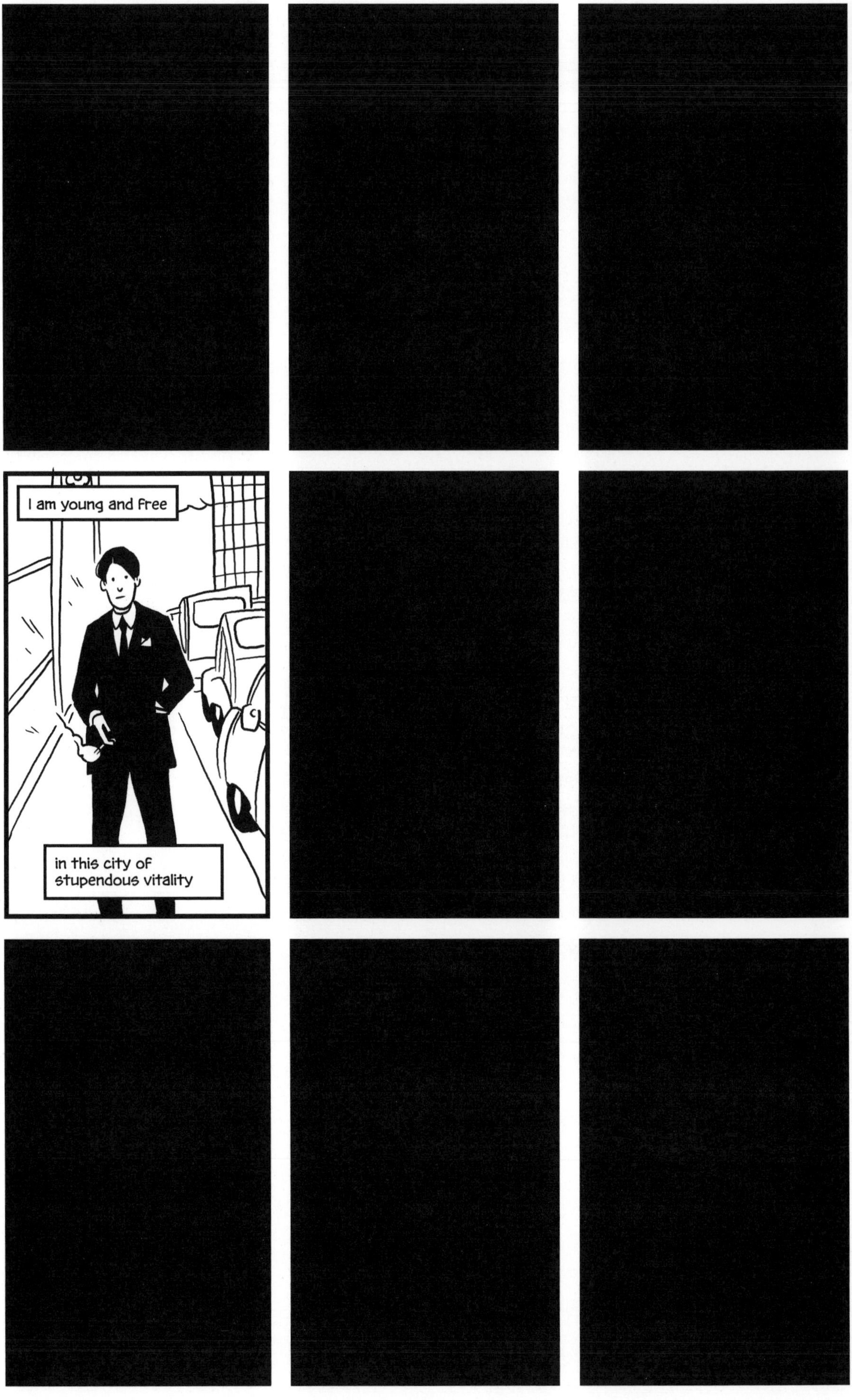
I am young and free
in this city of
stupendous vitality

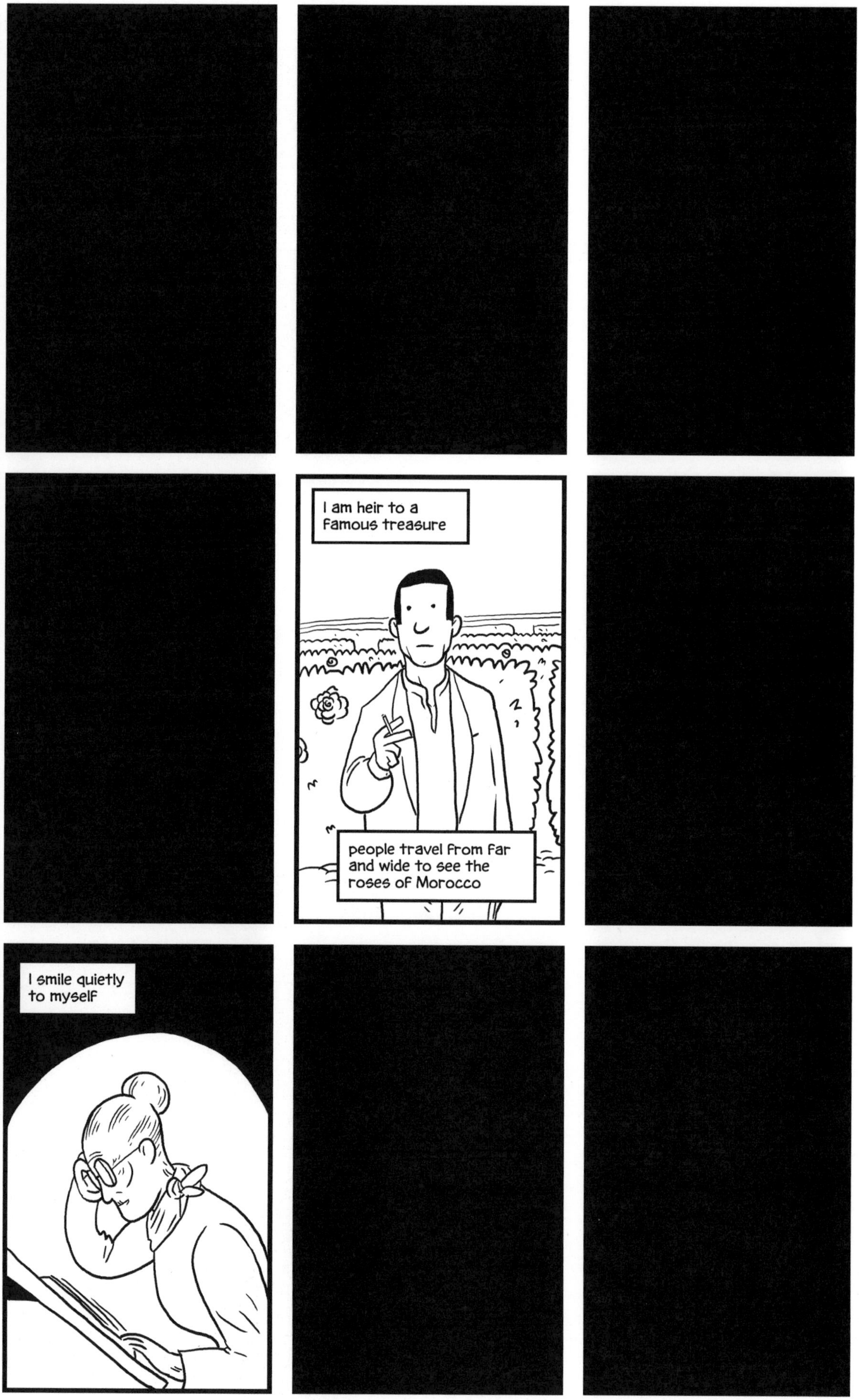
I am heir to a famous treasure
people travel from far and wide to see the roses of Morocco
I smile quietly to myself

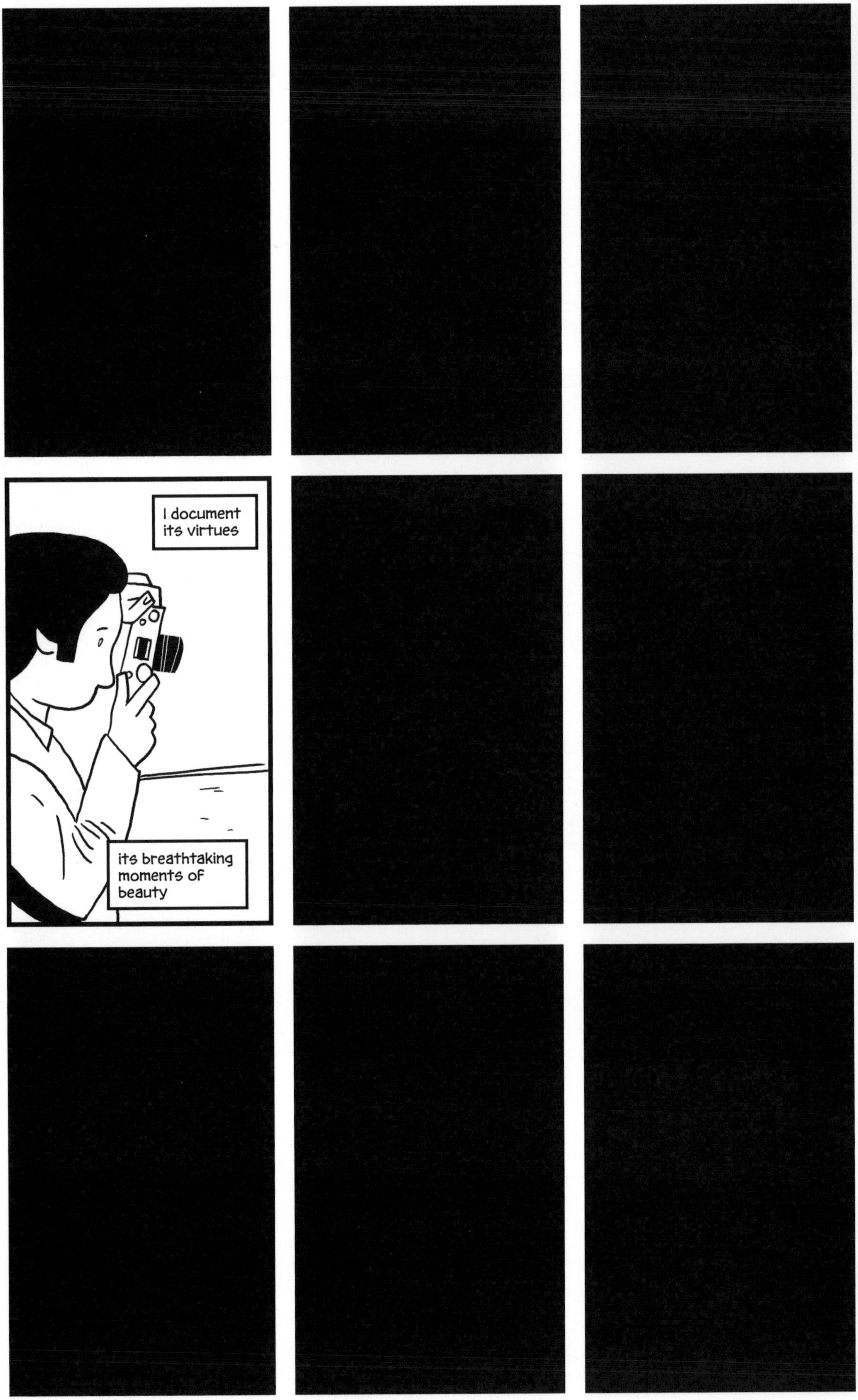
I document its virtues
its breathtaking moments of beauty

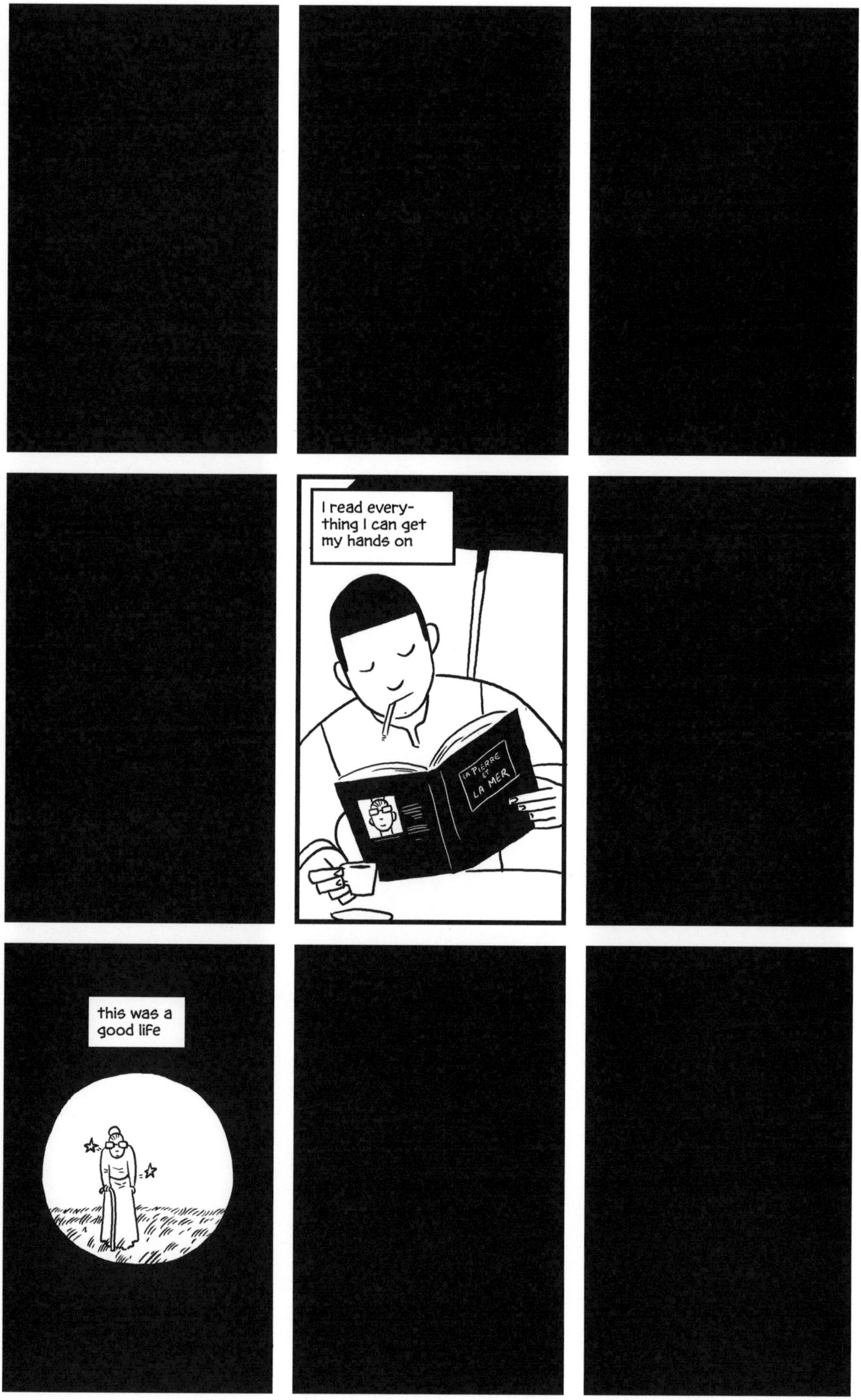
I read every-
thing I can get
my hands on
LA PIERRE ET LA MER
this was a
good life

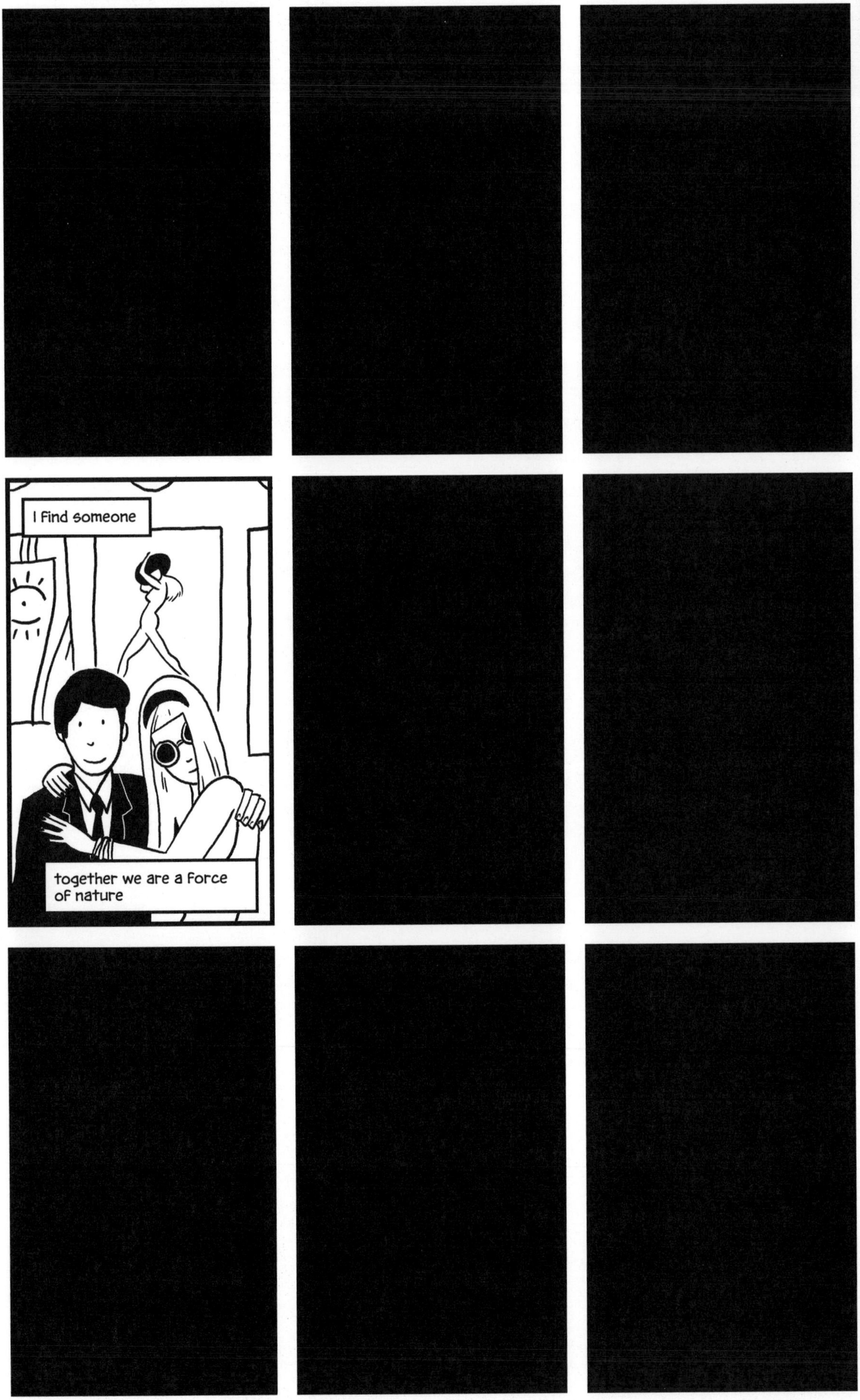
I find someone
together we are a force of nature

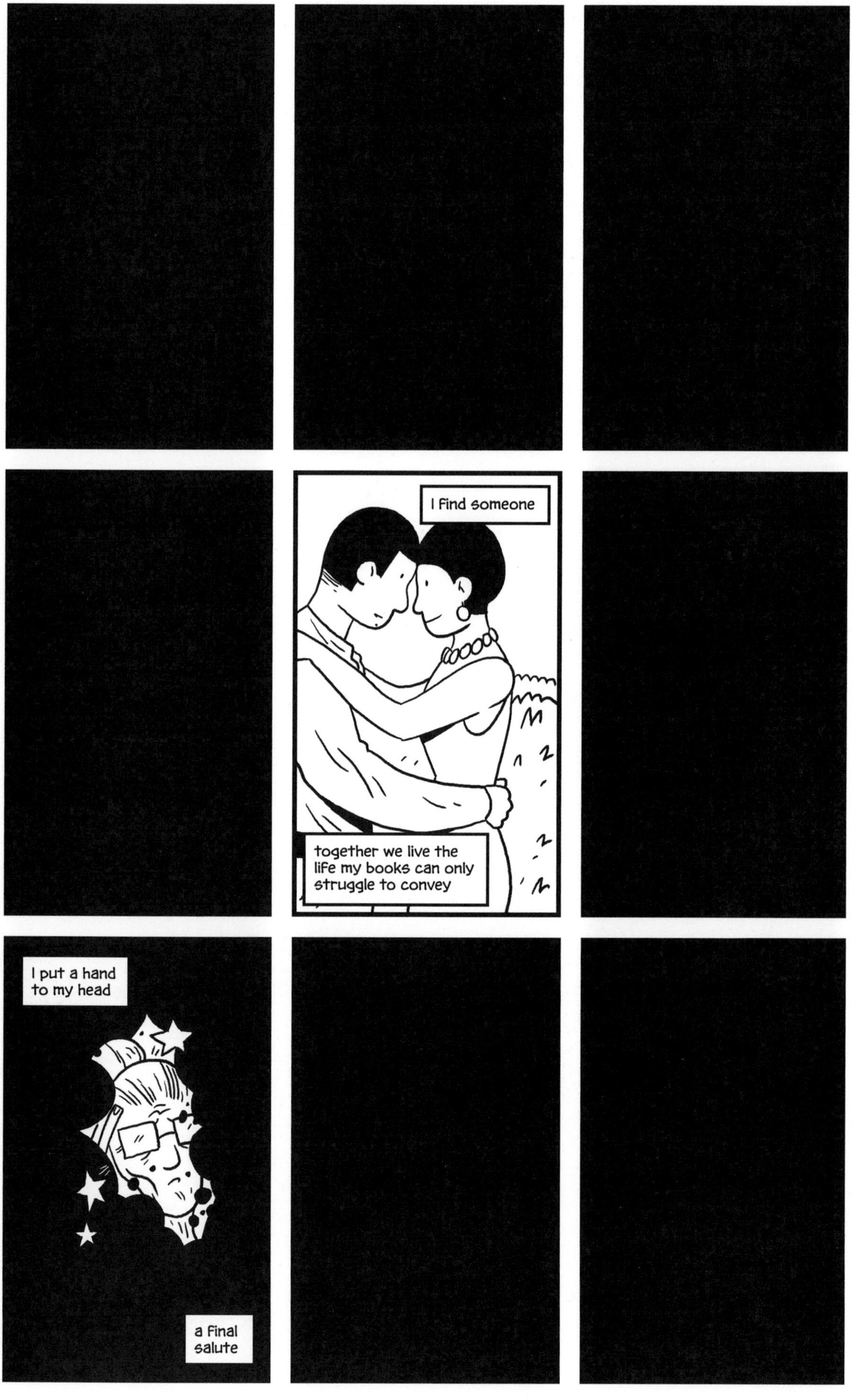

I find someone
together we live the life my books can only struggle to convey
I put a hand to my head
a final salute

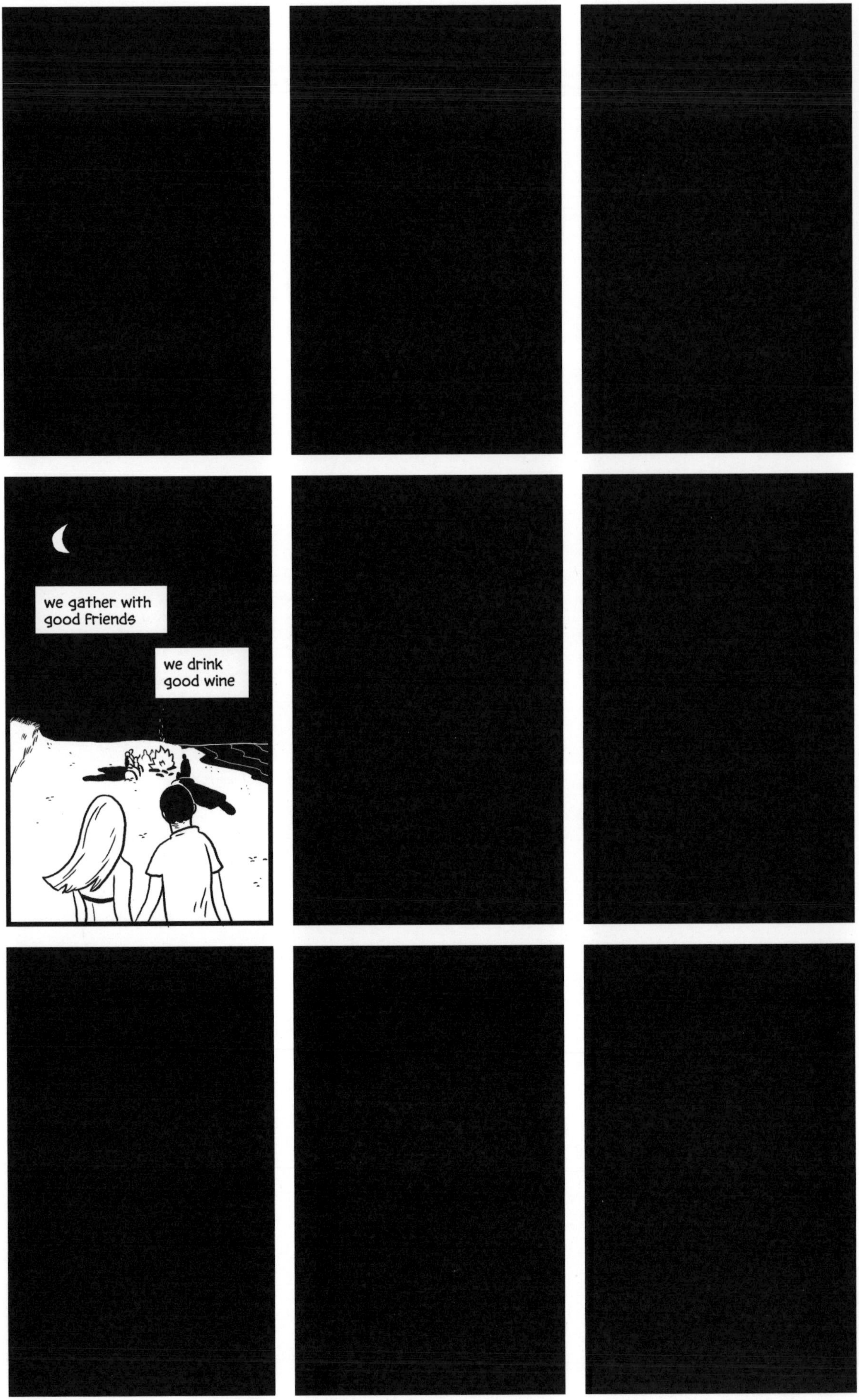
we gather with good friends
we drink good wine

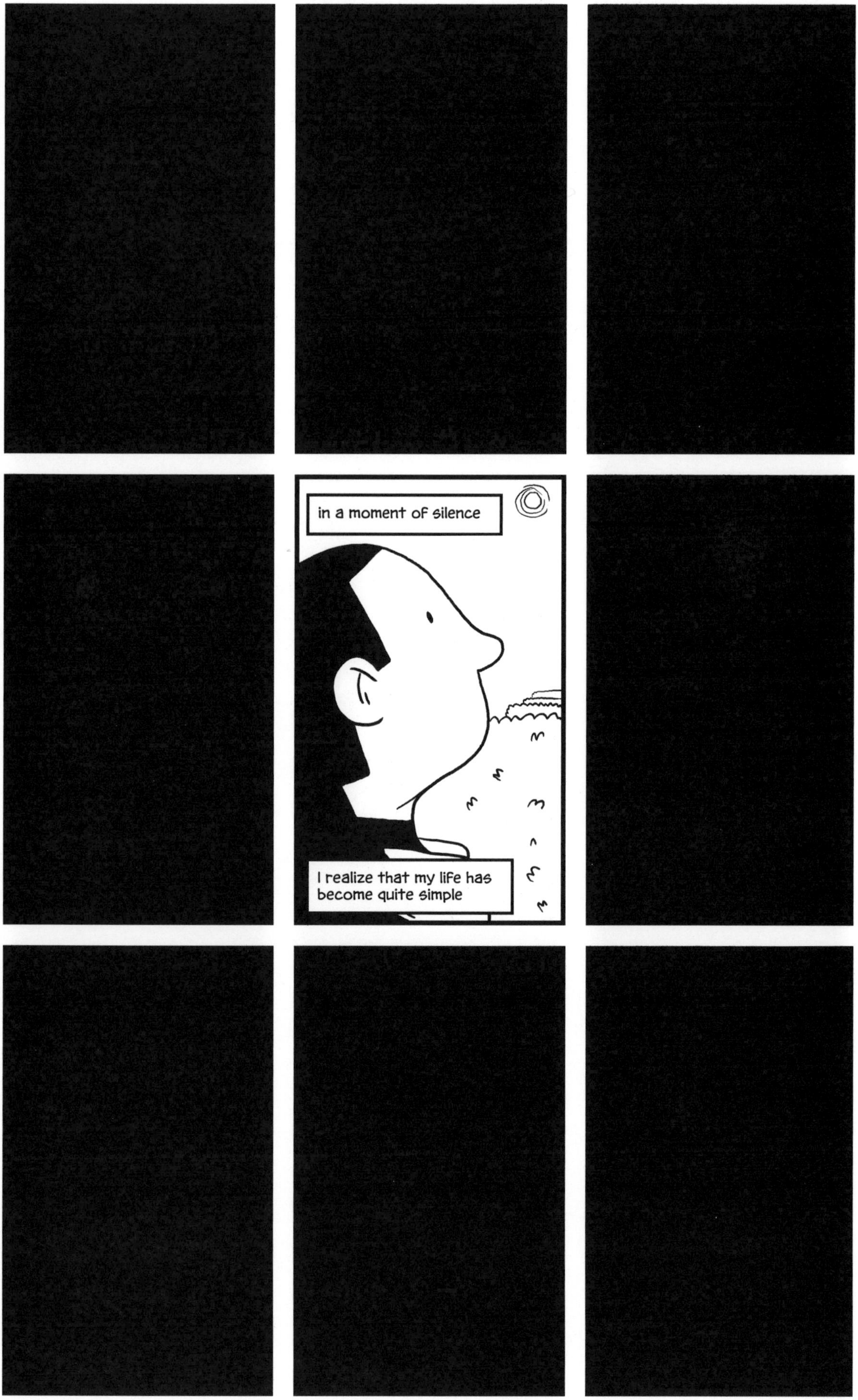
in a moment of silence
I realize that my life has become quite simple

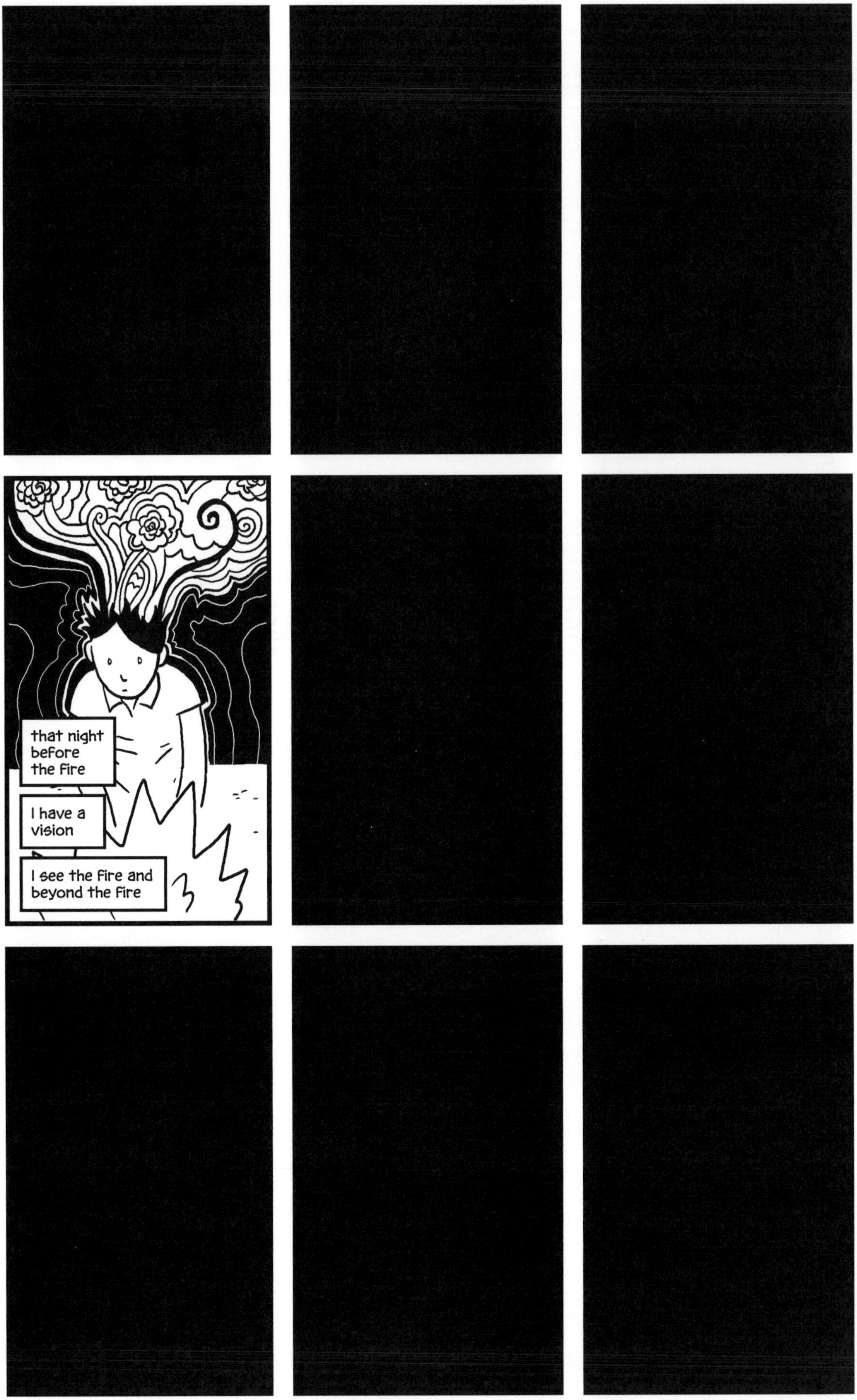
that night before the fire
I have a vision
I see the fire and beyond the fire

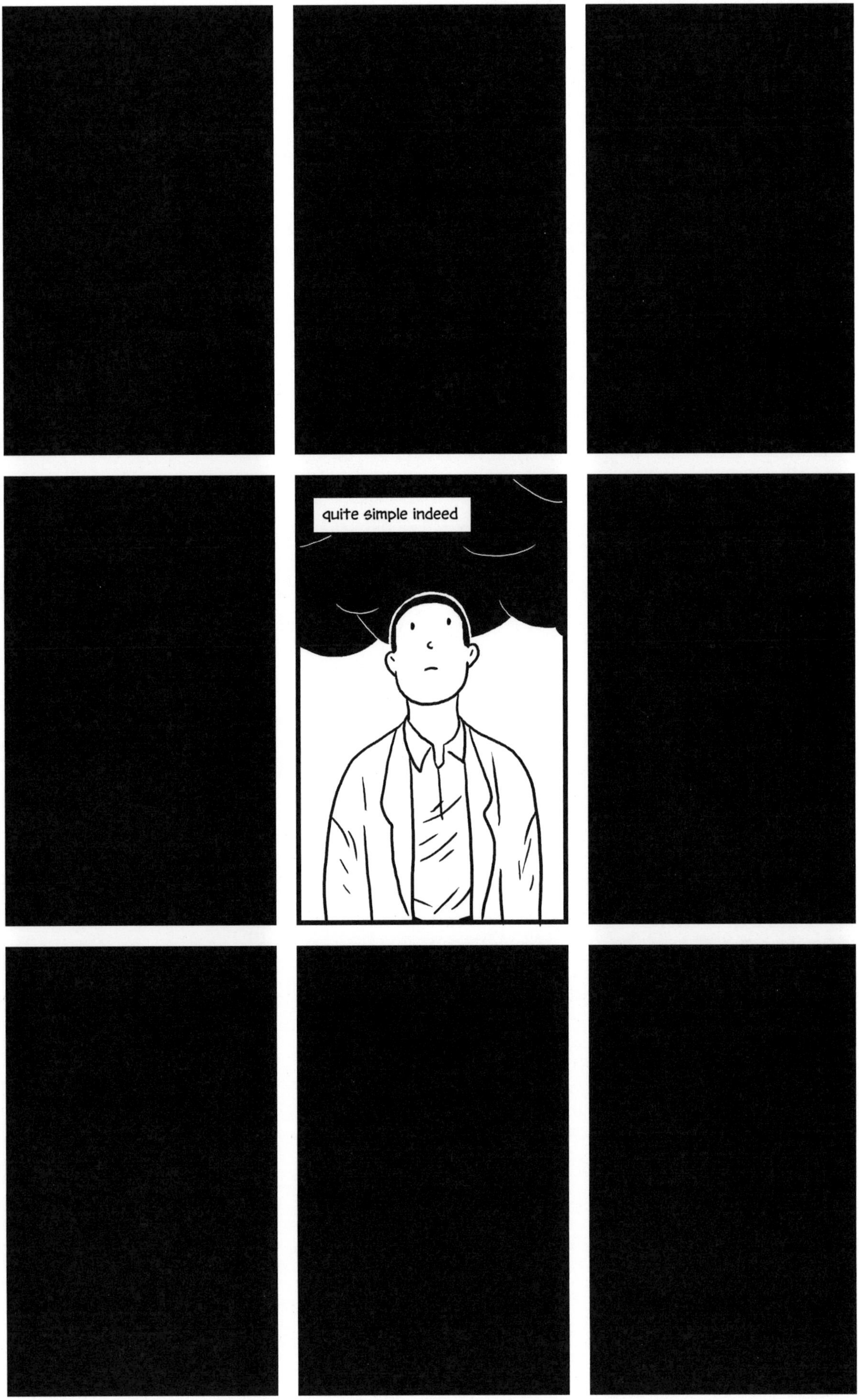
quite simple indeed

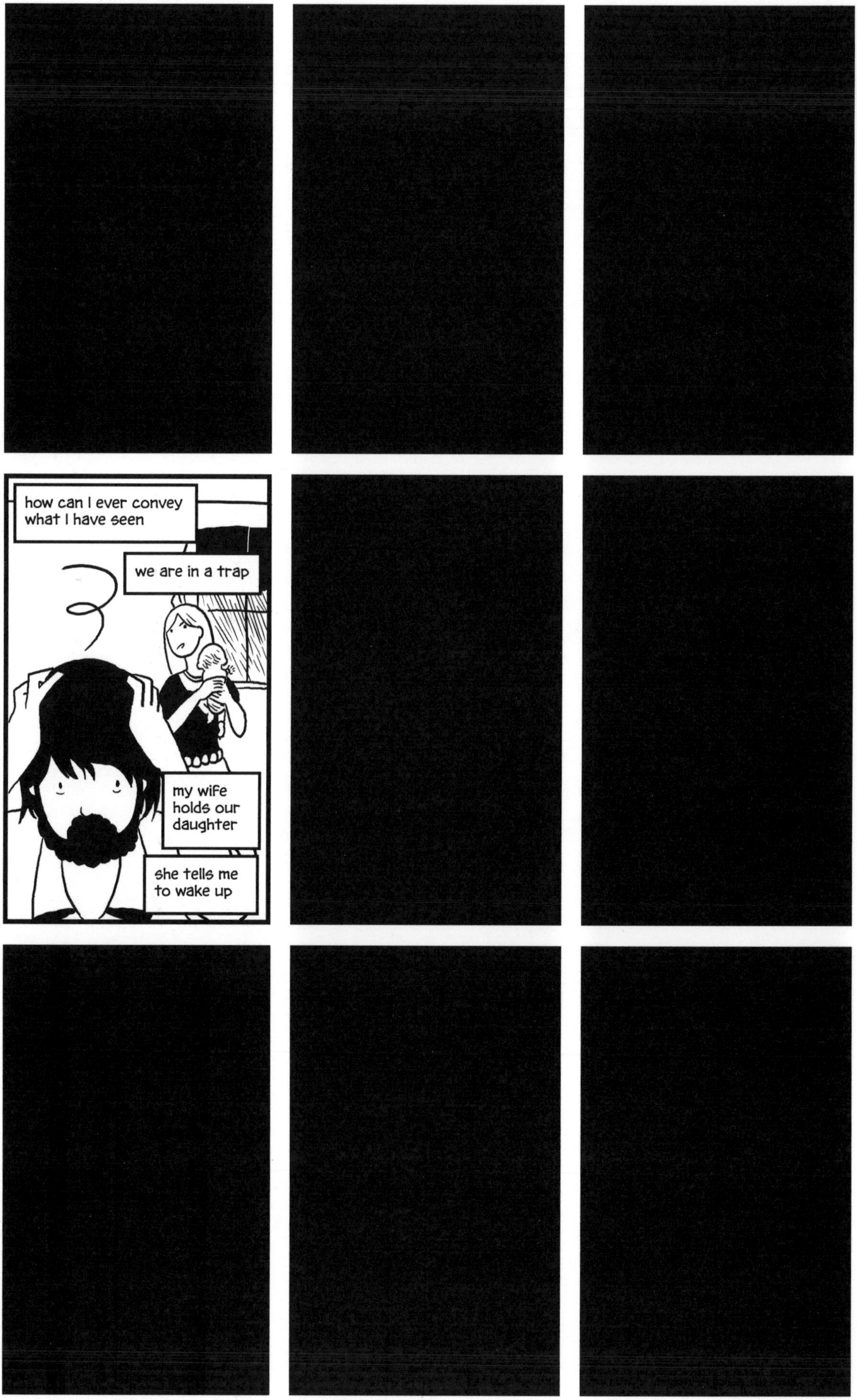
how can I ever convey what I have seen
we are in a trap
my wife holds our daughter
she tells me to wake up

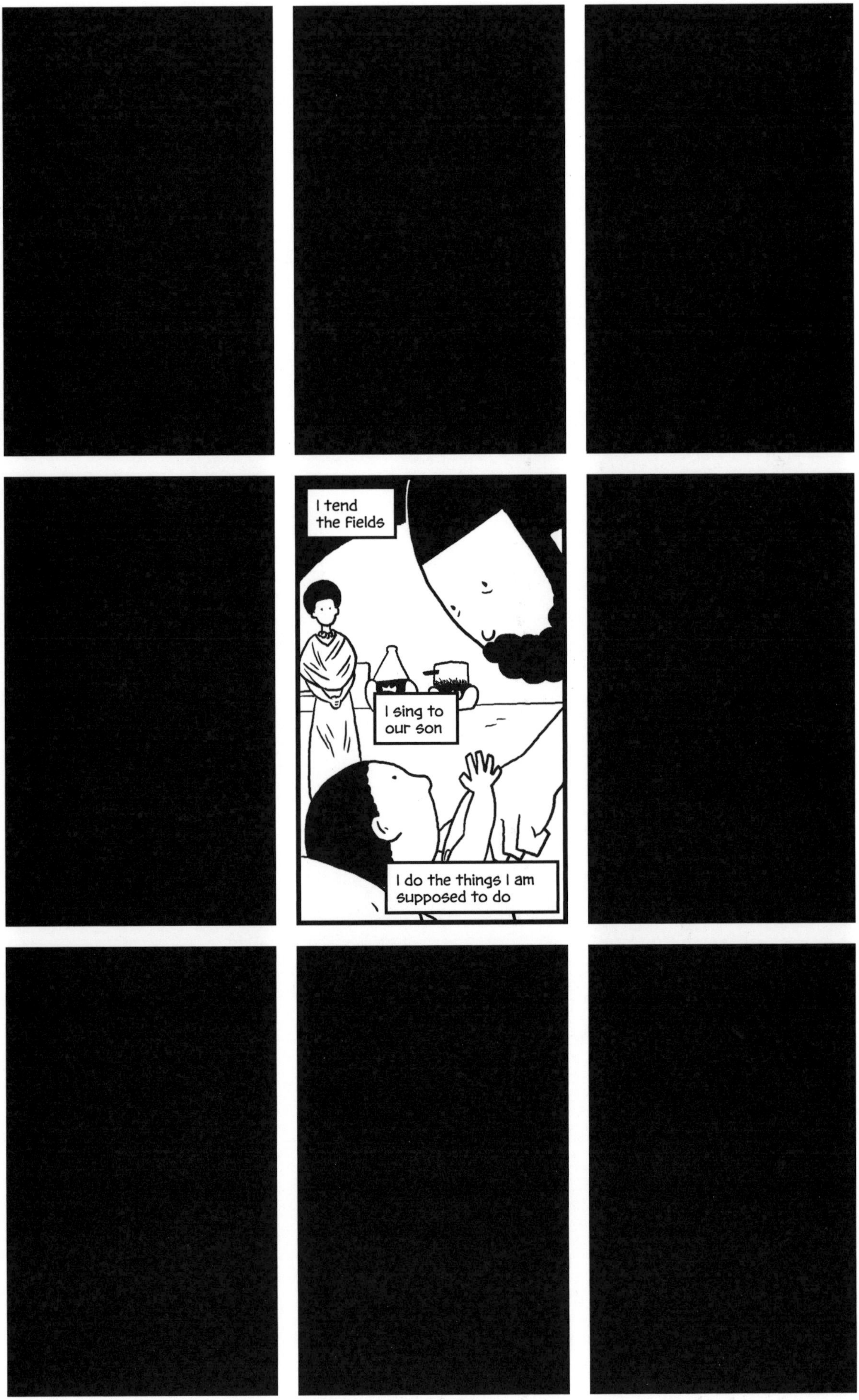
I tend
the fields
I sing to
our son
I do the things I am
supposed to do

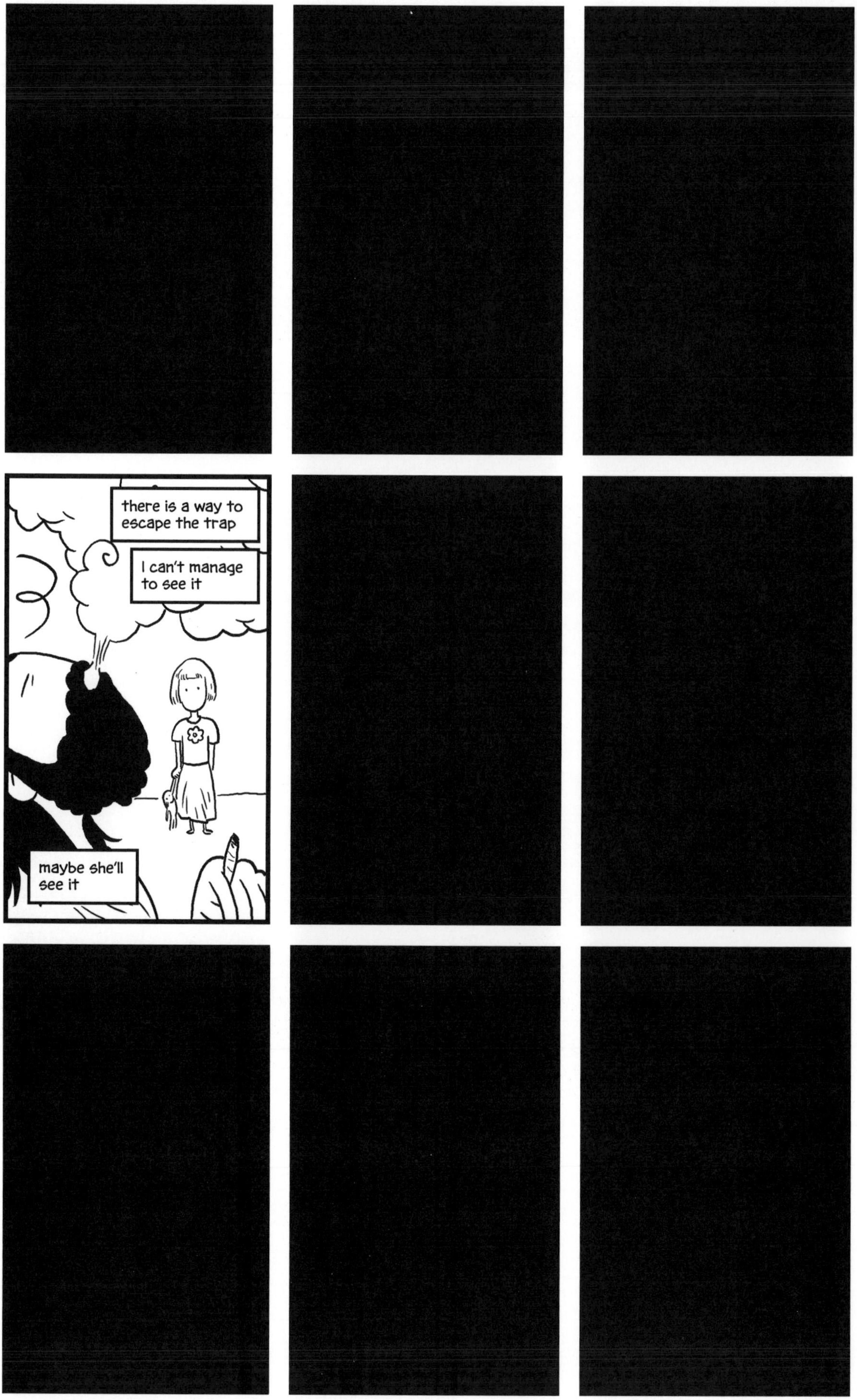
there is a way to escape the trap
I can't manage to see it
maybe she'll see it

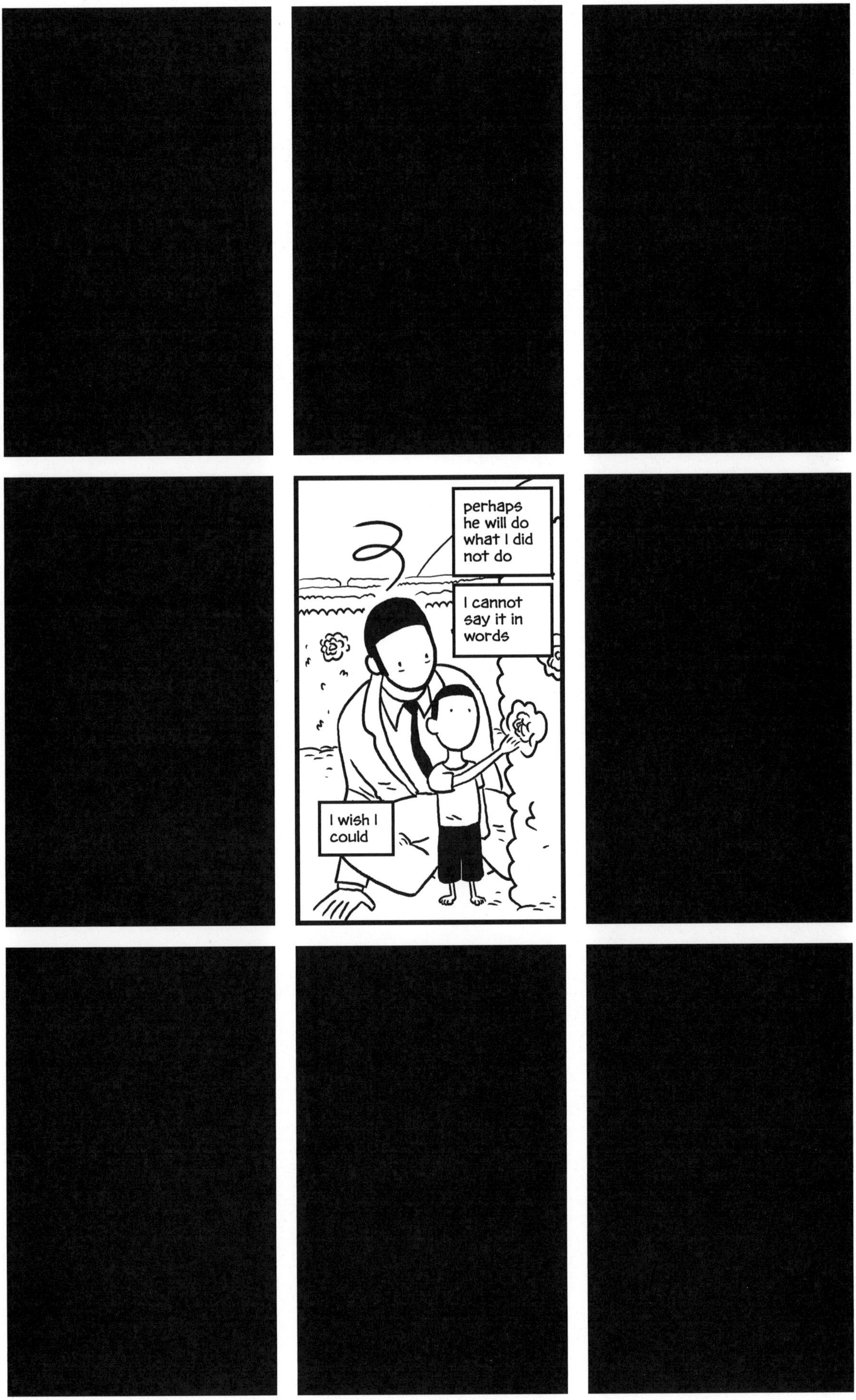
perhaps he will do what I did not do
I cannot say it in words
I wish I could

PART SEVEN

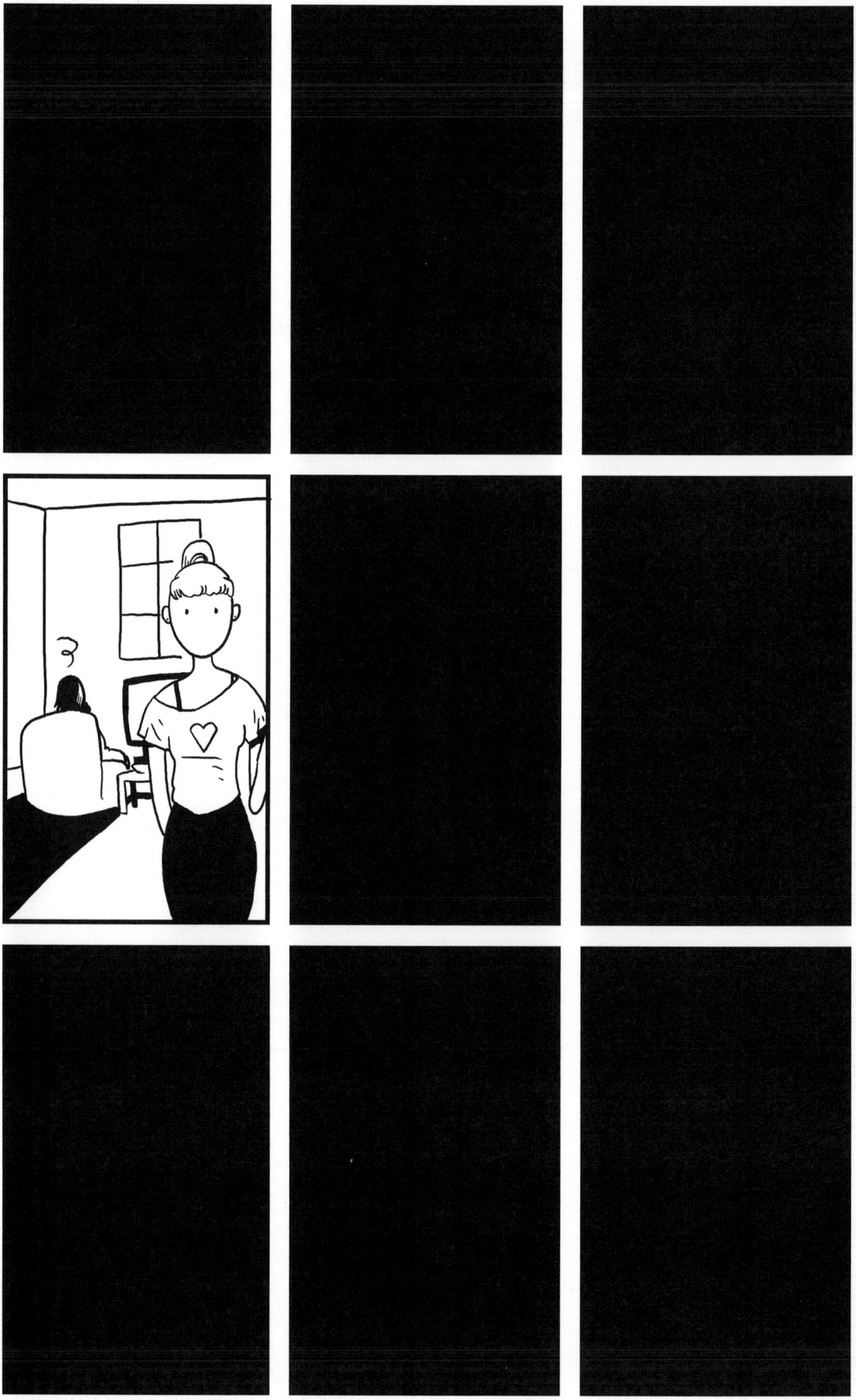

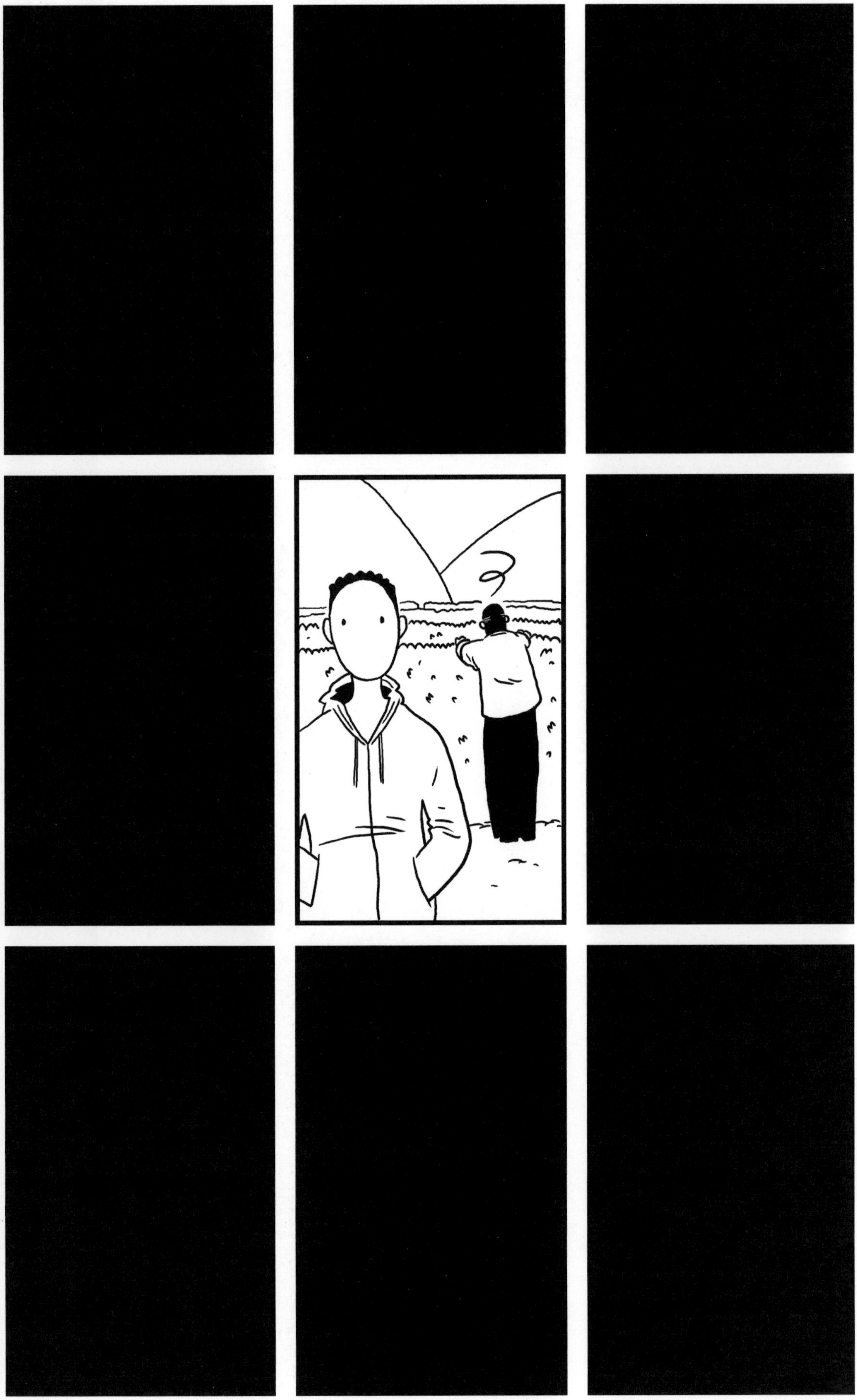

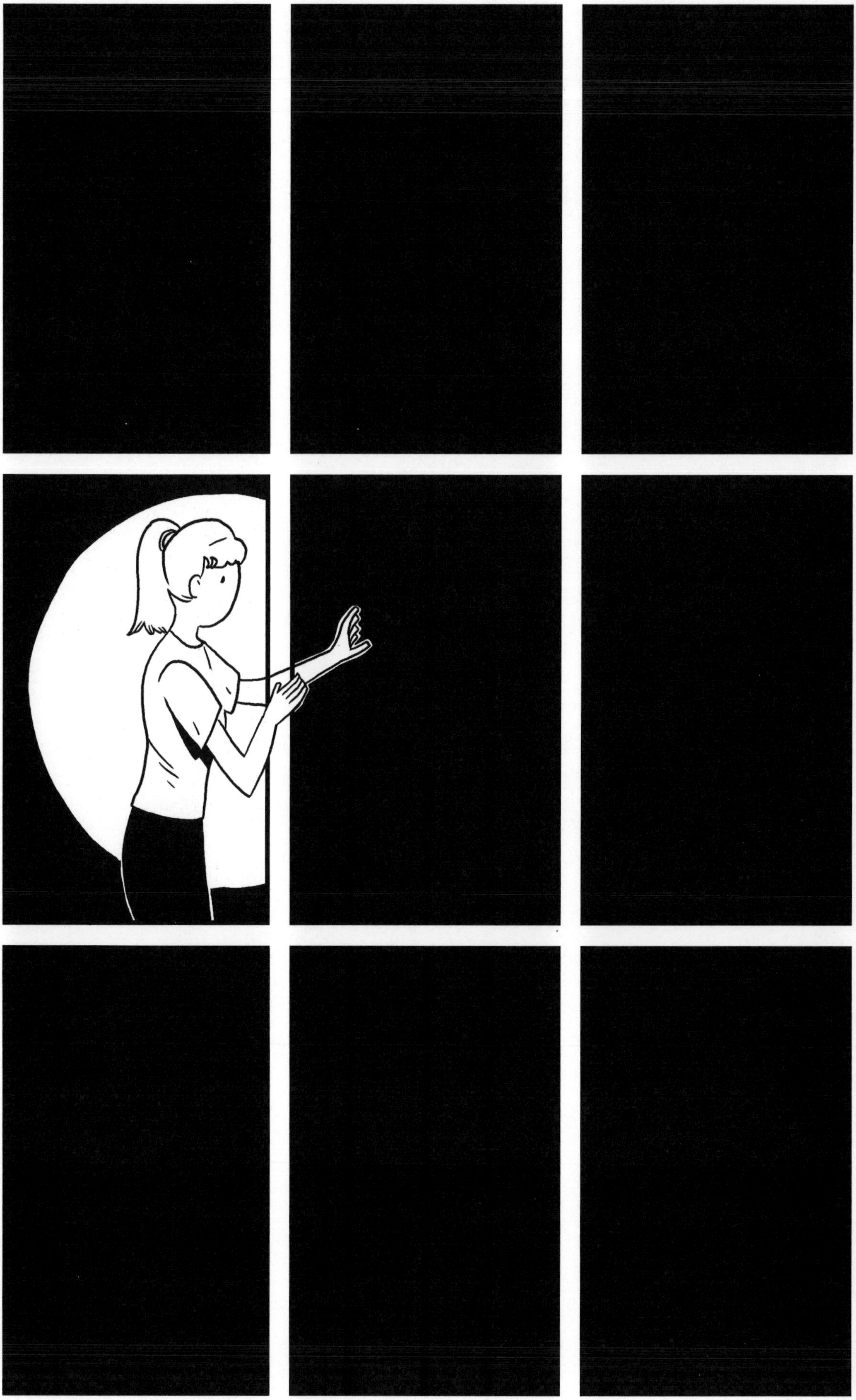

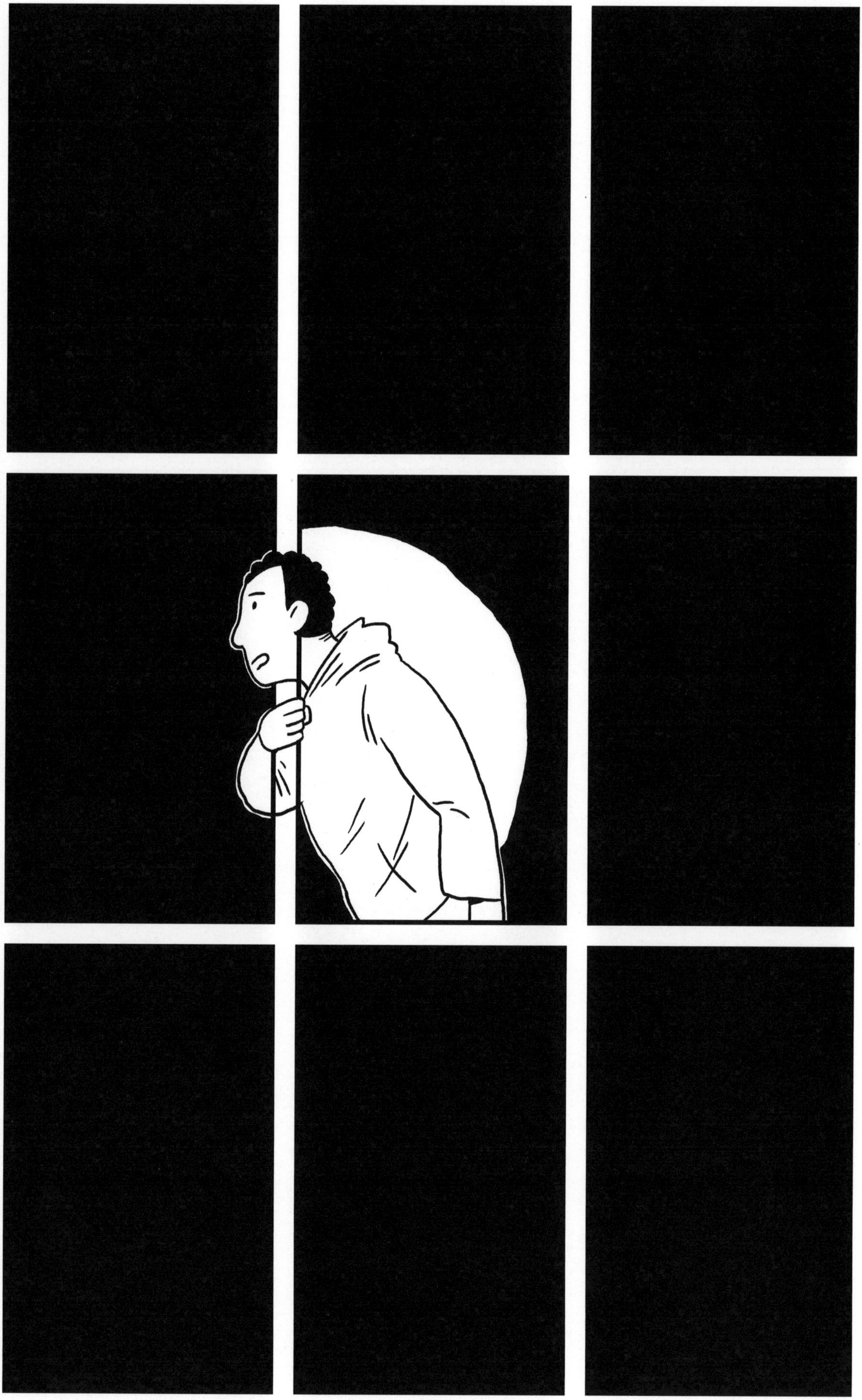

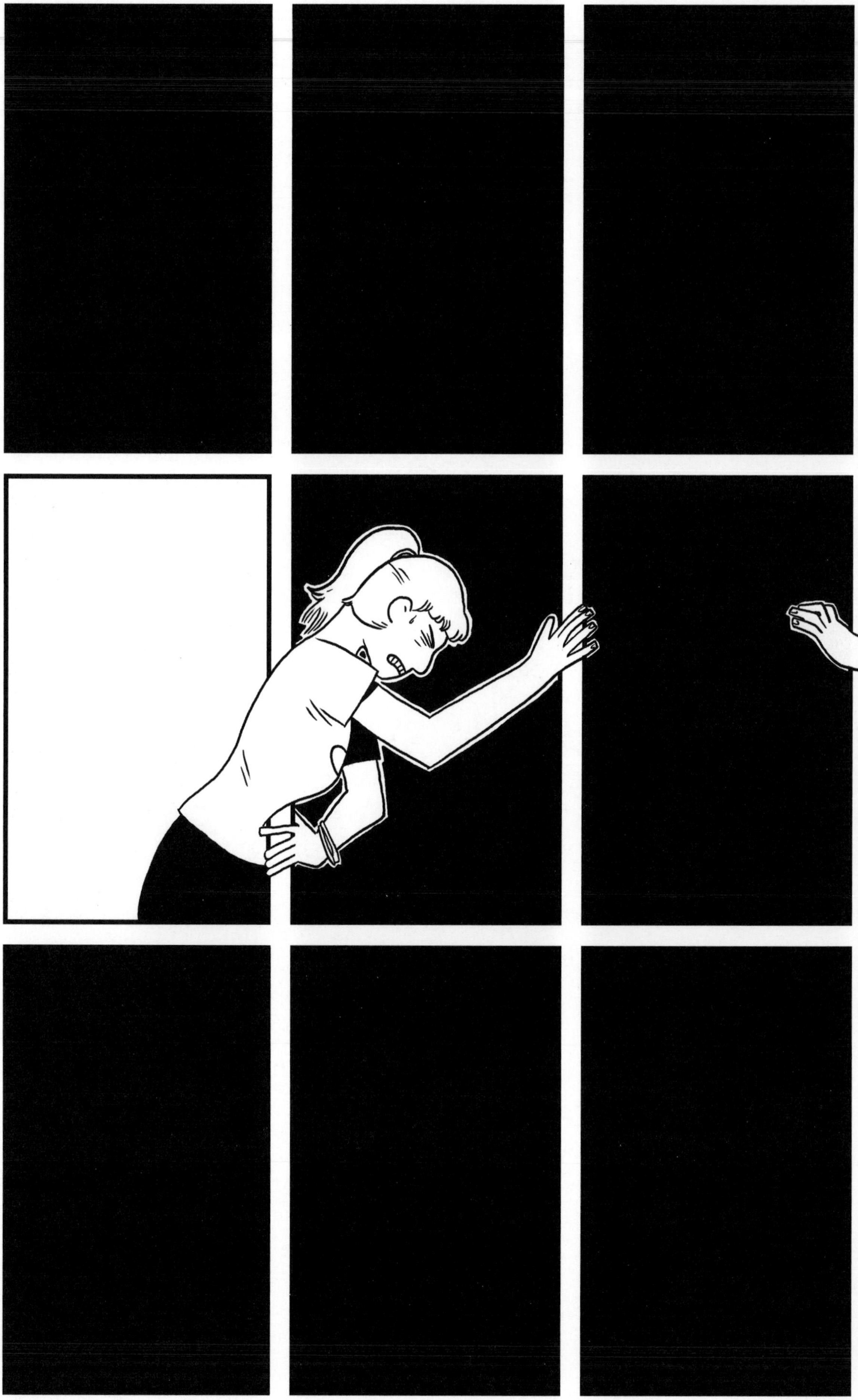

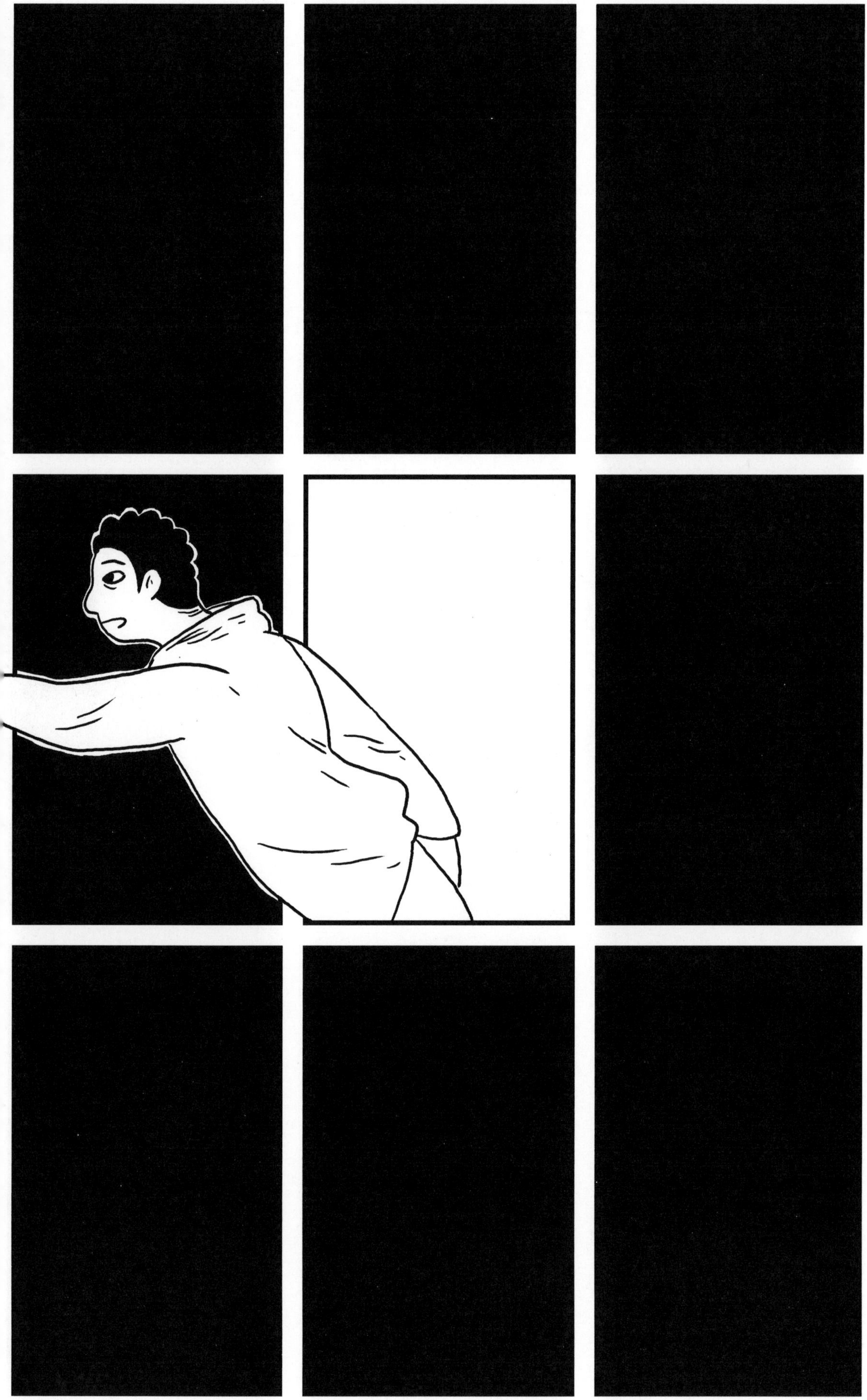

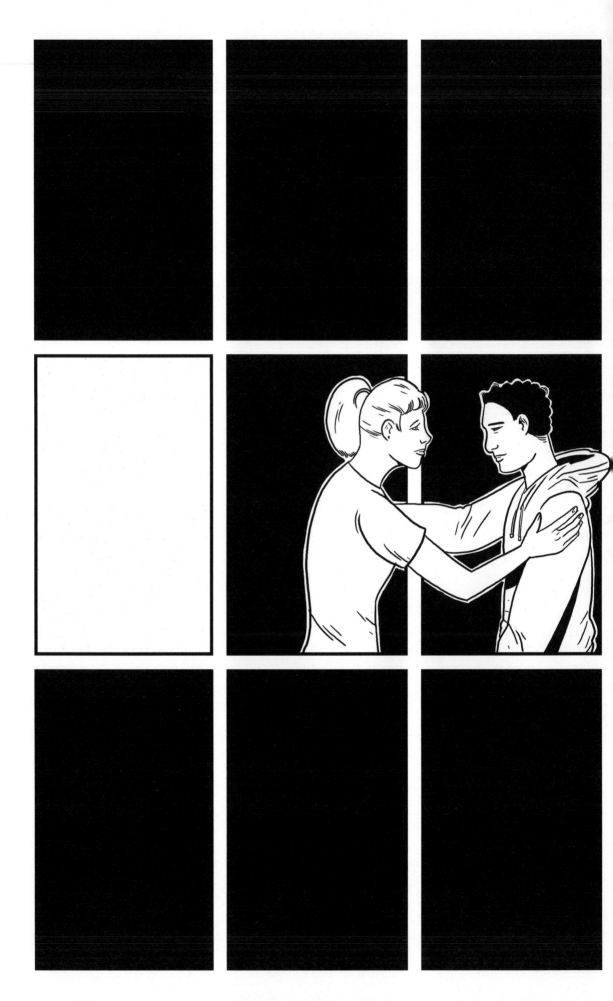

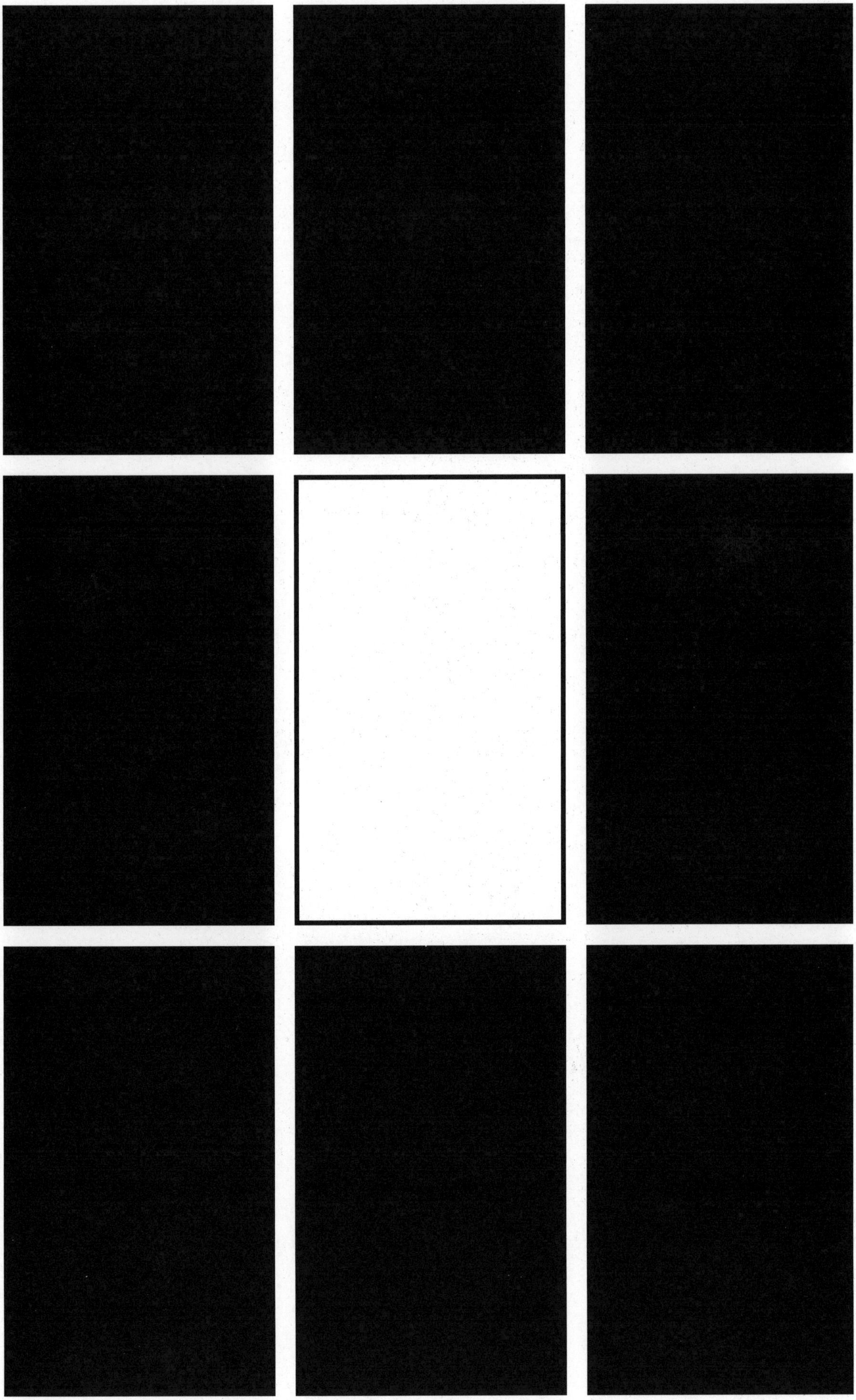

AFTERWORD

THIS BOOK, and the ones that preceded it, and every book I have ever written, are the product of my own ambitions and of a need to communicate that is muddy in its origin. And inherited talent and self-discipline. And what else? The stories that were read to me as a child. The stories I read for myself. The works of Lao Tse and Meister Eckhart and D.T. Suzuki and Robert Anton Wilson. The works of Kurt Vonnegut and Cormac McCarthy and J.D. Salinger and Alan Moore. The world around me and its histories, as they are known to me. I came of age in the 20th century, with all that entails, and am a father in the 21st, with all that entails.

To the consternation of every business-minded person I have ever known, I consider one of my books a success if it is available to read, and at least one of the people who happens to pick it up does read it, and it means something to them, and they find a way to say so. Sometimes they say thank you. When they do, I say thank you in return. Success!

Now: Thank you to my mother and father. Thank you to my children. Thank you to my editors, James Lucas Jones and Shawna Gore. Thank you, Lao Tse and company. Thank you, Alan Moore and company.

And at risk of jumping the gun: Thank you, reader.

-RAY FAWKES

Toronto, Canada

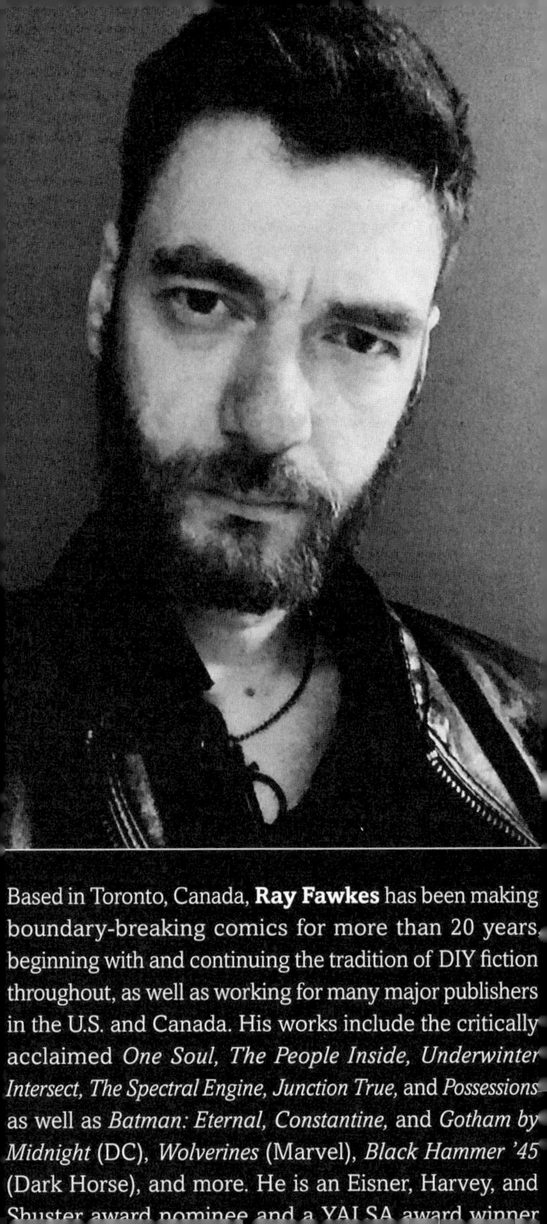

Based in Toronto, Canada, **Ray Fawkes** has been making boundary-breaking comics for more than 20 years, beginning with and continuing the tradition of DIY fiction throughout, as well as working for many major publishers in the U.S. and Canada. His works include the critically acclaimed *One Soul, The People Inside, Underwinter Intersect, The Spectral Engine, Junction True,* and *Possessions* as well as *Batman: Eternal, Constantine,* and *Gotham by Midnight* (DC), *Wolverines* (Marvel), *Black Hammer '45* (Dark Horse), and more. He is an Eisner, Harvey, and Shuster award nominee and a YALSA award winner

Published by
Oni-Lion Forge Publishing Group, LLC

James Lucas Jones
president & publisher

Sarah Gaydos
editor in chief

Charlie Chu
e.v.p. of creative & business development

Brad Rooks
director of operations

Amber O'Neill
special projects manager

Margot Wood
director of marketing & sales

Devin Funches
sales & marketing manager

Katie Sainz
marketing manager

Tara Lehmann
publicist

Holly Aitchison
consumer marketing manager

Troy Look
director of design & production

Kate Z. Stone
senior graphic designer

Sonja Synak
graphic designer

Hilary Thompson
graphic designer

Sarah Rockwell
graphic designer

Angie Knowles
digital prepress lead

Vincent Kukua
digital prepress technician

Jasmine Amiri
senior editor

Shawna Gore
senior editor

Amanda Meadows
senior editor

Robert Meyers
senior editor, licensing

Desiree Rodriguez
editor

Grace Scheipeter
editor

Zack Soto
editor

Chris Cerasi
editorial coordinator

Steve Ellis
vice president of games

Ben Eisner
game developer

Michelle Nguyen
executive assistant

Jung Lee
logistics coordinator

Joe Nozemack
publisher emeritus

Designed by
Kate Z. Stone

Edited by
Shawna Gore

Rayfawkes.com
instagram.com/fawkes.ray

onipress.com
facebook.com/onipress
twitter.com/onipress
onipress.tumblr.com
instagram.com/onipress

ONI-LION FORGE PUBLISHING GROUP, LLC.
1319 SE Martin Luther King Jr. Blvd. Suite 240
Portland, OR 97214 USA

First edition: July 2021
ISBN 978-1-62010-934-2
eISBN 978-1-62010-947-2

PRINTED IN CHINA

Library of Congress Control Number: 2020947307

10 9 8 7 6 5 4 3 2 1

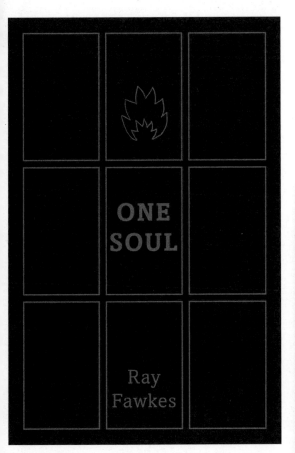
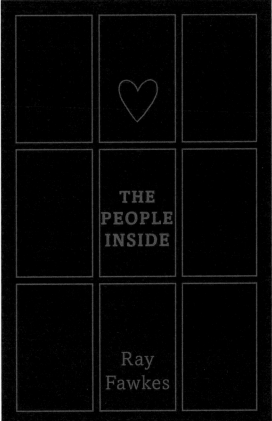